The Broadwater Farm Inquiry

The Broadwater Farm Inquiry

Introduction by Lord Gifford Q.C.

Report of the Independent Inquiry into disturbances of
October 1985 at the Broadwater Farm Estate, Tottenham
Chaired by Lord Gifford QC

Karia Press

The Broadwater Farm Inquiry

Report of the Independent Inquiry into disturbances of October 1985 at the Broadwater Farm Estate, Tottenham
Chaired by Lord Gifford Q.C.

With an Introduction by Lord Gifford Q.C.

First published in 1986 by the Broadwater Farm Inquiry.

This edition with an introduction published by
Karia Press

ISBN 0 946918 59 7 Pb
ISBN 0 946918 60 0 Hb

Copyright © The Broadwater Farm Inquiry, 1986
Copyright © Introduction Lord Gifford Q.C.

Typeset by Hive Photosetting and Calverts Press
Cover Design by Karia based on design of original cover by Eve Barker.

Printed by Whitstable Litho Ltd., Kent.

Karia Press
BCM Karia
London WC1N 3XX
United Kingdom

Terms of reference

To inquire into and report on the disturbances on Broadwater Farm Estate, London N17, on 6–7 October 1985 and in particular to consider:—

(a) social and economic conditions within the London Borough of Haringey;

(b) the policing of the area before and after the disturbances;

(c) the racial and other aspects of the relationship between the police and the residents of the area;

(d) the role of the relevant statutory and voluntary agencies concerned with policing and community relations.

To make recommendations.

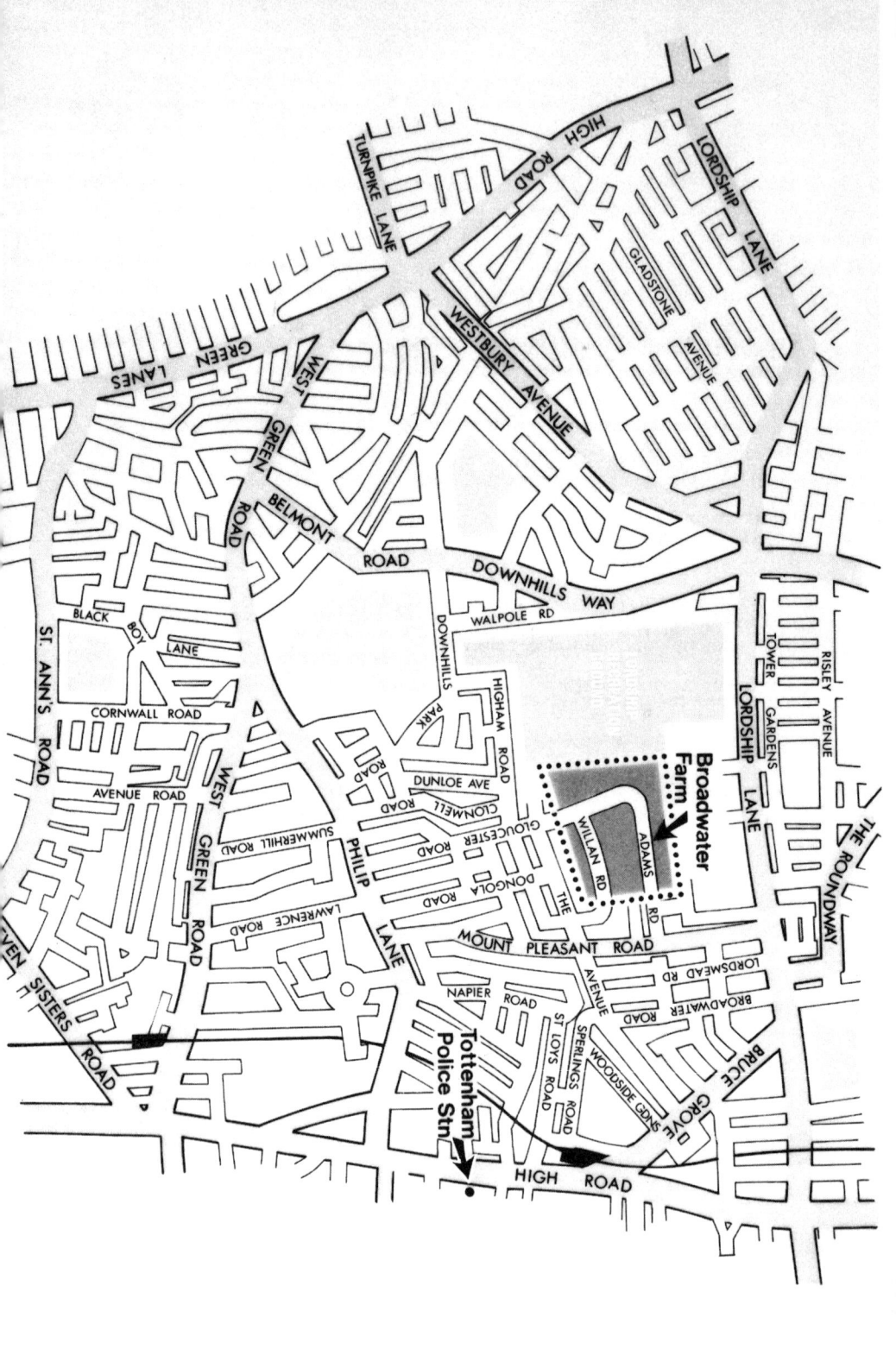

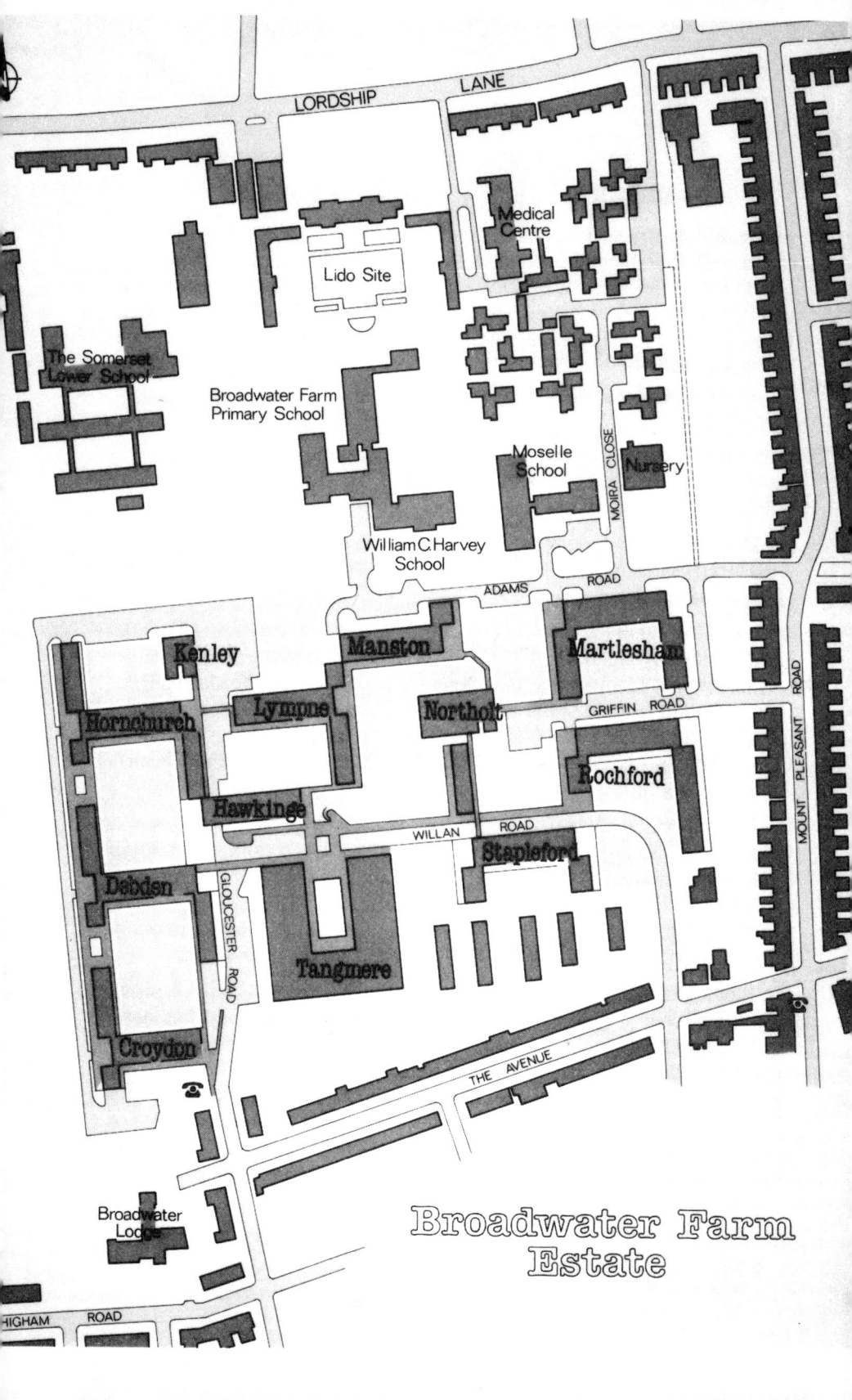

BIOGRAPHIES OF PANEL MEMBERS

Lord Gifford: Practising barrister since 1966. QC since 1982. Co-founder of Britain's first neighbourhood law centre in North Kensington in 1970. Has lived in Haringey since 1976. Active in human rights issues in Britain and abroad. Has conducted inquiries into "supergrasses" in Northern Ireland in 1983 and "political policing" in Wales in 1984. Vice-chair of the Defence and Aid Fund (UK) which provides assistance to political prisoners in South Africa and Namibia.

Rev Canon Sebastian Charles: Canon of Westminster Abbey since 1978; chair of the City of Westminster Police Consultative Committee; was assistant general secretary and secretary of the division of Community Affairs, British Council of Churches 1967-74.

Rt Rev Philip Harvey, OBE: Nominated by Cardinal Basil Hume; Auxiliary Bishop of Westminster; Bishop in North London since 1977. Has specialised in social work.

Dorothy Kuya: Director of Affirmata, an Equal Opportunities Training and Consultancy Agency; 1970-77, first senior community relations officer for Merseyside Community Relations Council; 1979-84, Principal Race Relations and Ethnic Adviser, London Borough of Haringey; 1983, member of the Home Office Police Training Working Party on Community and Race Relations & Training. Chair of Cardinal Hume's Advisory Committee on Race Relations.

Dr Paul Corrigan: Social scientist; has written books on social work, welfare issues and secondary education; 1980-84, Head of Applied Social Studies Department, Polytechnic of North London. Carried out a research project into "Understanding British riots" after the disturbances of 1981. Currently engaged on a survey of the living standards of Londoners – a survey to coincide with the centenary of Booth's survey of 1886.

Mr Randolph Prime: Teaches science at the Norwood Comprehensive School for girls; a specialist in education in urban areas, and has done research into problems in education for people of Afro-Caribbean origin. He was born in Trinidad, where he taught before coming to Britain in 1962. An active member of the Seventh Day Adventist Church, he is a member of the Education Committee and played a part in the setting up of London's first black school, the John Loughborough School in Tottenham. Married with four children, he lives in Crawley, West Sussex.

THE COMPLETE INQUIRY TEAM

Panel Members

LORD GIFFORD Q.C.
RT. REV. BISHOP PHILIP HARVEY OBE
REV. CANON SEBASTIAN CHARLES
DOROTHY KUYA
DR. PAUL CORRIGAN
RANDOLPH PRIME

Counsel to the Inquiry

ANESTA WEEKES

Administrator

HOWARD HANNAH

Office Staff

ROGER BRYAN
SARAH FIDDIAN
CATHY HISLOP
STELLA JOSEPH
DENISE ALDRED

Interviewers

BARBARA McKELLAR
RANA SAKAR

Researchers

TOMMY MOHAJANE
EDWARD OTENG

Press and Publicity
CLIVE STEELE
ANGELA COBBINA
CAROLYN DEMPSTER
PETER LANG
KEN WHALEY

Proof Reader
MARGUERITE DE SOUZA

Middlesex Polytechnic Survey
DR. JOCK YOUNG
TREVOR JONES
JOHN LEA

Consultants
EQUINOX

Computer Technology Consultant
DOUGLAS BAYFORD

Sound Recordist
TONY O'LEARY
(SICOM CONFERENCE SERVICES LTD)

Transcription Service
TAPE TYPING (WEST END)

Stewards
JOHN DAVIS
JON ALEXANDER

Cover Design
EVE BARKER

Photosetting
HIVE PHOTOSETTING

LIST OF ORGANISATIONS WHO MADE WRITTEN SUBMISSIONS

London Borough of Haringey.
Haringey Independent Police Committee.
Broadwater Farm Defence Campaign.
Haringey Trades Council.
Haringey Sports Council.
William C. Harvey School.
Broadwater Farm Junior School.
Broadwater Farm Clergy Group.
Post Office.
Haringey Community Relations Council.
West Indian Standing Conference.
Inquest.
Middlesex Area Probation Service.
Haringey Co-operative Development Agency.
Tottenham Communist Party.

We wrote to a large number of other organisations who did not respond with evidence. We are concerned that in some cases their reason for not responding was a lack of interest in or awareness of the problems which surfaced at Broadwater Farm. We therefore ask every local organisation to study this report and examine whether they can be more involved in future in the issues which have been raised.

CONTENTS

	Page
Terms of reference	(v)
Map of Broadwater Farm	(vi)
Map of Tottenham	(vii)
Biographies of Panel Members	(viii)
The full Inquiry Team	(ix)
List of organisations submitting evidence	(xi)
Contents	(xiii)
List of illustrations	(xvii)
Introduction by Lord Gifford Q.C.	(xix)

PART 1
Chapter 1 The Inquiry Process

Why have an Inquiry?	3
The work of the Inquiry	6
The sub judice question	8
The Inquiry and the police	9

Chapter 2 The Estate and its People

The conflicting views	13
The building of the estate	14
The problems of the 1970s	18
The Youth Association	24

Chapter 3 The Police and the Community

The background of injustice	35
1981 – The chance for a new start	38
The police and the Youth Association	39
A failure of leadership	42
Police on the estate	45
Crime on the estate	49
The police and the council	52
The summer of 1985	56
Rumours of riot – true or false?	61

	Page

Chapter 4 The Death of Mrs Jarrett
Introduction 65
The arrest of Floyd Jarrett 66
The decision to search the house 69
The warrant 70
The search 74
The medical evidence 79
The verdict of the jury 80
The Police Complaints Authority 81
The evening of 5th October 87

Chapter 5 October 6 What Happened?
Reactions to the tragedy 89
The deployment of the police 96
The outbreak 98
The fighting spreads 104
The actions of the crowd 106
The actions of the police 109
"Lakes of petrol" 113
Gun shots and firearms 115
The shops on Tangmere 116
The entry of the police 119
Conclusion 121

Chapter 6 The Aftermath
The first week 123
The arrests and searches 130
Detention and questioning 135
Broadwater Farm since October 1985 142

**Chapter 7 Who lives on Broadwater Farm –
What do they think?** 151
Who lives there? 152
Yearly household income 154
Employment 155
Voting patterns 156
Community organisation 157
Problems on the estate 158
Police accountability 159

	Page
Assisting the police with their inquiries	161
How well do the police perform?	161
What should the police concentrate on?	162
How do residents view police activity?	164
Fairness and the police	165
Policing by consent?	166
The community view of crime	169

PART 2:
Chapter 8 Looking Forward – Justice from the Law

Justice from the Law	189
Why did it happen?	189
Policing in Tottenham	193
A comprehensive training programme	197
A commitment to eradicate oppressive and racist policing	202
Policing Broadwater Farm	206
Consultation and accountability	207
The prevention of disorder	213
Police complaints	214
Police investigations	215
Courts of law	218
Education in legal rights	219

Chapter 9 Looking Forward – Building a Self-reliant Community

Building a Self-reliant Community	221
The role of central government	223
The creation of jobs	225
The estate and its environment	233
Participation in education	237
Media reporting	240
Conclusion	243
WITNESSES	245
INDEX	251

LIST OF ILLUSTRATIONS

	Page
Pensioners lunch on the Farm	175
Princess of Wales visits – 1985	176
Drawing of Prince and Princess of Wales	176
Dawn over the estate	177
Welcome to Broadwater	177
Lord Gifford QC	178
Rev. Phillip Harvey	178
Rev. Canon Charles	178
Dorothy Kuya	179
Dr. Paul Corrigan	179
Randolph Prime	179
Anesta Weekes	179
Sir Kenneth Newman	180
PC Keith Blakelock	180
Opening meeting	181
People shield faces from TV cameras	181
Clasford Sterling	182
Stafford Scott	182
Dolly Kiffin	183
Martha Osamor	183
Cynthia Jarrett	184
Mrs Jarrett's house	184
Riot (1)	185
Riot (2)	185
Councillor Bernie Grant	186
Ernie Large	186

Introduction

INTRODUCTION

This Report was first published on 7th July 1986. We now publish it in a new edition for wider circulation. There has been a demand from many parts of the country to obtain the Report, which rapidly used up the 3,000 copies which were originally printed. Members of the Inquiry panel have been invited to speak at meetings and conferences. There are, we believe, lessons to be learned from Broadwater Farm, about policing, about racism, and about the building of communities, which can be of general value, and fully justify taking the Report to a wider public.

THE IMPACT OF THE REPORT
There was a major response from the media. I gave seven television and five radio interviews in the course of the day. Questioning by the interviewers was serious and in no way hostile. The *Guardian* described the Report as "a document worthy to be set alongside Lord Scarman's report on Brixton"; but the *Times*, in a leader headed 'A Partial Report', considered that it was "unlikely to be helpful" in improving relations between the ethnic communities and the police.

All the national papers gave prominence to the Report (except for the *Sun*, which although it had devoted pages to its own view of Broadwater Farm, allowed only six lines at the bottom of a page to the Report's very different view). Provincial papers in cities throughout Britain printed extensive summaries. The *Economist* and other papers emphasised that the Report's conclusions were underpinned by the objective survey carried out by the Middlesex Polytechnic (see chapter 7). The view of the *Times* was not shared by the head of the Tottenham police, Chief Superintendent Alan Stainsby, who ordered 50 copies of the Report for his officers to read, and wrote to me a letter which is worth quoting in full:–

"I have now had the opportunity to read your report into the disturbances of October 1985 at the Broadwater Farm Estate.

You will appreciate that I cannot comment about your description of the events which led to the disorder, the manner in which it was resolved or the police enquiry which followed.

We are proud of our record with regard to the education and training of our officers, our commitment at all levels to eradicate oppressive and racist policing and the steps we have taken to provide effective consultation. I look forward to further advances in these areas which you correctly identify as the 'three principal ingredients' to make co-operative policing a reality.

This being said, I view the report as a valuable contribution to police/community relations in Tottenham and, in particular, the

THE BROADWATER FARM INQUIRY REPORT

part it will play in stimulating dialogue between the local authority and ourselves."

The Government also appeared to take the Report seriously. Speaking in Parliament on 11th July 1986, Mr Giles Shaw, Minister of State at the Home Office, said:
"I understand that Lord Gifford's report raises several important issues. One of them involves Haringey council's participation in the consultative group. Lord Gifford agrees with the council's claim that at present the group is insufficiently representative but said that its boycott is misguided. However, I shall invite Lord Gifford to see me to discuss the report, as I recognise that there are issues that we should discuss."

The meeting, which took place on August 13th, was serious and constructive, with no attempt made by the Minister to discredit or even criticise the Report. Lord Scarman was reported as endorsing the main points of the Report, while appearing to express reservations about its style. He said:–
"Stripped of some of its rhetoric, it is saying very much the same as the Brixton report five years ago. Many of its proposals are no more than a repeat of the proposals you will find in the Brixton report."

In summary, there was a recognition by many in authority that there were serious grievances about the policing of the Black community in Tottenham which had to be put right. The labelling of Broadwater Farm as a criminal community seemed to have been effectively stopped.

THE COMMISSIONER'S REVIEW
The Report came out five days after the Commissioner of Police, Sir Kenneth Newman, had published his own account of the disturbances, entitled "Public Order Review – Civil Disturbances 1981–1985". Its 27 pages, plus appendices, claimed to be the result of "an extensive and thorough review" of the Brixton and Tottenham events.
Half of the eight-page chapter on Tottenham is taken up with a "history" of Broadwater Farm, of which these are some extracts:–
"By the autumn of 1980 . . . the estate saw an increase in the proportion of households comprising those from the 'New Commonwealth' and young single parents. A brittle relationship

INTRODUCTION

developed between some of the white, predominantly elderly tenants, and some of the newer residents."

"In 1981 the tenants' association on the estate asked the police to open a police office to help combat the rising crime rate and to reduce the anxiety felt by many residents about their safety. This move was not altogether welcomed by young Black residents, and was seen by them as constituting an oppressive presence on the estate. Consultation and discussion to counter this perceived threat did little to allay the animosity and fear felt by Black youths."

"It would be difficult to define 'normality' in respect of Broadwater Farm. It has an unenviable reputation and normal policing methods are resisted by a vociferous ill-disposed minority. Gratuitous abuse and violence towards the police became an almost daily occurrence during periods of tension. The throwing of bricks, bottles, beer barrels and lumps of concrete became so frequent that police officers had to be as concerned for their own safety as for their general policing responsibilities."

The first of these quotations makes an implicitly racist suggestion that elderly white people were entitlted to be uneasy about the arrival of Black tenants. But having said that, the Commissioner made no mention in the review of the outings and meals provided to pensioners, nor to any of the achievements of the Broadwater Farm community which we describe in chapter 2. Then in the second quotation it is suggested that young Black people were blocking a move to combat crime out of an unreasonable "animosity and fear" which the police tried in vain to allay through "consultation and discussion". It is not recorded that the police themselves never wanted a police office on the estate (see paragraph 2.32); nor is there the slightest recognition that the misconduct of police officers might have in any way been a contributing factor to the attitudes of Black youths, as we demonstrate in Chapter 3.

The third quotation, which repeats the words used by Deputy Assistant Commissioner Richards in his earlier Report, is intended to put the definitive label on Broadwater Farm. Our analysis of the history in chapter 3, which deals with incidents of misbehaviour both by police officers and by residents of the estate, demonstrates how grossly distorted is the picture conveyed by these words.

In his treatment of the disturbances themselves, covering 1¼ pages, the Commissioner repeated much of what had been written by

THE BROADWATER FARM INQUIRY REPORT

D.A.C. Richards, with two notable changes. First, the Commissioner did not suggest that barricades of blazing vehicles were erected at the entrances to the estate *before* the police arrived on the scene (see paragraphs 5.32–5.41 for this allegation and our analysis of it). The erection of these "barricades" had been claimed by D.A.C. Richards as being proof of a pre-arranged plan. But if, as several witnesses told us, the cars were set on fire *after* police in riot gear were deployed, then it is more likely that such action was taken as a spontaneous response to the police surrounding the estate.

Secondly, the Review did not repeat D.A.C. Richards' allegation that basement garages had been flooded with "lakes of petrol", to be set alight if the police moved in. But as we show in paragraphs 5.61–5.63, D.A.C. Richards had himself resiled from this allegation.

The Commissioner's Review contained nothing which made us want to change the conclusions made in our Report. It did however greatly reinforce our belief that the independent Inquiry which we conducted was thoroughly necessary. It would have been a scandal if the Commissioner's Review had stood uncorrected as the official view of Broadwater Farm.

THE VIEW OF THE COMMUNITY
People living on Broadwater Farm have been generous in their praise for the Report. Clasford Sterling, Vice-President of the Youth Association, has said to me that for him the Report records a history which needed to be written, a history which portrays the community truthfully with its strengths and its faults. He said that the past had been set straight; it was now up to the people of the Farm to build the future. Others, while paying tribute to the work done, remained sceptical whether it would change anything. How can a Report, they said, do anything to alter the mentality of racist police officers? It is a fair question to ask, especially after the London programme on Thames TV on 11th July 1986, in which officers in the Broadwater Farm were saying openly that some among them wanted victory next time.

Before attempting to answer the question, I would like to describe an incident which took place on August 12th 1986, for it demonstrates both the seriousness of the present situation and the possibility of improving it. The account given below was later accepted by police officers as being broadly correct, with certain areas of dispute which I mention.

On August 11th a party of young people had arrived from Clarendon, Jamaica. It was the return visit following the trip made by

INTRODUCTION

Broadwater Farm youths in 1985. Clarendon had been devastated by the recent floods, and the Youth Association were organising a number of functions both to raise funds and to welcome the visitors.

There was therefore a lot of extra activity around the Tangmere precinct on August 12th, and the home beat officers appeared to be unusually curious, standing about and staring at the groups of people on the precinct.

The officer in charge was Sergeant Palmer, who was deputising for Inspector Hudson who was on holiday. During the afternoon it seems that he had received a report that two of his officers had passed a group of people and smelled a smell of cannabis. They had taken no action, but claimed to have identified one of the group as a member of the Jamaican party.

Sergeant Palmer decided to take action. Half an hour after the alleged smelling, he went onto the precinct with a number of officers, with a reserve squad of police from another division in the background. Several plain clothes officers were also seen about the area.

Sergeant Palmer went up to a group of men outside the Youth Association and said that he wanted to search one of them for drugs. Stafford Scott tried to intervene, saying that the man (a Broadwater Farm resident) had been inside the building with him, and there must be a mistake. He asked Sergeant Palmer, whom he knew, to explain matters to him as a youth worker. Sergeant Palmer pushed him aside, then grabbed him by the shirt front and said, "You're nicked". Sergeant Palmer then drew his truncheon.

A struggle followed, with people trying to pull Stafford Scott back into the Youth Association building. Other officers were said to have drawn truncheons, but this was denied by the police. A bottle of Guinness was thrown from the Youth Association, spilling over some of the officers. Stafford Scott was cut on the back of the head. He did not know what had hit him; the police say firmly that it was the bottle, but other witnesses said it was a truncheon.

There was then a serious danger of a major eruption. A police helicopter was flying overhead, and tensions were high. The officers on the precinct withdrew, without making any arrests, but people remained angry at what had happened and fearful that a stronger force might return.

Dolly Kiffin was particularly incensed that it was being suggested that one of the Jamaicans may have been smoking cannabis. She feared that rumour would be spread that her guests were involved with drugs. She telephoned to councillors and community leaders, and to me. When I arrived, Dudley Dryden of the West Indian

THE BROADWATER FARM INQUIRY REPORT

Standing Conference was talking on the telephone to Superintendent Sinclair, who was in charge at Tottenham while Chief Superintendent Stainsby was on holiday. Superintendent Sinclair agreed to come down to the estate himself.

For the next two hours there followed a meeting involving Superintendent Sinclair and his colleagues, including Chief Inspector Horne, the new Community Liaison Officer; two of the home beat officers; the deputy leader of the council, Councillor Steve King, with several other councillors; Dolly Kiffin, Stafford Scott and his parents, and other Youth Association staff and members; representatives of the Standing Conference; community workers and other council officers; and myself. Accounts of the incident were given and disputed on both sides. Assurances were sought, and given, that the incident was not pre-planned by the police. Fears were expressed as to what would happen next.

What emerged from the discussion was that Sergeant Palmer should never have provoked the incident in the first place, and certainly had no cause to draw his truncheon – as was confirmed at the meeting by one of the home beat officers who had felt obliged to restrain him. On being pressed as to what he would do, Superintendent Sinclair agreed that there was a serious matter to be investigated, that he would consider it at once, and that, although he could not announce the outcome in advance, the community "would not be dissatisfied" with the investigation.

Appeals were made to the police to keep a low profile during the visit of the youths, and to let people enjoy themselves without interference. The police in turn appealed for people to be calm and not let the incident get out of proportion. By the end of the meeting the atmosphere was much more relaxed. In the following days I attended two functions on the estate, and noticed that the police patrol was keeping very much in the background.

On the negative side the incident shows that there are officers around who are happy to call in reinforcements and risk a major confrontation on Broadwater Farm on the most spurious of pretexts. The danger of a further provocation must always be there.

But there are positive sides of the episode to be emphasised. It had echoes of the night of 1st November 1982, when another man was arrested for a reason which people believed to be false. Then a bitter chain reaction was set in motion – arrest, protest, assaults on the protestors, further arrests, assaults on the police the next day, riot police on the estate (see paragraphs 3.26–3.29). Now the matter was handled differently. First the senior officer in the Division was prepared to come at once to meet with the community. Secondly, a junior officer had the courage to speak out and criticise the conduct

INTRODUCTION

of his superior. Thirdly, effective assurances were given; a police investigation is still in progress, and the officer who was criticised is no longer on the estate team. There was, in short, a real dialogue in which both police and community were ready to participate.

A chance for dialogue at another level will come next month, since the Commissioner of Police has accepted an invitation to visit the Youth Association. After all that he has written, one may comment that it is not before time. Even so, it may be another sign of a readiness to listen and learn.

If there turns out to be an enduring shift in attitude – and it is still too early to say – then the Inquiry will have played a role. The incident of Broadwater Farm took place a day before my meeting with Mr Giles Shaw MP at the Home Office. Superintendent Sinclair had been aware that this appointment had been made, and he reported on the incident to the Minister before my meeting. Here was, perhaps, an element of accountability in practice.

THE MESSAGE OF THE REPORT

The main thrust of our proposals for police-public relations in chapter 8 was contained in our call for co-operative policing, which we defined as a policing strategy by which the police at all levels co-operate, on a basis of mutual respect and equality, with those various agencies which represent the community, in order to deter and detect those crimes which the community believe to be priority evils. We said that this could be brought about by an intensive training programme for police officers of all ranks; by a commitment from the top leadership of the police service downwards to eradicate racist and oppressive policing; and by an effective system of consultation and accountability. Under the present law, any hope of real local police accountability must depend on the effective operation of the police/community consultative process. We describe in paragraphs 8.40–8.51 how serious has been the failure of the present Community and Police Consultative Group in Haringey. We appealed to the Group to withdraw its ultimatum to the Council (paragraph 8.51) and it did so. We appealed to the Council and to the Group to re-think their position, and in response the Council has resolved to meet the Group "to insist that it meet the Inquiry's concerns about its unrepresentativeness and lack of anti-racist commitment".

The future of the Consultative Group still gives great cause for anxiety. It was interesting that in our meeting with him, the Minister stressed the flexibility of the consultative arrangements. He mentioned that in Southwark a system of proportional representation had been worked out – an idea which could well be

THE BROADWATER FARM INQUIRY REPORT

applied to Haringey so as to avoid the present dominance of neighbourhood watch scheme representatives. For example, 50 neighbourhood watch schemes may represent less people than 10 ethnic minority organisations, but under the present constitution of the Group every one of them has an equal vote. A new voting system could be the way out of the impasse.

THE COUNCIL'S RESPONSE

The Council accepted the Inquiry's comments, including the criticisms of several Council services, as "a basis for action", and resolved that these would be fully considered by appropriate Committees at their next meetings, and detailed proposals drawn up for implementation of the Inquiry's recommendations, subject to the principle of full consultation, involvement and control by the community. It specifically endorsed the urgent need for a new comprehensive community centre for Broadwater Farm and the surrounding neighbourhood. At the Council meeting at which we presented the Report, there were some allegations by Conservative members that we had been one-sided, but many aspects of the Report were accepted by them also.

Finally, the Council invited the Inquiry "to review progress in police/community consultation and the Council's response to its criticisms, and to report further in 12 months". In reply to this, we have said that we did not think it right that we should remain in being as a continuing body, but we have agreed to re-convene the Panel next summer. Subject to what may have happened meanwhile, we will ask all interested parties to comment on the Report and on what has been done since, and hold a limited number of public hearings. We have in particular asked that the Police should participate in such a review.

THE FACTOR OF RACISM

As well as the many favourable reactions to the Report there were letters from the public which were overwhelmingly hostile. The hate mail which we received was revelation of the dark and unreasoning elements of race hatred which persist in our society. Much of it was so unpleasant as to be unprintable, but a flavour can be gained from these extracts:

> "can you wonder that the public wants to abolish the House of Lords if theres a lot of STINKERS LIKE YOU AND SCARMAN seems to me you and Scarman must have mixed blood (no Im not a Rascist)"

INTRODUCTION

"You, have never worked with them, or lived near them, you do not know, what life is all about. The likes of you, are Traitors, and have sold us, and our Country, out, to Blacks. You do not believe in Honesty, truth, or FAIR PLAY."

"Cowson's like you who condem the Police Force is nothing but a traitor to Britain. To think we lived in peace and solely relied on them until the blacks came and needed control. While we have so called people like you in office life is hell when you sympathise with the blacks. This country will never be the same and will get worse thanks to your type."

"You dirty cowardly homosexual looking filthy bastard I am getting on a bit but I am going to find out your private address and give you a dam good hiding."

"The whole world needs a nuclear war and the sooner the better. It is so polluted and I see no remedy for it. The religious leaders are a disgrace and even some of them are homosexuals."

For every one who wrote there must have been hundreds who thought the same, and some of them would be in the police service. The prejudices which they expressed have been fanned, as we show in chapter 9, by racially distorted reporting in many parts of the British press.

THE FUTURE
As we say in the concluding paragraph of the Report, we were privileged to have taken part in the Inquiry and we have a belief that there are people of courage and good will who can build unity where is now bitter division. It will need the participation of many agencies: the resources of central government; the commitment of local government departments; the constructive energy of people in the community; and above all, co-operative behaviour between the police and the public.

The future of Britain as a multi-ethnic society depends on these aims being achieved, both in Broadwater Farm and elsewhere. The events of October 1985 show that when co-operation breaks down, the consequences are appalling: the loss of human life, the alienation of people from each other, and the overriding of basic human rights that a democracy is intended to protect. We can and we must learn why such consequences occur, and act to prevent them from ever occurring again.

Tony Gifford
September 1986

Part 1

Chapter 1
THE INQUIRY PROCESS

WHY HAVE AN INQUIRY?
1.1 On 5th October 1985, four Tottenham police officers entered the home of a Black woman, Mrs Cynthia Jarrett, and searched it. During the course of the search Mrs Jarrett collapsed, and soon after she died. On the following afternoon a demonstration outside Tottenham police station passed off without any serious incident. But during the evening and night of 6th October, a violent disturbance took place at the Broadwater Farm Estate, Tottenham. A police officer, PC Keith Blakelock, was killed. Several buildings were set on fire, as well as many motor vehicles. Guns were alleged to have been fired at the police. Officers armed with plastic bullets and CS gas were deployed but not used. In a television interview, the senior officer for the North London area, Deputy Assistant Commissioner Richards, claimed that the disturbances were "the most ferocious, the most vicious riots ever seen on the mainland". In the weeks and months following 6th October, police officers remained on the estate in considerable numbers, and raids were carried out by large squads of police upon dozens of homes.

1.2 The disturbances were the third to have happened in the space of a month. On the night of 9th/10th September 1985 two men had died in a Post Office which had been burned in the course of disturbances which stretched over two days in the Handsworth and Lozells districts of Birmingham. The local authorities for that area acted swiftly to investigate the causes of the disturbances. Following the refusal of the Home Secretary to set up a public inquiry, the Birmingham City Council set up an independent public inquiry under the chairmanship of a barrister. The West Midlands police force participated in that inquiry. The Race Relations and Equal Opportunities Committee of the West Midlands County Council sponsored a review panel to establish the nature and extent of legitimate grievances of the Black community, and to make recommendations for urgent action. Both of these inquiries published their reports in the early months of 1986.

1.3 On 28th September 1985, Mrs Cherry Groce, another Black woman, had been shot and paralysed inside her home in Brixton by a police officer carrying out a raid. Disturbances broke out on the streets of Brixton over the following day. A police officer was suspended and later charged, and awaits trial on a charge of causing grievous bodily harm to Mrs Groce with intent.

1.4 On 14th October 1985 the council of the London Borough of Haringey called for "a thoroughly independent public inquiry into the death of Mrs Jarrett and subsequent events and into the break down in police/community relations in Tottenham". The council resolved that if there was not an adequate Government response, it would set up its own independent public inquiry. The Home Secretary again decided not to exercise his powers under the Police Act 1964 to set up a public inquiry. In a letter to Haringey's chief executive, the Home Office referred to Lord Scarman's inquiry, and said:—

> "The Home Secretary does not believe that a rerun of such an inquiry would be likely to cast a new perspective on the situation: The broader issues raised by the disorders continue to be the subject of widespread public debate and in the Home Secretary's view there are no grounds for believing that there are radical new solutions waiting for an inquiry to uncover."

The Home Office claimed also that a public inquiry would cut across the investigation of the Police Complaints Authority into the death of Mrs Jarrett.

1.5 There then followed a delay of several months while the council tried to find a person who would be willing to be chair of the independent inquiry which they wished to set up. Mr Mark Bonham–Carter said publicly that he would not serve as chair because the Commissioner had indicated that the police would not participate. In our view this was not a good reason; the issues raised by the disturbances and the grievances which were being voiced demanded urgent investigation. But the delay was unfortunate — by the time we began our work, memories had faded and some of the impact which the Inquiry could have had was lost.

THE INQUIRY PROCESS

1.6 In early February 1986, Lord Gifford QC was asked to take on the chairmanship of the Inquiry and accepted. Some of the other members of the panel had already been approached; others were invited by the chair himself. The aim was to bring together a broad based panel of people who had personal and professional experience of the issues which the Inquiry would have to confront. From the outset the Inquiry Panel asserted its independence; we did not, for instance, accept the terms of reference drafted by the council, but drew up our own terms of reference to enable us to conduct a wide-ranging inquiry into the underlying causes of the disturbances. The qualifications of the members of the panel and the terms of reference of the Inquiry are given in the preface to this report. The council approved the appointment of the chair and four members of the Inquiry Panel, and its terms of reference, on 18th February 1986. The membership of the Inquiry Panel was finally completed with the appointment of Mr Randolph Prime at the end of February.

1.7 At a well-attended opening meeting on 21st February 1986, the chair explained why the members of the panel had agreed to take part:—

"Why have we taken on this task? Because we believe that an inquiry is needed. We believe that you in this community want an independent and fair inquiry. Your presence here indicates that this is so.

"People do not attack the forces of the law out of mere wickedness or a sense of fun. As Lord Scarman said only last week in a televised broadcast, 'Public disorder usually arises out of a sense of injustice.' There are causes to these events going back over many years. They must be recorded and made known.

"When there is conflict in society it is always the powerful institutions which find it easy to put out a version of the events which — even if it is only based on hearsay — is reported by the mass media as if there were no other truth.

"Those without power have no such voice. Our task is to listen to the powerless as well as the powerful. To listen to the ordinary people of this community and the organisations which represent them. And having listened to everyone, to produce recommendations which can be used to bring about change."

1.8 In the particular context of the Broadwater Farm, there was a need to provide a channel for the grievances and complaints of the local community, and to investigate a number of disputed issues. There was bitter dispute about the circumstances of the death of Mrs Jarrett, and a widespread distrust of the Police Complaints Authority, which was then investigating the conduct of the officers who entered her house. There was bitter dispute about the way in which the disturbances broke out, with accusations of deliberate planning and provocation on both sides. And beyond all that, there was bitter dispute about the record and the reputation of a whole community. As we shall show, a large section of the police and mass media saw the Broadwater Farm as a centre of well organised criminality. To many others in authority, both in central and local government, Broadwater Farm was a showpiece, a model of what a responsible and hard working community could do to better the conditions of all its members.

1.9 The Inquiry set itself four objectives:—
(1) To seek out evidence in the most thorough way possible and from the widest possible range of opinions;
(2) To reflect that evidence objectively and impartially in our report;
(3) To make an independent and logical analysis of that evidence;
(4) To make sensible proposals for the future which can be studied by those who have responsibilities to bear for the welfare of the community.

THE WORK OF THE INQUIRY

1.10 At the outset of the Inquiry, during the opening session on 21st February, we became vividly aware of a cloud of fear which hung over Broadwater Farm. Some who attended sat far away at the back of a gallery. Others shielded their heads when a television crew tried to film the audience. Many more, we were told, would stay away and not come forward. During our first full hearing we asked Floyd Jarrett how we could approach such people. He replied:—
> "I can't really see a solution because you see they have become so frightened that they don't know who to trust in the system."

Joanne George, social service community worker at Broadwater Farm said:—
> "I think people are still afraid to talk to anybody, because they fear being arrested. Even though the Inquiry has explained about confidentiality, they just feel that they can't risk doing that. And unfortunately it is probably those people who know more about

THE INQUIRY PROCESS

what happened on 6th October than any of us who are free to come and talk here."

To us, this climate of fear was itself a matter of intense concern. It is deeply disturbing if people not only have strong grievances, but dare not speak out about them.

1.11. To secure our first objective, we went far beyond the normal inquiry process whereby any interested person or organisation was invited to put in written submissions and give evidence at public hearings. We turned the Inquiry into an active process. Members of the Inquiry Panel themselves, as well as the Inquiry staff, knocked on doors, held interviews, and attended meetings in the community. We published two newsletters, which were distributed throughout the Broadwater Farm Estate and neighbouring streets. At the public hearings, we encouraged participation by members of the public. In all these ways, we reached out into the community. We could not remove the cloud of fear, but by treating people's fears as being serious and reasonable, we believe we obtained far more information than a formal "judicial" inquiry would have done.

1.12 The statistics of our work show that we invited evidence from 116 organisations, and from all members of the Haringey Council. We held 22 public hearings, at which we heard a total of 77 witnesses. We held recorded interviews with 80 people. At meetings and visits to the estate, we listened to many more who wished to speak without fear of being identified. We were also aware of the danger of relying solely on the views of those who chose to come forward. Since it was apparent that people living in a number of the Broadwater Farm blocks would have had a clear view of the disturbances, we called on 178 homes and received a number of accounts of what people had seen. We believe we were able in this way to build up an objective picture of what took place.

1.13 We were aware also that there were disputed views about who represented the "community" of Broadwater Farm. While there were organisations which the council accepted as being representative, others, including the police, appeared to dispute that they were. Deputy Assistant Commissioner Richards in his report on the disturbances (the Richards report) spoke of normal policing methods being resisted by "a vociferous minority".

1.14 We wanted as far as possible to ascertain objectively who were "the community" on Broadwater Farm and what they thought about the key issues before the Inquiry — the police, crime, the estate, the Youth Association. We therefore commissioned a survey to be carried out by a team from Middlesex Polytechnic, headed by Dr. Jock Young. The survey drew a large sample of 700 adults out of a total of about 1800 adults on the estate. We asked for people's co-operation in responding to the survey, and got it — the response rate was 75.2%, which is far higher than other surveys in similar areas. The results are analysed in Chapter 7 of the report.

1.15 The Inquiry also undertook or commissioned three further pieces of research: —
(1) Members of the Inquiry and staff carried out a study of the treatment by the media of the Broadwater Farm Estate and of "riots" in general.
(2) The Inquiry employed its own research worker to make a independent evaluation of Haringey's economic and social conditions, and the policies of the council in relevant areas.
(3) The Inquiry commissioned the consultancy firm, Equinox, to consider initiatives aimed at assisting in the economic development of the Broadwater Farm area in the field of small businesses and co-operatives.

This research provided material which we use in making our proposals in Chapter 9 of the report.

1.16 By gathering evidence in these forms, we believe that we have obtained as full a picture as was possible in the time available. We have only been able to achieve this through the strenuous and devoted work of the staff of the Inquiry, the interviewers, transcribers and researchers, and more important still, through the co-operation of the hundreds of people who gave time to speak to us.

THE SUB JUDICE QUESTION
1.17 The days from 5th to 7th of October saw two tragic deaths, those of Cynthia Jarrett and Keith Blakelock. Both had been greatly loved and admired. Their deaths, and the need to prevent such tragedies from recurring, were in our minds continually and underlined the seriousness of the Inquiry. In the case of Mrs Cynthia Jarrett, the inquest into her death has been concluded, and we have been free to comment on the evidence given and the verdict recorded.

THE INQUIRY PROCESS

Regrettably, we cannot deal with the circumstances surrounding the death of PC Keith Blakelock. A number of people are awaiting trial for his murder. It would be unlawful to discuss, even in general terms, how he was killed and who was to blame.

1.18 However, PC Blakelock had died in a place removed from the main areas of action, following a particular incident of which most people involved in the disturbances would have been unaware. The pending proceedings do not preclude a discussion of all the other issues relating to the outbreak of the disturbances and the course they took.

1.19 By the end of May 1986, 162 people had been charged with offences alleged to have been committed on 6th October. 13 people have now been charged with riotous assembly, of whom six are also charged with murder. 56 are charged with affray, some of whom face other counts of burglary, throwing petrol bombs, and of manufacturing petrol bombs. Most of the others were charged with lesser offences such as threatening behaviour and burglary. Only three of the riot or affray cases have been dealt with by the court. We mention in Chapters 5 and 6 that these trials also prevent us from expressing a conclusive view on the legality of certain actions and on certain aspects of the police investigation after the 6th October.

THE INQUIRY AND THE POLICE

1.20 From the outset we made it clear that we wanted to have the full participation of the Metropolitan Police in the Inquiry. Even before his appointment became public, Lord Gifford asked for an informal meeting with D.A.C. Richards, in order to assure him of the independence and serious purpose of the Inquiry. This request was not accepted. On 20th February 1986, Lord Gifford wrote to the Commissioner, Sir Kenneth Newman:—

> "I am most anxious that the police view should be fully put to the Inquiry, particularly on the general questions which are certain to arise about police/community relations. I would wish to be entirely flexible in the way in which that view should be made known. I understand that it may not be appropriate for the police to be officially represented in the public sessions of the Inquiry — though we would welcome such representation if it were desired. I hope, however, that you and Mr Richards will leave the door open for

other forms of communication with us, whether written or oral, public or private."

1.21 On 26th February, the Commissioner wrote giving three reasons for declining to give evidence to the Inquiry: —
(1) He referred to the inquiries which were already taking place, namely the inquest into Mrs Jarrett's death; the report of D.A.C. Richards; the investigation of the Police Complaints Authority; and the internal review undertaken by the Metropolitan Police. He said that "a further inquiry would be likely to add little to those already undertaken".
(2) "The statutory procedures for accountability laid down for the Metropolitan Police are to the Home Secretary and the borough consultative groups. Your inquiry cuts across those lines of accountability."
(3) He referred to the pending criminal proceedings which he claimed would be "an effective barrier to investigations under some of your terms of reference."
The Commissioner ended that "in all the circumstances, I am not persuaded that any useful purpose would be served by our meeting."

1.22 On 4th March, Lord Gifford replied to these three points: —
(1) "The inquiries which you mention are all limited in scope. Those which are independent of the police, are limited to the circumstances of Mrs Jarrett's death. The report to the Consultative Group (The Richards report) has aroused considerable controversy and cannot be regarded as presenting the full account of the causes of the disturbances. The internal review concerns policing procedures rather than the underlying causes of disorder. I am convinced that it is right to probe further.
(2) We do not set ourselves up as a body to which the police should be accountable. Rather we are a group of concerned citizens, seeking to discover the truth as best we can, and to make recommendations which might prevent a recurrence of the tragic events of last October.
(3) We accept that there are limitations imposed by the sub judice rules. But there are considerable and important areas of the Inquiry which do not require findings to be made about specific sub judice incidents."
Lord Gifford concluded by asking the Commissioner not to close his mind to the possibility of an exchange of views at some stage, if there

were developments in the Inquiry which made it reasonable to approach him again.

1.23 On 6th May, after we had heard ten days of evidence, Lord Gifford wrote again asking for the view of the Metropolitan Police on key questions which had by then emerged. The questions were put under ten headings: —
(1) Police co-operation with the Broadwater Farm Estate.
(2) Police intelligence about Broadwater Farm.
(3) Drug trafficking in September, 1985.
(4) Police deployment around 7.00 p.m. on 6th October 1985.
(5) Police tactics during the disturbances.
(6) Methods of making arrests.
(7) Levels of policing.
(8) Racist behaviour by police officers.
(9) Police training.
(10) The future.
Lord Gifford concluded: —
"I urge you to respond as fully as possible to these questions. It would seem to me that your reasons for not wishing the police to participate in our Inquiry would not preclude you from commenting on these important issues over which my colleagues and I — both as an Inquiry Panel and as London residents — are deeply concerned."

1.24 Sir Kenneth Newman's reply on 28th May was brief: —
"Thank you for your letter of 6th May 1986, the contents of which have been noted.
"My letter of 26th February set out the reasons in declining to give evidence to your Inquiry into the Broadwater Farm disorders. Nothing has occurred since which leads me to alter that reasoning, and your letter contains nothing which causes me to reconsider that decision."

1.25 We deeply regret the decision of the Commissioner and find his reasons to be unconvincing. Because of the position which he took, it was difficult for a number of police officers whom we knew to be anxious to talk to us, to do so openly. However we have not been short of material from which we can discover the views of police officers about issues relevant to our Inquiry. The Richards report is clearly intended to be the definitive statement of the police command about the disturbances and their causes. Very different perspectives from junior officers have been expressed in numerous articles and letters in the *Police Review*, the *Police* magazine and *The Job*. The accounts given by the officers who searched Mrs Jarrett's home are available to us from their evidence to the inquest. Finally, we have been able to have a number of informal personal conversations with police officers of different ranks.

Chapter 2
THE ESTATE AND ITS PEOPLE

THE CONFLICTING VIEWS.
2.1 One of the most remarkable features of this Inquiry has been the extraordinary conflict of opinion about the estate itself and its community organisations. In the view of most witnesses from the estate and from the local authority, the estate had realised enormous achievements, benefitting young and old alike, principally because of the hard work and caring approach of the organisers of the Broadwater Farm Youth Association. Their achievement had been recognised by the personal support of Sir George Young, Minister of State at the Department of the Environment, and by the visit of the Princess of Wales in February 1985.

Tricia Zipfel, consultant to the Department of the Environment summed up this view:—

"For the community to have achieved what they have achieved, over four years of hard, hard work, is highly significant and gives enormous hope to other people. We have brought tenants from all over Britain to look at Broadwater and talk to the Youth Association. I do not feel I would be honest if I undersold the achievement of what has happened there."

2.2 But a negative and condemnatory view has also been expressed. As we shall see, it has come from sections of the press and from people living in streets near the estate who rarely go there. It is also the view of a great many police officers, who, while recognising that a point of view of the estate existed, claimed that it was entirely false. As the leading article in *Police*, the monthly magazine of the Police Federation, put it in November 1985:—

"The official picture of Broadwater Farm Estate as a beehive of flourishing rehabilitation and positive community involvement, which was fostered by skilful propaganda from the Department of the Environment and Haringey Council (and swallowed by TV and

THE BROADWATER FARM INQUIRY REPORT

the press) cloaked the ugly reality of criminal gangs ruling the estate, robbing and terrorising the inhabitants, and making daily war on any police officers who dared to venture near."

D.A.C. Richards, the officer in charge of Number 1 area, which includes Haringey, shared the view of the rank and file:—

"The estate has earned an unenviable reputation over recent years as one where normal policing methods are resisted by a vociferous minority and where unprovoked attacks on police are all too common."

2.3   We have no doubt that these conflicting perceptions of the estate were of central importance in the build up to the disturbances, and that they continue to have a divisive and dangerous effect on police/community relations. It has therefore become central to our Inquiry to trace the history of the Broadwater Farm Estate and its community, to assess how such extreme and opposite views have come to be formed.

THE BUILDING OF THE ESTATE

2.4   Broadwater Farm was built on open land which had been used for allotments. Local residents were angry at the plan, and hired a lawyer to fight against it. Running through the site was the Moselle river, which flooded at times of heavy rainfall — one of the reasons for building the blocks on stilts above ground level. Another reason was the stipulation by the council that there should be car parking for one car for every flat, plus a further 10% for visitors. Since the council also required a high density development, car parking could be provided at ground level with the blocks interconnected with walkways.

2.5   In 1965, when the brief was given to the Borough Architect, the new Labour Government was encouraging local authorities to achieve a target of one thousand new units a year. Scandinavian industrialised building schemes were in fashion. The contract for Broadwater Farm was won by Taylor Woodrow using the Larsen-Neilson method of system building. One consequence of using such systems is that the design of the estate is largely taken out of the hands of the council's architects. The head of the team of architects at the time was Salem El-Doori, who said:—

"Once the contractor is nominated and selected they have the ultimate say, because they are guaranteeing the constuction, it is

THE ESTATE AND ITS PEOPLE

their system, it is their patent. You are aware that a great deal of the control is being taken out of your hands. But for local authorities such systems were very attractive because of the speed of building, economy of resources, and the difficulty of finding skilled building labour."

2.6 Contrary to widespread belief, the estate did not receive any architectural award. But it was built with the highest hopes. In the words of Roy Limb, Haringey's Chief Executive: —
"The chair of Planning in those days thought Broadwater Farm would be an everlasting memorial to him and his committee — that was a genuine belief. I have talked to him about it since then. What they were trying to do seemed the right thing at the time."

Most of the new residents were rehoused from slum clearance schemes. But 34 flats were made available to the ordinary waiting list, and lots were drawn to choose the people whom the local press described as "the lucky 34 who will be given tenancy of brand new flats in the Broadwater Farm Estate."

2.7 Construction started in the middle of 1967 but was held up for a time in 1968 after the Ronan Point disaster. Flats became available in successive blocks as they were completed, with the last block finished in February 1973.

The reactions of the early inhabitants were enthusiastic. As Ernie Large, chair of Housing until 1968, explained: —
"What we were doing was clearing slums in South Tottenham and other parts of the borough, so that people who actually went into the Broadwater flats originally found them palaces compared with what they were living in previously i.e. back to back slums."

2.8 The quality of the flats themselves has been stressed by many witnesses. They were spacious, peaceful, and above all warm. Sheila Ramdin, now chair of the Residents' Association, said: —
"I love this flat. There is no way I would go when this flat is so hot. You don't have to wear no jumper or no socks or anything in doors. You can just go about in your T–shirt. That's how warm these flats are."

Dolly Kiffin, founder of the Youth Association, described her feelings when she moved in: —
"There was a lot of peace there. The front room was quite big, and it was so warm for the kids. You did not have to bother with

heaters like paraffin heaters. It was all nice and clean. And especially at night when you sit on the patio and look all over, it's a beautiful sight."

2.9 When finally completed in February 1973, the Broadwater Farm Estate contained 1063 properties in 12 blocks, each of them built off the ground and connected by raised walkways. Ten of the blocks are low rise, having four or six storeys. Two (Northolt and Kenley) are high rise blocks of 18 storeys. The central block, Tangmere, was built in the form of a ziggurat, consisting of flats with balconies surrounding a shopping precinct. The estate also includes a small group of two storey houses on the higher ground close to The Avenue; otherwise the accommodation was in flats and maisonettes of one, two, and three bedrooms. The housing was built over 21 acres of land at a density of approximately 140 persons per acre.

2.10 What was lacking were the essentials for making the estate into a living community for over 3000 people. The original design provided for shops, pub, a launderette, and a doctor's and dentist's surgery. Only the shops survived. As Mr Murray of the council's Building Design Services explained:—
"What happens when tenders come in, is that the tenders are always high, things are cut out, and what is cut out is thought to be the froth or the icing on the cake. And these will always be things like pubs and community centres."
As a member of the panel observed, and Mr Murray agreed: "What we know now is that they are not the icing on the cake. They are the fruit itself."

2.11 In an unattractive location under one of the walkways on Willan Road, a small clubroom was built for the Tenants' Association. It was not part of the original design. The club cost £16,000 to build, and the council's decision in December 1972 to spend £8,000 in a grant to the Tenants' Association to fit it out as a bar was strongly opposed by the opposition party. **"DOWN THE HATCH – IT'S ON THE RATES"** was the headline in the local paper. For years the club was the only facility on the estate. It was used as a lunch club for pensioners and in the evening as a bar. We will return to consider the role which it played in the community.

2.12 The estate not only lacked amenities but was cut off from the

THE ESTATE AND ITS PEOPLE

surrounding areas. Transport facilities were poor; the walk to the buses in Lordship Lane was inconvenient, particularly for older people. Attempts were made by the council as early as 1972 to persuade London Transport to run a bus service through the estate. But to this day no such service exists.

2.13 On the edge of the estate were built the Broadwater Farm Infants and Junior Schools, which conveniently served the families on the estate. (For secondary schooling, children go to almost all of the ten schools in Haringey). But in addition there were three buildings, constructed close to the estate which had no relationship to it; the William C. Harvey School for children with special educational needs arising from severe learning difficulties, and the Moselle School for children with moderate learning difficulties, both situated to the north of the estate; and a hostel for older children in care, situated on Willan Road near the entrance to the estate. Witnesses from the Education Department told us that the siting of these schools "doesn't make sense"; Roy Limb explained that these institutions had been put where they were in order to be "part of the community", but recognised that on Broadwater Farm "things got out of balance". No thought appears to have been given to the design of any of the schools to enable them to be available for general community use.

2.14 The estate does have access to the open space of the Lordship Recreation Ground — a facility which could have been put to far greater use than it has. The Haringey Sports Council, in a strong submission to us have pointed out that over the last few years the open air theatre on the recreation ground has been little used; the cricket pitches have become unusable; the boating lake and children's waterfall have disappeared; and the changing facilities and toilets have fallen into a disgusting condition. There was also the Lido swimming pool to the north of the estate, which was closed in 1983.

2.15 The residents in the nearby terraced streets had opposed the plans and disliked the reality. A nearby resident of 20 years standing described to us his view of the estate as "like a wart on one's hand, a monstrosity, out of character for the area". From the beginning, there began to emerge a dangerous polarisation between the estate and its neighbours.

THE PROBLEMS OF THE 1970S
2.16 The high hopes of the planners were confounded almost from

the start. The history of Broadwater Farm through the 1970s is a spiral of deterioration. Its reputation became so bad that virtually nobody accepted a offer of housing on the estate unless they were homeless and had no choice. In 1980, less than ten years after it had been built, the estate featured in a Department of the Environment report of an investigation into difficult to let housing. It described how "Lakeside Estate", a pseudonym for Broadwater Farm, had gone into a "catastrophic slide" in popularity. Its conclusions were pessimistic:—

"At best the local authority can hope to make it tolerable for the next decade or so, but eventually, because the estate is so monolithic and comprises such a large portion of their total housing, the possibility of demolition is one that will have to be considered."

It is one of the features of our Inquiry that this forecast has been confounded, and that the bleak picture has radically changed. Before describing the change, we must assess the reasons for such a rapid decline.

2.17 In the first place, there were severe problems arising from structural defects and disrepair. Water penetration had affected some flats from the early 1970s. Cockroaches were found to take advantage of easy passages through the gaps between the industrialised building slabs. Above all the council's response to complaints about maintenance and disrepair was shoddy. The council's evidence to us describes a petition presented by tenants in 1981:—

"(The Petition) complained of poor security and a major burglary problem, frequent lift breakdowns, graffiti, poor repairs service, a poor cleansing service, unfair allocation policies, water penetration and inadequate spending on estate improvements. Most of these complaints speak for themselves and were certainly justified by the situation existing on the estate at that time."

2.18. Many of those who have been closely involved with the estate recalled the situation which had developed by 1981.

Russell Simper, now the estate supervisor, was then a caretaker:—

"The youths used to hang about, people used to break the windows, doors were hanging off, the wood frames were rotten and it generally started to become a run down place. In the end, tenants just get disheartened and they just want to move."

He said that there was a meeting in the late 1970s when tenants "threatened to lynch the council if the council didn't come down and

THE ESTATE AND ITS PEOPLE

start doing some repairs on the estate and making people have somewhere decent to live in".

2.19 Joanne George, who has played an important role as chair of the Tenants' Association and is now a social services community worker on the estate, arrived in 1980 as a homeless parent:—
> "The first thing that actually hit me was the condition of the estate and the flat that I was first offered itself. The estate was dirty, there was lots of vandalism, lots of glass, the flat I was allocated was in a really bad state of repair. There was no kitchen sink, there was no kitchen cupboard, there was a hole in the floor. It was just horrendous. It looked to me like squatters had lived there. All the passages had graffiti and stains all over it. It was absolutely disgusting and I was told, 'sorry, no money for decorations'."

2.20 The problems became exacerbated in the mind of the public by sensational reporting in the local press. The tenants, who might have welcomed a serious inquiry into the real problems which existed, hit back against what they felt to be a smearing of the estate and its inhabitants. The first of a number of "shock reports" was published by the *Hornsey Journal* on 11th May 1973, under the headline:—
> **"MARRIAGES ON ROCKS AMONG THE CONCRETE SAYS REPORT ON HIGH RISE LIVING."**

The "report" had been written by a junior school teacher and leaked to the newspaper, which published it with many photographs and described it as painting a "scarifying picture". One quotation reads as a first example of the racist labelling which was to become more frequent:—
> "'Problem' families — many of them single parent families — were seen to be placed together," claimed the author. "The sight of unmarried West Indian mothers walking about the estate aggravated racial tension."

However tenants on the estate were reported by the newspaper as disagreeing vehemently with such a view of the estate.

2.21 On 30th April 1976 the *Tottenham Weekly Herald* published a "survey" carried out by two of its reporters under the headline:—
> **"'FAMILIES WHO LIVE IN THE SHADOW OF VIOLENCE'.**
> Fear haunts the gloomy passages, lifts and entrances of Broadwater Farm Estate."

Again the residents, led by the president of the Tenants' Association, protested at "total mis-representation of the facts".

THE BROADWATER FARM INQUIRY REPORT

2.22 On 6th October 1978 under the headline **"EXPERT RAPS TERROR FLATS"** the *Weekly Herald* reported:—
"An explosive survey carried out by a sociologist appointed by Tottenham Liberals claims that the 1,063 tenants on Broadwater Farm Estate are living in a 'sub-culture of violence'. The sociologist says there is complete social disorganisation."
There was a strong reaction from residents who wrote to the paper, such as one who stated:—
"I can speak from personal experience. I am a woman. I do not suffer from tension or depression and have many friends like myself and am extremely lucky to live on Broadwater Farm."
Others set up a "Broadwater Farm Council Tenants' Protection Action Group" in opposition to the Tenants' Association, but it was short-lived and seems to have attracted little support. The local home beat officer was reported in the press as expressing little anxiety about the situation:—
"PC Stratton said that crime was no worse on the estate than anywhere else. 'And you are more likely to get mugged at Bruce Grove than here.' He added that Broadwater Farm is being adequately policed and most relations with the Tenants' Association are very good."

2.23 Thus we see as the contributory factors to the terrible image to the estate, a combination of on the one hand real grievances, such as the poor maintenance, unrectified structural defects and the inadequate facilities, and on the other hand an unjust labelling from outside, from the press and from neighbouring residents. The labelling became attached not just to the buildings but also to the people, as if they too were undesirable. Residents on the estate had severe problems with hire purchase or T.V. hire facilities, or obtaining goods from catalogues. Deposits were required for the installation of gas and electricity. There was even a kind of social ostracism, as illustrated by evidence from on the one hand Russell Simper:—
"It gets blown out of proportion. People from outside read the paper, they say: 'Cor, what a flipping place, Broadwater Farm.' They've never been on Broadwater Farm, they've never lived on Broadwater Farm, but they get the wrong impression of Broadwater Farm. Then when people who live on Broadwater Farm go on a bus and someone says: 'Oh, hello,' and they start talking they say: 'Where do you live?' 'I live on Broadwater Farm'

THE ESTATE AND ITS PEOPLE

'Oh, I wouldn't live over there for a pension'. This makes people disheartened. It's making out that I'm no good because I live on Broadwater Farm."

Then on the other hand we had the view of a nearby resident: —

"I don't want to have friends on that estate. I wouldn't go there to make friends. I would like to see you go round the houses and say: 'What do you reckon should be done?' They would all say: 'Raze it to the ground'. That would be the answer."

2.24 The image of the estate inevitably affected the pattern of lettings. The numbers of those who wanted to transfer were double the borough average – 20% of all tenants by 1976. The numbers refusing an offer of a place on the estate was also far higher than the average. Borough Housing Officer Barry Simons made a comprehensive report on the situation in October 1976, which said:—

"Since very few tenants wished to transfer to Broadwater, and many housing applicants refused accommodation there, dwellings tended to be left to those whose need was most urgent, and the estate has received up to now an unusually large share of homeless and single parent families. In all, 75% of acceptances on voids on Broadwater in 1975 were by homeless families, compared to 24% of voids elsewhere in Haringey."

In a thoughtful section on race relations the report discussed the dangers of such a trend, and the need for consultation about allocation policies:—

"A policy which has the effect of dispersing an ethnic minority away from unpopular estates can be justified if it accords with that minority's wishes and takes account of individual preferences."

2.25 The council adopted recommendations in the report designed to broaden the social mix on the estate. They resolved that no more homeless people or one parent families should be allocated to Broadwater for two years; only one void in three should be offered to furnished tenants (who were predominantly Black); and one void in seven would be offered to households outside the waiting list, such as key workers. But these policies did not last. In September 1979 the council reverted to a policy of allocating vacancies on Broadwater Farm in accordance with boroughwide housing policy. It was considered that it was not possible to alter the composition of an estate through allocation policies, and that the image of an estate created by press publicity had more impact on the choices which people made.

2.26 Throughout these changes in policy a large proportion of new lettings were made to homeless families: 70% in 1980, decreasing to 48% in 1982. They went to Broadwater Farm because they had no choice; before November 1981, a homeless family was only given one offer. They had needs for themselves and their children for which the council failed to make provision. Dolly Kiffin described their situation:—

> "It was just young people with children, unemployed, that was coming onto the Broadwater Farm to live. They hadn't got any carpet, furniture, anything, and there is problems for social security to give them these things. So they struggle, and the struggle get harder and harder. You could see the frustration in the young people there."

2.27 We have tried to discover to what extent the lettings on the estate were being made to Black people. One Black resident from 1973 described the trend to us in direct terms:-

> "As the Black people came in, the Whites went out."

The difficulty is that the council's Housing Department has not carried out any ethnic monitoring of lettings to their housing stock. So they have deprived themselves of the information which would be essential to consider whether there were discriminatory practices in decisions being made by council officers about the estate. For as William Trant, speaking on behalf of the West Indian Standing Conference, said to us:-

> "I do not feel that there is anything that is horribly bad about having large concentrations of Black people in a particular area, because I believe that it provides the strength and support that we need. But at the same time what I am saying is that it ought not to be the case where the less desirable estates are allocated to Black people"

We agree. As we shall see, it was Black people on the estate who led the fight against the estate's decline.

2.28 The best information which we have about the numbers of Black and White people on the estate is that in the 1981 census, 42% of the residents of Broadwater Farm had heads of households who were born in the new Commonwealth. Our own survey shows that the ethnic breakdown of adults is now as follows:—

White	49%
Afro-Caribbean	42%
Indian subcontinent	3%
Other	6%

2.29 The only community facility on the estate, the social club under the walkway, offered little welcome to Black people. It did provide a friendly environment for some residents of the estate, and we have heard from older people who enjoyed coming down for a regular evening drink. But it was dominated by a few individuals who did not operate it for the whole estate. As Malcolm Sargison, community worker on the estate from 1978 to 1981, said: "They saw themselves as a social club and not a community centre." Around 1981, serious financial irregularities had emerged. These were investigated by the Community Development Department and led to the sacking of staff. While some have claimed that there was no discrimination against Black people in the club, there was too much evidence to the contrary for us to accept that claim. The following quotations describe the real position:—

"There were requests from within the Black community that for only one night a week they could have some kind of chance to do something pertaining to different cultures, and this request was always turned down. The social club actually became a pub. There were several occasions where Black people were assaulted and bodily beaten in there, badly beaten." (Stafford Scott).

"I went for membership and I was turned away – I did not know why." (Clasford Sterling).

"It's fair to say that in 1976-80 before the emergence of the Youth Association, the social club appeared to be predominantly White." (Ernie Large).

"There was a social club downstairs – White people and the token Black. If you wasn't part of that token, you go in there, you soon get out of it. There were a couple of times you would get kicked out of there as well." (Black resident since 1973).

"There were only a few Black people on the estate that used to go down there regularly and there were quite a few who lived off the estate. The main thing there was playing dominoes. I used to hear racist remarks about them slamming down their dominoes." (White woman resident).

2.30 So the estate before 1981 offered nothing to young Black people except a home. They were effectively excluded from the social club. They had no other facilities on the estate. The young men, many of them unemployed, had nothing to do. The old people were afraid of them, the police suspected them. The young women with children were isolated and lonely. The teenagers had the use of a flat in Hawkinge block which operated on three evenings a week, but nothing more. The physical appearance of the estate was run down and ill maintained. In 1981 a new organisation – the Broadwater Farm Youth Association – was formed in order to face these massive problems.

THE YOUTH ASSOCIATION
2.31 Having noticed that many people at the Youth Association were young adult men, we asked, who is a youth? Stafford Scott gave a reply which reveals much about being unemployed in Britain today: –
 "When we say youth, this is funny because most of them are not really youths in the conventional use of the term. They are actually young men, some of them well into adulthood, but because they are not in employment, because they don't have total control of their future, they don't really see themselves as being men in the conventional use of the term. They allow themselves to be called youth because they believe they are in a kind of transitional period."
The Youth Association, he explained, had catered for people from eight years old right up to 30.

2.32 The events which sparked off the Youth Association started with a meeting called by the Tenants' Association to discuss the increased number of burglaries on the estate. About 20 people were there. Only one or two of them were Black. Councillor Bernie Grant was in the chair. People were complaining about the time which it took to get the police in. Community worker Malcolm Sargison suggested that if there were a small police sub-office on the estate, the police could come straight in when needed, and be accountable to the community. The proposal was well supported by the tenants, although the police did not think it would be helpful. Councillor Grant recalled his reaction from the chair: –
 "I said that the meeting was not representative, and I wanted to

THE ESTATE AND ITS PEOPLE

hear the views of the Black residents on the estate, before I could agree to such a move."

Malcolm Sargison wrote up a minute suggesting that the council would support the mini police station idea. *The Tottenham Herald* picked up the story, and stated that Councillor Grant was in favour.

2.33 Dolly Kiffin recalled her response:–

"My son bought a newspaper article saying 'Mini police station for Broadwater Farm' And that was when I talked to the youths. It wasn't very hard to talk to youths because they were always in the corridors and on the precinct in Tangmere, hanging about there from day to day . I called a meeting in my front room....You have to go around to ask how would they feel, would they be happy with it or not? Or would they rather to have a centre where they can play a part, and to see if life could be changed on the Broadwater Farm? And that was when they said they rather to get together and start up a centre of themselves and work together on it."

Clasford Sterling, Vice President of the Youth Association, described the spirit of the early meetings:–

"The concerned people in the community came together and said: 'What you really need is some resources and facilities'. And that is how the Youth Association actually started. It came about to prove the point, that if the community were involved in the decision making around their lives, they would actually have a better community to live in."

2.34 Barry Simons, then Director of the Mid-Tottenham Housing Office, recalls the first meeting with the new association:—

"There must have been 30. Dolly was there, but they were largely youths and all Black. They really went for the council. I got a significant lot of heat put on me. They talked about not having access to the social club, the Tenants' Association being a White association, and the police station. And their need for youth facilities on the estate. And they said to me: 'We want the fish and chip shop'."

2.35 The fish and chip shop was an unused shop on the Tangmere precinct. Barry Simons had decided in his own mind that it was essential to meet the aspirations which the youths had expressed. He was able to get the necessary approval from the committee chairs and cut through the bureaucratic red tape. The shop was open for use by the Youth Association within three weeks.

2.36 There was no heating in the shop and it was filthy. The youths got together and scrubbed it out. Dolly Kiffin went around and begged for things to put into it. Malcolm Sargison helped to find them some chairs, a cooker, fridge and typewriter. For Christmas 1981, Dolly Kiffin cooked a meal in her flat and brought it downstairs:—
"It was so cold some of the youths caught cold in that little place. But the atmosphere was good and you could see the determination in them."

2.37 In the view of Howard Simmons, who was then Principal Community Development Officer, the opening of the Youth Association premises was "a major symbolic base of achievement". The youth could see that their influence was actually delivering the goods, that the council were responding. But in some quarters there was discontent. Malcolm Sargison felt that the decision had been railroaded:—
"For years the Tenants' Association and other people on the estate had negotiated with the council in various guises, and they had never been forthcoming with anything. Suddenly the chip shop was turned over in a fortnight. No tenants on the estate had been consulted. For me that really harmed relationships on the estate."

2.38 Within a short time the Youth Association had taken an initiative which demonstrated their desire to make links across the whole community. They began serving meals and arranging outings for pensioners on the estate, and have continued ever since. Today, 60–70 pensioners are involved, some getting meals in their homes, some coming to the Youth Association for lunch. Dolly Kiffin explained how it started:—
"The older pensioners was afraid of the youths. They would hold their bags underneath their arms and you could see they were frightened. So we called a meeting and we said, it's time that with the little money that we was making, we have outings for them, parties to take them out of their home. And that built up closer links and more understanding between the pensioners and the youths. And that was the greatest achievement, I think, for us on the Broadwater Farm."

2.39 Many people on the estate paid tribute to this work. For

THE ESTATE AND ITS PEOPLE

Russell Simper, the estate supervisor: —
"It's a thing I never thought I would see, the elderly people going into the youth club in Tangmere. But they do and they enjoy it, and there are always compliments regarding their meals."

Andy Sansom, a caretaker on the estate for seven years, said: —
"Before the club you had the youth doing their thing and you had old age pensioners going down to the social club for their dinners, and they never mixed. They wouldn't know each other if they fell over. Now some of the older people are going into the club, they can see the youths. They can be boisterous, but they will hold the chair for them. And they get to know that they are not yobbos, they are just people."

A lady whom we interviewed, well into her 80's, who had been knocked unconscious on the estate some years ago by an unknown attacker, happily goes to the Youth Association for lunch every day. She looks forward to it very much because she meets so many of her friends. She spoke warmly about the Christmas functions. Even in the week after 6th October, when the Youth Association was ringed with police officers, the pensioners still came in.

2.40 When it started, the leaders of the Youth Association had no idea how to deal with the council system or apply for grants and keep detailed accounts. There was little enough money — a £300 grant from the council at the beginning, and contributions from the pockets of the members. Gradually they became aware of the various funding sources and how to deal with them — the council, the Urban Aid programme and the Greater London Council. The fish and chip shop was far too small, and an application was made for Urban Aid funding to convert a derelict shop in the corner of the precinct. Sir George Young gave personal support to this initiative, and the new premises were opened in 1984.

2.41 In 1982 the Youth Association was pressed for space for a day nursery for young children. They had been looking at the hostel in Willan Road run by Social Services, for older children in care. It was under used, with only three or four teenagers living in it. The Chief Executive, Roy Limb recalls how he was approached by Dolly Kiffin and her colleagues. They wanted it for single women who had children and could not get out: —

"They were quite determined about it. My little bit in it was to try and create a climate of opinion to overcome the resistance that obviously existed within the bureaucracy. It was not the normal thing to do in those days, handing over this professional institution to unpaid volunteers. I told some minor white lies like saying, well it was only a temporary thing. I knew damned well that once Dolly Kiffin got her hands on it we would never get it back."

2.42 The Willan Road premises became a day nursery on the ground floor providing for 25 children on the estate. In 1984 the mothers' project started on the upper floor, (funded by the Greater London Council), providing a shopping centre for women, a library, activity rooms for women's groups, and a range of activities including keep fit sessions, crafts, English classes, advice sessions, and a Turkish women's group. Joanne George worked with the team which set up the Willan Road nursery, recruiting staff, getting equipment etc:—

"In general a lot of women were very isolated, just fed up, because of many reasons, because of poverty, because of unemployment, because of bad housing conditions, because of having nowhere to go. The general feeling was: 'We are fed up now, this is the last straw, we want something better for us and for our children.' Becoming involved changed the lives of many young people."

As the Youth Association premises on Tangmere were frequented mainly by men, the Willan Road building was very necessary for the needs of women. By October 1985 about 50 women came to the mothers' project everyday, both from the estate and surrounding streets.

2.43 The other valuable new facility for children, and thus for parents also, is the play centre, located to the north of the Kenley block. It was opened in 1984 and caters for children from five to 11 after school and during school holidays. Children are picked up from school and stay at the centre until they can be collected by their parents around 5.30 pm. Around 40 children attend – up to 100 in the holidays. It is financed by the council as another response to the demands which were being voiced for proper facilities for families on the estate.

2.44 Every summer the Youth Association has organised a festival on the Lordship Recreation Ground – a mixture of music, dance, fashion, stalls, sports and side shows, all with an African/Caribbean flavour. It has become a major local event with a carnival

THE ESTATE AND ITS PEOPLE

atmosphere. The Youth Association organised a number of stewards with special T—shirts to ensure that nothing went wrong, and persuaded the police to keep in the background. The press reported it with headlines such as **'FUN DAY DOWN AT THE FARM'**. Many witnesses spoke of the good feelings which the festival had generated:

"It's a time to enjoy, a time to reflect on the whole work we have done over the year." (Clasford Sterling)

"It is a festival that is aimed at bringing together the community, and allowing the community to understand each other's culture." (Stafford Scott)

2.45 The formation of the Youth Association led to major changes in the composition of the Tenants' Association. A new committee was voted in with an equal number of Black and White members. A new constitution was adopted, with a system of representatives on each block on the estate.

2.46 Finally, the Youth Association set up a number of co-operative enterprises; a community launderette, a food and vegetable co-operative, a hairdressing salon, a photographic workshop, and a sewing workshop. In late 1985 a co-operative development worker was appointed with funds from the GLC, now taken over by the Haringey Council. All of the co-operative's projects continue to function, although some are in difficulty. We return at the end of the report to the needs for the future in this field.

2.47 The achievements of the Youth Association in under five years have been remarkable. They have succeeded against all the odds. They lived in a depressed and divided estate, and they brought to it co-operation and real benefits. They faced the massive unemployment of young people on the estate, and provided for them activity and a number of real jobs. They have been true to their motto "Success Through Caring". Their efforts were deservedly recognised when in February 1985, they were rung directly from Buckingham Palace and asked if they would welcome the Princess of Wales.

THE COUNCIL RESPONDS

2.48 The Youth Association had been formed at the right time. The council was already moving towards policies of real consultation with local people. Its Community Affairs Department was formed in 1982, in order to make the council's services more community orientated and responsive, more accessible to the wide range of interests and needs within the borough. The Housing Department was moving its services into more accessible local offices. The revival of Broadwater Farm has therefore been a partnership of a community eager to work hard for change joined with a council which in many of its departments was changing also.

2.49 A number of concrete decisions were made in the 1980s to bring council services into a closer physical and co-operative relationship with the people of Broadwater Farm: —
(1) In 1981 the Mid-Tottenham Housing Office was set up, combining management and repair teams, and with a priority to respond to the complaints of tenants on the estate. We have described the prompt action of its senior officer over the Youth Association request for premises.
(2) In 1982 an estate based repairs team was established, which now completes 90% of its jobs within the targeted time limits — by far the best performance in the borough.
(3) In 1983 the Broadwater Farm neighbourhood office was opened on the Tangmere precinct. It provides for management and repair services and housing benefit claims. It is the base for the two community workers, and since October 1985 for a team of social workers. It will soon have a five person team from the Building Design Service to study building defects, consult over and plan a building strategy, and oversee new building projects.
(4) In 1984 the Broadwater Farm Panel was set up as a sub-committee of the council, chaired by Councillor Bernie Grant, to bring together the council, the Tenants' Association, the Youth Association, and other agencies into discussion and decision making on issues of concern to the estate.

2.50 Neale Coleman of the neighbourhood office, spoke of an atmosphere of co-operation between housing staff and tenants which astonished some visitors to the estate: —
"As you know, our office is completely open plan in its reception area, and we've often had people come from other boroughs who have been asking us: 'How do you manage without thick plate glass screens to hide you from the public?' We have never had problems of that nature in dealing with the public in the office."

But he stressed the difficulties of getting other council officers in other departments who were accustomed to a rigid departmental hierarchy, to be accountable to local meetings as well as to their departmental superiors: —

"It was necessary for us to establish very firmly the principle that all services would report regularly at every meeting of the Broadwater Farm Panel. That was important because it provided a focus of accountability which people could key into. We are making more progress there, but it is still a difficult area."

2.51 To ease the problems of co-ordination, an Inter-Agency Working Party meets regularly under the chair of the neighbourhood officer. A meeting attended by one of the Inquiry panel, included representatives of eight local authority departments and several local groups. The meeting dealt with a very large amount of material in two hours. People were clearly working with co-ordination, and were used to members of the local community being actively involved, both in criticising and supporting what they had to do and say.

2.52 Community leaders recognised that these changes were a real attempt to respond to community needs. As Dolly Kiffin put it: —

"Councillors must get off their backsides and come and see the community before they sign anything. Officers cannot just come and write a report to the council unless they now consult the community. That's what we do on Broadwater Farm and that's what we changed."

Leonardo Leon, Treasurer of the Tenants' Association, drew a distinction between the council as an institution and the neighbourhood office:

"We have a really good working relationship with the neighbourhood office. Most of the officers there have been working with us and helping us to develop our initiatives but at the same time we have met some difficulties when we go higher and have to deal with the chairs of committees, or whoever is involved at the higher level."

2.53 The new partnership between council and community produced a number of concrete results. In a million-pound maintenance programme all broken windows, woodwork and communal glazing were repaired or replaced, and the exterior redecorated. Major steps were taken to improve security and prevent crime. Entry phones were

THE BROADWATER FARM INQUIRY REPORT

installed in the two tower blocks: the flimsy front doors to the flats were renewed and strengthened with metal plates. The areas around the bottom of the blocks, where thieves used to hide, were opened up.

2.54 Neale Coleman described how the changes were made:—
"We talked to the local crime prevention officer. We talked to tenants in a number of blocks in an intensive way and the initial change that we made was to replace all the front doors with solid core doors. We strengthened the frames by lining the frames with steel and providing a mortice lock that locked into the steel-reinforced frame. And on the other side of the door, the new doors had metal hinge bolts. And our experience was that this made an immediate effect, a dramatic effect on burglaries."

However there was still a problem because the area around the lock was a point of weakness, and some burglars were able to push the lock through the door with a hard blow. Neale Coleman continued:—
"So again we talked to the police and we talked to tenants and we talked to community groups and we came up with the solution of fitting two steel plates bolted through to sandwich that part of the door together and give it extra strength. We carried out that work again across all the flats on the estate. And since then the burglary rate has again been very, very low indeed, as is accepted by the police. It is far lower than for the rest of Tottenham."

2.55 Tricia Zipfel, who had studied the estate for some years on behalf of the Department of the Environment, summed up the achievements in a report to the Department in October 1985:—

"(The Estate) had become a training model for the Priority Estates Project, hosting visitors from estates all over the country. The neighbourhood office was dealing with over 900 queries from tenants each month, the refusal rate had been halved, more tenants were choosing to live on the estate, repairs were being done faster than in the rest of the borough. Voids had dropped from around 60 to 15, and the atmosphere and quality of service in the neighbourhood office was excellent. The estate was clean, there was very little graffiti or vandalism. Also, and perhaps most significantly, crime on the estate had plummeted. The police have acknowledged that burglaries on Broadwater Farm were lower than in the rest of Y district. Visits to the estate by Princess Diana and

THE ESTATE AND ITS PEOPLE

Sir George Young boosted the confidence and morale of workers and tenants alike."

In the evidence to us she provided a graphic illustration of the change: —

"When the D.O.E. investigators went on to the estate in 1978, there wasn't a single pane of communal glass intact. The whole place was littered with broken glass. By 1983 — 84 when I was on the estate, there wasn't a single pane of communal glass that was not intact. There was no broken glass on the estate anywhere."

2.56   Council officers give credit to the Youth Association, and to Dolly Kiffin in particular, for the turnaround that has taken place. The Chief Executive Roy Limb said: —

"The dynamism and enthusiasm of Dolly Kiffin has had everything to do with the way in which progress has been made on Broadwater Farm Estate."

An elderly resident echoed his words:-

"Well I don't know who this Miss Dolly is, but she has worked wonders for this estate."

We too praise Dolly Kiffin, but we would emphasise that she was not alone. Many people have made a wrong assumption that Dolly Kiffin was the only leader of the Youth Association — an assumption which led to serious consequences in the summer of 1985, as we shall describe. In reality there has been an extremely able and dedicated team of young people, both men and women, Black people and White, working for the Youth Association from the start.

2.57   In the 1980s the pattern of press reporting began to change. There were still a number of negative reports; but people in the community were now more organised, and able to insist that reporters from the local newspapers came down and reported in full on the positive achievements of the estate. On 14th October 1982 the *'Weekly Herald'* had on its front page published an article headed **"CALL FOR SLUM CLEARANCE SCHEME"**, in which a councillor was reported as saying that Broadwater Farm and some other estates should be pulled down. In the following week the newspaper printed a full page "news probe" headed **"BROADWATER FARM — WHAT IS ITS FUTURE? TENANTS INJECT NEW LIFE."** The report featured the projects of the Youth Association and also the tensions between youths and the police. There was a similar sequence of articles in November 1984. After a leaked report by a social services officer had been published in *The Journal* in which it was claimed that home helps were scared to go on the estate, Dolly Kiffin contacted the paper expressing anger at the report. The result was a full page report about the Youth Association and in particular its work for old people. A leading article said:—

"Broadwater now offers a community life to old and young alike, especially to the unemployed with time on their hands. Not only that: those who are housebound get hot dinners delivered by young volunteers."

2.58 While the success has been remarkable, it is important to recognise that the Youth Association has many obstacles still to overcome. As we show from the analysis of the survey in Chapter 7, the estate is not a fully integrated community. Many people praised the work of the Youth Association and other new organisations, but few are actually involved in them. There are sections of the estate that do not feel that the Youth Association caters for their needs. There have been considerable improvements in the housing field, but in other areas, such as education and economic development, the participation of the community has scarcely begun. We return in Chapter 9 to consider various ways forward for the future. We now turn to consider how the various ranks of the Metropolitan Police responded to the community of Broadwater Farm.

Chapter 3
THE POLICE AND THE COMMUNITY

THE BACKGROUND OF INJUSTICE
3.1 Black people who settled in Britain in the 1950s and early 1960s were strongly supportive of the police. But over the 1970s, as a generation of Black people born in Britain grew up, the attitudes of their parents to the police changed dramatically. The change came about because they saw what was happening to their sons and daughters. They saw them picked on in stop-and-search operations and arrests under "Sus". When they complained to the police, whom they believed to be the protectors of the law, they were rebuffed and sometimes mistreated.

Mrs Scott, the mother of five children, told us how her experience changed: —
"In the sixties I was quite friendly with the police. We had a club on the Bruce Grove Road. I can't remember the name — there is a hairdresser's there now. And we used to gamble there and the police officers from Tottenham used to be there. We used to know and call each other by our first names. And sometimes when I'd get broke I would turn to one and say: 'I'm skint, have you got any money?' And they would turn to me the same way. It suddenly changed in the early seventies. It seemed as if all the decent police officers had left the area and there were all different people coming in. And you couldn't go to the police and make a complaint without being harassed. Although you are making a complaint, you are being harassed by the police."

Mr Jarrett described to us an incident in 1977 when he asked for the help of the police to deal with a boy breaking his windows, and ended up being arrested himself. He concluded: —
"These are all things which you have to look into. How much can you trust the police when you need help? There are several West Indian families who have gone to the police for help and been turned down flat."

3.2 The pages of Haringey press show that throughout the 1970s there was mounting concern about the behaviour of police officers to Black people in Tottenham. In August 1973 a meeting was held at the Civic Centre, chaired by the Mayor, to "ease strained relations between the police and the Black community". Bitter criticism of various aspects of police behaviour was voiced. The meeting launched a voluntary liaison scheme, organised by the Haringey Council for Community Relations, under which volunteers could be called into police stations in cases of difficulty.

3.3 In July 1975 there was an outraged reaction to the conviction of a Black sixth-form student for assaulting a police officer. Many witnesses had testified in court that police officers assaulted him. A reporter on the *Hornsey Journal* analysed the background of the case and concluded:—

"There must be a thorough investigation of the general complaints being made against the police, and action taken to see that the Black community have confidence in them. Anything less would be a whitewash, with untold consequences in a multi-racial society".

Concern about the crisis in police/community relations crossed party lines. At a meeting in the same month, a Conservative councillor, Robert Atkins, said:—

"There are frightening indications of a sudden and serious deterioration in relations between the immigrant community and the police."

3.4 In January 1978, a Labour Party inquiry was set up into racism and discrimination against Black people in the borough. The inquiry had been called for by the Tony Anderson Campaign — a campaign to expose police harassment of one Black youth, whose case was said by the inquiry chairman to be "the tip of the iceberg". Dolly Kiffin is Tony Anderson's mother, and she told us of her own response when her son came home and said the police had punched him:—

"I just grab him and take him down to the police station and demand: 'This police punched my son and I want justice'. Because although you read about it, you don't know this, don't believe that these things happen, because you believe they are supposed to keep the law. I personally did not realise that they break the law."

3.5 Witness after witness to our Inquiry spoke of the indignities which they have suffered at the hands of police officers for no other reason than that they were Black. The bitterness of their experience was shared by old and young, men and women, professional people and unemployed: −

"I have never been unemployed. I have a reasonable standard of living. However as a Black person individually, it's been my common experience to be stopped, searched, questioned by the police, and treated with suspicion and hostility." (Michael Hutchinson-Reis, social worker).

"I have had my toes stepped on, I have been backed into corners, policemen have spoken to me with a filthy mouth full of spit. I have stepped out of that and I have handled the situation, but I can see that young people can't keep their patience, and quite a lot of the times they have exploited that, and then they get a hammering and a hiding." (Norton McLean, Principal Youth Officer).

"They stopped me by St. Paul's cathedral once, twice in one night. Two different lots of police. They said: 'Well what are you doing in St. Paul's? We don't usually see Black people in St. Paul's.' So I asked him: 'Is that the only reason why they stop me, just because I'm Black and in St. Pauls?', and they said: 'Yes'. At which point I got a bit angry, because I thought that was a fucking insult" (young Black man).

It is because of experiences like this that people so often get charged for what are called "knock-on offences"; they get stopped, searched or arrested for a reason which turns out to have no foundation, but are then charged with some other offence − obstructing or assaulting the police, or threatening behaviour − which has arisen only because of the contact between the "suspect" and the police.

3.6 There should be no surprise at this evidence. Throughout the 1970s there were reports written and inquiries made into the maltreatment of Black people by the police. Finally in 1981, the evidence was brought before the official inquiry made by Lord Scarman into the Brixton disorders. Lord Scarman said of the evidence of which he had heard: −

"Whether justified or not, many in Brixton believe that the police routinely abuse their powers and mistreat alleged offenders. The belief here is as important as the fact. One of the most serious developments in recent years, has been the way in which the older generation of Black people in Brixton has come to share the belief of the younger generation, that the police routinely harass and ill-treat black youngsters".

3.7 We differ in one central respect from the conclusion of Lord Scarman. It deliberately avoided the central question — was the "belief" of Black people based on fact or fiction? The belief is not "as important as the fact"; it is the fact which is supremely important. If the belief of Black people was based on fact, it meant that great numbers of Metropolitan Police officers were racist in their thoughts and actions. If the belief was based on fiction, it meant that Black people were being over-credulous and were naively accepting unfounded rumour. From the mass of reported evidence, which was available to Lord Scarman, we have no doubt that the conclusions of Black people were deeply grounded on true experience of racially prejudiced police behaviour.

1981 — THE CHANCE FOR A NEW START
3.8 In 1981, the year of the Brixton and Toxteth disturbances, the Borough of Haringey had also experienced confrontations between police and people. On Easter Monday there had been a brief but violent clash at the Finsbury Park funfair. Commander Dickinson, the head of Y district which covered the boroughs of Haringey and Enfield, suffered a broken nose and a fractured cheek bone. The Hornsey *Journal* carried an emotive report:—

"They did it again. About 500 Black youths stampeded the Finsbury Park funfair last Monday — as they did last year — and terrified the mixed race groups, who until then, were happily mingling on the swings and roundabouts. And today people in Haringey are asking: **"WHO IS GOING TO STOP THESE RIOTS?"**

On 7th July shop windows were broken and missiles thrown at the police in the Wood Green High Road. It was reported that 59 shops had been damaged or looted, and 8 police officers injured.

3.9 The publication of the Scarman report in November 1981 offered to all the chance of a fresh start. Lord Scarman had made a series of recommendations to deal with the crisis in police/community relations: action against racist behaviour by police officers, improvements in police training, compulsory in-service courses, close supervision of stop-and-search operations, and a setting up of immediate consultative arrangements, in advance of a statutory

THE POLICE AND THE COMMUNITY

scheme. In Brixton immediate steps were taken to bring in a new leadership to the police force which was prepared to carry through the Scarman proposals. Such leadership was desperately needed in Tottenham.

THE POLICE AND THE YOUTH ASSOCIATION

3.10 On Broadwater Farm, the newly formed Youth Association was ready and willing to enter into dialogue with the police, and at some levels, at least, the police were ready and willing to enter into dialogue with the Youth Association. It is central to our Inquiry to discover why the dialogue failed to develop trust and confidence between the police and people on the estate.

3.11 At a certain level, the contact was close. Three officers in particular came frequently to the Youth Association office in the period between 1982 and 1985:
– Chief Superintendent Couch, the officer in charge of the Tottenham division from 1984, and a man generally recognised to have been committed to community policing. We will have to examine how he interpreted the concept of "community policing", and whether he operated it effectively. But we have no doubt that he genuinely wanted to work in collaboration with local community leaders.
– Chief Inspector (later Superintendent) Dick Stacey, the Community Liaison Officer, and a man who also made great efforts to be available for meetings with local people. Councillor Martha Osamor, who has been prominent in campaigns against police abuses in Tottenham for many years, said of him:–
   "We don't see them all as bad people, wicked people. There's some good ones. Inspector Stacey was one of those that we could rely on, call him day and night and he will visit the families."
– Inspector Paul Gee, who worked as Superintendent Stacey's assistant in community liaison work.

3.12 On the side of the Youth Association, there was also a desire for co-operation. A football match was played between the Broadwater Farm team and a team from Tottenham Police station. Police had an open door invitation to come into the Youth Association Office. High ranking officers from abroad, such as Superintendent Henry De Geneste of the New Jersey police, were entertained for lunch. The accusation made by D.A.C Richards that "normal policing methods are resisted by a vociferous minority" – an accusation which is plainly levelled against Youth Association leaders — is preposterous. Indeed it is completely belied by Chief Superintendent Couch's words in a television interview after the disturbances: —

> "Up till about June of this year, the Broadwater Farm Estate was a pleasant place to work on for our police officers. In fact, they said you really don't need so many of us any more. And things were working very well. And we worked in good co-operation with the housing department, and with Miss Kiffin, who was on the Broadwater Youth Association."
>
> (*The London Programme,* 11th October, 1985)

3.13 The problem was that the constructive ideas discussed at meetings with Messrs Couch, Stacey, and Gee were not translated into reality. There were two areas of difficulty. First, the local command appeared to have no control over the activities of special units such as the Special Patrol Group and the instant response units. Attempts at building good relations were regularly set back by the insensitive and unnecessary actions of these units which enraged local youths. Haringey's Chief Executive, Roy Limb, who helped to arrange many of the meetings, described what used to happen: —

> "It did seem to us that when we had had a good meeting and things were going quite well, all of a sudden there would be another incident on Broadwater Farm and that would damage the relationships. Now I still don't believe in the conspiracy theory, but I do actually accept that these incidents occurred. On one occasion, it had all been agreed that 15 youngsters were going to go over to Hendon (the police training college) and have a look at what goes on there, and be really straight with policemen about police-youth relationships. That had all been arranged for a Saturday morning, and the police were to provide the van. Sure enough, as God made little apples, on the Friday an instant response unit came screeching down onto the estate. Out leapt policemen and a number of youths were detained, questioned and so on, and sure enough that was the end of the visit to Hendon."

3.14 The second difficulty was that the Youth Association wanted, above all, to build a co-operative relationship with the regular patrolling officers on the estate, who had been increased into a team of eight. But this never happened, except briefly when a young Black woman officer joined the team. As one witness said: "There was a

THE POLICE AND THE COMMUNITY

lot of ribbing and she accepted that and at the end of the day there was some kind of vibes between her and the youth." But to everyone's annoyance she was transferred after a few weeks. The police said that she needed to continue her training elsewhere, but many took it as evidence that good community relations at rank and file level were not to be encouraged.

3.15 Stafford Scott, a youth worker with the Youth Association, gave a vivid picture of how the Association pressed for contact with patrolling officers, only to be confronted with two men who plainly had no intention of being community policemen: —
"Although we had what at times seemed to be very good meetings with senior police officers, what we found was, in the day to day relationships with the beat officers, there was no change. At one stage we actually had to demand that they come and visit the Youth Association. We told them:'You do not need to phone; come in and see what we are up to; come in and play pool with us, come in and talk to the members'."
Question from Panel: —
"Has that ever been done?"
"The first time it ever happened, we had Billy the Kid and the Sun Dance Kid — anyway they were cowboys. They actually kicked open the Youth Association's door and stood with hands on hips holding truncheons, and they just looked in, in a very aggressive and antagonistic manner."
Neale Coleman, who as Neighbourhood Officer had regular dealings with the patrolling officers, confirms: —
"It was certainly my impression that the complaints that the Youth Association made about a comparative lack of response from the patrolling officers to invitations to come into the centre, to become involved, were, by and large, justified. Obviously there were other pressures on those officers, other tasks that they had to carry out, but I think it is fair to say that not very much progress was made in establishing links between the patrolling officers and the community as a whole."

3.16 If proof were needed of the failure of the patrolling officers to relate to local organisations, it came from a remarkable piece of evidence provided by Tricia Zipfel. She had attended a meeting with police officers on 1st October 1985. Present were Chief Superintendent Couch, his deputy, Superintendent Sinclair, and

Sergeant Gillian Meynell, who was in charge of the Broadwater Farm home beat team. Tricia Zipfel's record of the meeting states:—
"A further significant point emerging in our discussions was the fact that, although very committed to community policing, the sergeant who had been in charge of the home beat team since May 1985, had rarely been on the estate and had never met with Dolly Kiffin or any other key people. In fact, she stated that she and the home beat officers were not allowed to meet with community groups."

3.17 We find it quite deplorable that the police officer in charge of the patrolling team should make no effort to meet key people on the estate — especially during a period in which, as we will see, there were causes for increased tension and therefore a real need for police/community understanding. As for the statement that "she and the home officers were not allowed to meet with community groups", we find it even more appalling. Tricia Zipfel felt that it was not so much an order, but an implicit assumption that the job of negotiating with the community was left to senior officers, and the people on the ground were not part of that process. We find that to be profoundly disturbing. The Broadwater Farm home beat team had cut themselves off from any hope of co-operation with the community they were meant to serve. They had — and their later published reports prove it, as we shall see — begun to regard local people as the enemy.

A FAILURE OF LEADERSHIP
3.18 When senior and junior officers are found to have such conflicting views of their role, it becomes important to look at the person in overall charge, who from 1981 to May 1985, was Commander Dickinson. He has been mentioned by many as a man who had no desire to consult seriously with local people. Ernie Large was a councillor in the Bruce Grove ward until May 1986, and was involved many times in trying to improve relations between his constituents and the police. He was himself a former military policeman and magistrate, and not a man who would make judgements lightly. He gave us this view of Commander Dickinson:—
"He was the grey haired, old fashioned type police officer. We both came from the East End. He actually had knowledge of the criminals in the East End, and a kind of mutual respect. What the Commander could not handle was the openness of community relations with the council, with its felt need to protect the community from all injustice. In all my political life I have not

THE POLICE AND THE COMMUNITY

really had a serious argument with anybody on the council. The only battles I have had have been with that particular Commander. I found an iron curtain came down, and every time we wanted something, the retort was invariably, we don't have to tell you anything, we are only responsible up the road at the Home Office, and therefore we are totally separate. The insularity of the police vis-a-vis the community was created by the attitude of that one Commander. If there could have been a different type of character there in terms of human relationships, he would have found that moderate and left-wing Labour councillors might have been no different to anyone else, in human terms, in getting things right for the community. But there was this total blockage."

3.19 Commander Dickinson was responsible for starting a petty minded procedure whereby, when written to by the chair of the council's police sub-committee, he invariably replied to someone else. In one such letter, written on the 10th April 1985, to Mr Limb in reply to a letter from Councillor Makanji, the contempt for the council was scarcely veiled:—

"The proposals in a letter dated 2nd April signed by a Councillor Makanji are not acceptable."

Not surprisingly, Councillor Makanji told us that this form of reply was regarded as a snub to the elected leaders of the council. According to Nick Wright, head of the council's Police Research Unit, Commander Dickinson had issued an instruction to his subordinates not to talk to any of the staff of the unit:—

"We would talk to an officer and when they found out who we were, they put the phone down. That was a consistent pattern until April or May of last year."

3.20 As regards the Broadwater Farm Estate, Commander Dickinson made no secret of his attitude in an interview on the *"Black on Black"* programme, broadcast in early 1983:—

Commander Dickinson:

"Certainly the crime rate as far as street crime is concerned, that's robberies and mugging in the modern parlance, had gone down as opposed to last year, and it needs to go down because it was extremely high last year, but this hasn't gone down because we are walking away from the problem. It's gone down because of effective policing that we are displaying around the area."

THE BROADWATER FARM INQUIRY REPORT

Interviewer:
"How do you reply to the youths that say that the decrease in the crime rate was because of their specific action, in other words they had taken youths off the streets, provided them with some sort of special centre and so on?"

Commander Dickinson:
"Well if that is the case, if they claim that, very good, and I give them great acclaim for that, but it only proves that they were responsible for it in the first place, if that's what they say".

For a senior officer to make such a remark, on a programme designed for a Black audience, reveals a frightening lack of understanding and sensitivity.

3.21 We are bound to conclude that with Commander Dickinson in charge, the opportunity of taking a new, post-Scarman look at police/community relations was not on. Chief Superintendent Couch must have felt himself caught between junior officers who had no sympathy with his approach and a Commander who was unwilling to give him support.

3.22 In May 1985, the reorganisation of the Metropolitan Police command structure began to take effect. The districts disappeared, and instead London became divided for police purposes into five areas, each under the command of a Deputy Assistant Commissioner. D.A.C. Richards took on the overall command of Area 1, a huge wedge of North London from the centre to the outer suburbs. He had little time before October to know much about Broadwater Farm, but he appears to have adopted the negative view of his predecessor. In an interview on the *"Diverse Reports"* programme, broadcast on 27th November 1985, he had this to say about the estate and its people:—

"No, they've long since been alienated, I'm afraid. It's long been a haven for the wrongdoer. It's long been the place to which people go from outside to gain comfort and support from people of a like ilk."

There are some nasty connotations to this description, which we do not believe were shared by the Chief Superintendent of Tottenham, who had direct knowledge of the estate and its people. It seems to indicate that the new top leadership was no more open-minded than the old.

THE POLICE AND THE COMMUNITY

POLICE ON THE ESTATE
3.23 We turn now to the particular clashes which took place on the estate. Prior to 1982, a single home beat officer, PC Brian "Ginger" Stratton patrolled the estate. He was liked by many residents. Russell Simper, now the Estate Supervisor, described him as a decent police officer, dedicated to the people on the estate. But there was discontent about the problems of getting police assistance after the all too frequent burglaries and vandalism. As one resident said:-
"You would have a job getting a policeman if you phoned the police. But when they did come, they would come in droves."

3.24 The friendly attitude of PC Stratton contrasted with the activities of the special units that came in from time to time. Malcolm Sargison, community worker at the time, described the two kinds of policing:-
"Whenever there was a spate of burglaries on the estate, they'd send in the SPG and clamp down on everybody, especially Black people. I could see that there was something missing in it all. We had Ginger, and he was a friendly sort of chap. He didn't seem to realise the effects of the SPG being sent in."

3.25 A number of incidents occurred in 1982 which served to harden attitudes on both sides. On 12th August 1982, PC Andy Holland, who five months before had joined PC Stratton as a second home beat officer, was struck on the head with a bottle while inside the office of the Youth Association talking to Dolly Kiffin. Dolly Kiffin agreed that this happened. She explained that there had been a heavy police presence on the estate shortly before, but that did not excuse what was done:-
"We called a meeting as an effect of that, because as we said at the meeting, that should not ever happen. We called the meeting to say that two wrongs don't make a right."
PC Holland said later to the press: "How can you talk to people under those circumstances?" It was a disgraceful incident, which must have reinforced the view that the recently formed Youth Association was hostile to the police.

3.26 On the next occasion, it was the community that had cause for bitter complaint. Late on the evening of 1st November 1982, a group of police officers, with dozens more in support, ran into Tangmere and arrested Roger Scott, an active member of the Youth

Association, saying that he had just burgled the Social Club. There were dozens of other youths present who had been watching a film with Roger and knew that he could not have done it. The Social Club had been entered and messed up, though nothing had been stolen. The burglar alarm had not gone off, and Youth Association officers are convinced that it was not a genuine burglary. The police claimed later, according to the press, that they acted "as a result from a tip from a member of the public".

3.27 A crowd gathered outside Tottenham Police Station. Several witnesses have described to us how, because of the lack of trust in the police, it has become an important community reaction when an injustice is thought to have been done, for people to go to the police station and to demand information. Indeed, we shall see that it was this intention to make a stand at the police station itself, which directly led to confrontation with the police on 6th October. Clasford Sterling described what happened when he reached the police station in the early hours of the morning after securing the Social Club:-

"I just found myself being dragged backwards by police. Not only me, but all the people that were outside the police station, which were young kids, women, adult people as well. It was just disgusting really. I ended up with a broken nose and charged with obstruction."

What had happened was that a special unit of police in riot gear happened to return to Tottenham Police Station after attending a demonstration in Brixton. Seeing what they took to be trouble at the police station, they lost control. Four people were arrested for obstruction, all of them officers or active members of the Youth Association. Two, Clasford Sterling and Diane Anderson, were acquitted in the Magistrates Court at their trial over a year later. Roger Scott was released the same night without any charge.

3.28 This was a disgraceful case of a mishandled operation escalating into violence and inflaming an already tense state of affairs. It is to the credit of Clasford Sterling, who suffered a broken nose and false charge, that he continued to be a highly responsible vice-president of the Youth Association, seeking the maximum co-operation with the police.

3.29 On the following day, 2nd November, there were two attacks against the police. Two metal beer kegs were dropped onto a police

THE POLICE AND THE COMMUNITY

car off one of the overhead walk-ways. No one was hurt, but it was said afterwards that an inspector was fortunate to escape serious injury. More seriously still, the home beat officer, PC Brian Stratton, was struck on the head with a billiard cue while he was inside Manston block investigating a complaint by a Black woman about racist graffiti on her front door. There followed an immediate incursion onto the estate of riot police in large numbers. They remained for the next two days. Clasford Sterling recalled that period:-

"Every morning they would pull up, they would don their black gloves inside the van, and while they were putting on their black gloves they would be smiling at anyone who was around. They would come upstairs and they would position themselves totally around the deck of Tangmere. That was the only area of the estate they actually policed. They were just trying to incite and antagonise the youth as far as we see it."

3.30 From then on, the amount of police attention devoted to Broadwater Farm increased considerably. A team of eight home beat officers patrolled the estate on a continuous rota. PC Stratton never returned. Even before he left, secret surveillance had started from one of the high floors in the Northolt tower block. Millard Scott told us:-

"We could identify the windows because we saw the reflection from the sun on several occasions. We saw the curtain being moved and what looked like equipment being put in front of it. We have seen people actually looking from out of the windows. We got binoculars and we looked and we saw someone with binoculars looking at us."

Malcolm Sargison had been told by PC Stratton how the council co-operated with the police by allowing empty flats in tower blocks to be used during "surveillance weeks."

3.31 Sometimes there were flare-ups, when the risk of major trouble was averted by the intervention of senior people from the council, usually in the middle of the night: particularly Councillors Bernie Grant and Ernie Large, and the Chief Executive, Roy Limb, whose actions went far beyond the normal call of a Chief Executive's duty. We heard of three incidents in particular, two caused by insensitive policing and one by a criminal act. There was the case of the man who laughed at the police just after Easter 1983. Two men were working on a car. Two patrolling officers came by and one of them tripped.

The men laughed. Immediately they were questioned about the car; they refused to answer; others came over to see what was happening; the police called reinforcements; a van load came down, and the two men were taken off to the police station. The other insensitive incident could be called the case of the quiet football match. In the spring of 1985, when Chief Superintendent Couch's approach appeared to be working, three vans from special units swept down onto the estate and spread out in a show of force. The superintendent expressed his regrets at the incident, explaining that the officers had been at the Tottenham Hotspur football match where they had not had enough to do.

3.32 The criminal act, and in our view also a disgraceful incident, was the stabbing of a police officer, PC Betts, on 4th August 1983. Officers had gone to arrest a woman in the Manston block, a crowd gathered and the police radioed for assistance. In the melee which followed PC Betts was stabbed in the back. Great numbers of other officers were called onto the estate. Feelings were high on both sides. Councillor Bernie Grant, who arrived on the scene, was ordered to move on and almost dragged from his car before Mr Limb intervened. Mr Limb, Councillor Grant and Councillor Large then stood between the residents and the police and succeeded in preventing further trouble.

3.33 The more that incidents of this kind occurred, the more they created a vicious spiral of mistrust and fear. Conservative Councillor Andrew Mitchell described it as a "chicken and egg situation", since in his view it became impossible to discover who was originally to blame. He gave this analysis:—

"Conversations after the riot confirmed to me that there is an understandable perception that the police do not like the youths, and particularly did not like the organisations which were on Broadwater Farm. By the same token, giving a balanced view, there is a perception by the police that they cannot go to an area like Broadwater Farm to carry out normal policing, without being in some way attacked, victimised or abused. So you start to develop the chicken and egg situation. The police officers, because they are scared, rather than going in twos to investigate crime in the ordinary way, start to go mob-handed. Then those that are being investigated get the feeling that they are being victimised. You

THE POLICE AND THE COMMUNITY

want to say: 'Forget what's gone on in the past, let's start again and treat each other normally'."

We have described above how, in our view, the leadership of Commander Dickinson had made it impossible to make a fresh start, which Councillor Mitchell rightly said was needed.

CRIME ON THE ESTATE

3.34 The sad irony is that these dangerous clashes with the police were taking place over a period when crime on the estate was decreasing. Figures were provided from police sources to Haringey Council's police sub-committee, which have been often quoted and never disputed by the police. The figures were for the numbers of crimes reported, which occurred in or near the 12 residential blocks on Broadwater Farm Estate, during each six month period from June to November, from 1982–1985 (except that in 1985 the period taken was from June to October).

Year	Vehicle Crime	Beat Crime	Major Crime	Robbery	Burglary	TOTAL
1982	103	44	34	13	72	266
1983	122	59	68	34	135	418
1984	66	35	11	21	40	173
1985	48	31	22	30	30	161
Rate of increase 1984–5 Compared with 1982–3	50% Decrease	32% Decrease	63% Decrease	8% Increase	62% Decrease	50% Decrease

3.35 We have no doubt that the remarkable decrease in crime, which is revealed by these figures, was due to two principal causes:—
(1) The programme of security improvements such as the strengthening of doors and the installing of entry phones, which, in particular, was responsible for the decrease in the number of burglaries.
(2) The achievements of the Youth Association in providing activities for unemployed young men and a sense of purpose in the community generally. Stafford Scott described the effect of the Youth Association's work in terms which precisely echoed the sentiments of much more conservative witnesses speaking about the neighbourhood watch schemes:—
"We believe there was a rekindled community spirit. I used to

watch a lot of programmes when I was younger about pre-war Britain, when people used to come out of their houses and leave their front doors open, and everybody knew everybody on the street. And although people weren't actually leaving their doors open, there was a different kind of atmosphere."

Cliff Ford, an estate sweeper and member of the Tenants' Association Executive, as well as other witnesses, confirmed that the Youth Association was as concerned about crime as anybody else and was trying to get it down.

3.36 The police were annoyed that the Youth Association would not agree to a Neighbourhood Watch scheme being set up on the estate. Youth Association workers were concerned about such schemes in other areas. Their experience was that Neighbourhood Watch schemes targeted Black youths as objects of suspicion. In any case, they thought that they were making progress in reducing crime in the community in their own way, without the need for a formal scheme. On one occasion they had 'solved' a crime in a way which provoked considerable anger. Councillor Glenys Atkinson told Dolly Kiffin that her handbag had been stolen on the estate. Councillor Grant described what happened:—

"Dolly Kiffin had the youths going around trying to find her handbag, and apparently they found the handbag within five or six hours, and they brought it back intact, with the purse and so on in it. And the police were angry. I remember there was a meeting afterwards, and the police kept referring to this incident. Why was it that the Youth Association could do something like that and they couldn't?"

3.37 Chief Superintendent Couch and the Community Liaison Officers had some understanding of the achievements of the Broadwater Farm community in reducing crime. But most of the rank and file officers, we believe, were infected by a venomous antagonism towards the estate. The point was made politely in an article in the *Police* magazine:—

"It has to be said that the very high opinion of Mrs Kiffin's sense of civic responsibility and qualities of leadership, expressed by senior officers, appears to find little concurrence among rank and file officers dealing with the problems of the Youth Association's members on the estate."

THE POLICE AND THE COMMUNITY

One can only wonder how this view was expressed within the confines of the police canteen or the Instant Response Unit van.

3.38 It is necessary to stress the factor of racialism in the response of the rank and file police. The report of the Policy Studies Institute, *Police and People in London*, was based on a prolonged study carried out by experienced and reputable researchers. It was commissioned by the Metropolitan Police themselves. On the general level of racialist feeling within the police, they reported as follows: —
> "Our first impression after being attached to groups of police officers in areas having a substantial ethnic minority population was that racialist language and racial prejudice were prominent and pervasive and that many individual officers and also whole groups were preoccupied with ethnic differences... On the whole, our further research confirmed these initial impressions."

3.39 For the police, the characteristic feature of the Broadwater Farm Estate was that the prominent community leaders were Black people. Since no effective steps were being taken to educate junior officers out of their racialist feelings, or into some genuine understanding of the community, the prejudice intensified with every incident. The evidence which we have heard about the treatment of Black people is startlingly confirmed by the evidence of remarks passed to White people: —
> "Oh you've had some coons breaking in, have you? I don't know why you live around here with bloody nig-nogs trying to break in to your house." (Police officer to White woman after a burglary.)
>
> "We've been burgled four times. On each occasion when the police came to investigate, they have said automatically they had been done by Blacks. They said: 'Oh it must be somebody off the Farm'."
>
> "If we could have gone into the Youth Association we might have found the person who did this."

3.40 Over 1984-5, as Chief Superintendent Couch tried to exercise his authority, a new element entered into the attitude of the rank and file — one of discontent at their own superiors for not letting them deal with the people on the Farm as they wanted to. One officer said to a nearby resident, who had been burgled: —
> "It's a no-go area, we can't go onto there because we'll end up with a riot."

3.41 It is necessary to look closely at the use of this term "no-go area". It seems to reflect a perception which is felt at the highest levels of the Metropolitan Police. The Commissioner in his report for 1983 spoke of Broadwater Farm as one of:—
"Those areas identified as 'symbolic locations' where Black communities, often the young, come to view a particular location with something of a proprietorial attachment resenting intrusion, especially by the police to enforce the law."

He was claiming, therefore, that it was Black people who did not want the law enforced. Junior officers took up this theme, claiming they were not being allowed by their superiors to police the area properly.

3.42 But when we look at the reality of the actions and words of the representatives of the Broadwater Farm community, the idea of "no-go areas" or "symbolic locations" are seen to be a myth created by the police as far as Broadwater Farm was concerned. The Youth Association never asked the police to keep out. As we have seen, they wanted more contact not less. During the 21st public hearing of the Inquiry, Lord Gifford said:—
"We have not heard from anybody who is not pro law and order. We have not heard from anyone who does not want the police to do a job for the community."

His remarks drew applause from the largely Black audience in the hall. They reflected the evidence which we had heard. For in fact there were regular police patrols through the estate in the 1980s, and visits made frequently by senior officers, without molestation or opposition. The community did react in opposition to arbitrary policing, oppressive policing, and racist policing. But they did not, as alleged by D.A.C Richards in his report, seek to resist normal and lawful policing methods.

THE POLICE AND THE COUNCIL
3.43 Under the present law, the police authority for the London area is the Home Secretary. Local authorities have no legal role in the policing of their borough. In practice, however, there needs to be co-operation in many areas, and officers and members of the Haringey Council met frequently with the police. Chief Executive Roy Limb described the pattern:—
"There was a sort of myth around that Haringey Council never talked to the police. That's a load of nonsense, because going back

certainly as long as I have been Chief Executive, there have always been meetings with senior police officers. What usually happened if an issue arises on an estate or something of that nature, I would suggest, or be asked by a chair of committee or by the leader, to fix up a meeting with the local police chief, and I would."

There was, however, no structured basis for these meetings; they depended on ad hoc co-operation on each side.

3.44 Difficulties arose in Haringey because of the views held on both sides about police accountability. The council had resolved to support changes in the law which would make the police accountable to a locally elected authority. In 1983 they established a police sub-committee, comprising councillors and over 30 non-voting delegate groups representing Black and minority ethnic groups, youth and women's groups, the elderly, lesbian and gay communities, and a number of other recognised organisations such as the Haringey Community Relations Council. Its terms of reference included the monitoring of various aspects of policing, making recommendations upon matters relating to the police, and advocating democratic accountability of the police. Clearly it was hoped to achieve some form of accountability in practice, even though none was possible in law. From 1984 the sub-committee was serviced by a police research unit consisting of three officers.

3.45 The police through Commander Dickinson were invited to participate in the work of the sub-committee, but Commander Dickinson refused saying:—

"My constitutional position, as police commander responsible to the Commissioner and the Home Secretary, debars me from involvement in the schemes outlined in the letter."

This was not correct. The law precluded the Commander from being answerable to the local authority, but it did not prevent co-operation and consultation with the council through any appropriate channel. We understand that local senior officers in other areas co-operate with the council police committee and in at least one case attend meetings as observers. As we have said earlier, the attitude of Commander Dickinson in refusing to speak or write to the council's police sub-committee was petty-minded and unhelpful for community relations.

3.46 The next attempt at a structured dialogue involving the council, the police and the community concerned the Broadwater Farm Panel. The council were anxious to include the police in what was developing into a very useful forum for the discussion by different agencies of problems concerning the estate. The process was that each agency on the panel presented a brief report and answered questions from local residents. The chair of the panel, Councillor Bernie Grant wrote to Chief Superintendent Couch on 23rd January 1985, to confirm the invitation.

3.47   Chief Superintendent Couch replied on 5th February 1985: —
"I and my officers attend numerous meetings to respond to community issues and demands, and never has a request been made for a 'written report' in the council style. If we did, I and my staff would be permanently preparing reports instead of combatting the increasing crime rate, racial harassment and the problems of minority groups.

"In your position as ward councillor, I am always willing to inform you of current trends and issues affecting local policing, but I am not prepared to report in advance to the council-sponsored 'panel' which makes recommendations to the appropriate committee of the council."

This reply does little credit to the reputation of Chief Superintendent Couch as a community policeman, and rather bears the imprint of Commander Dickinson. Councillor Grant agreed to have further discussion at a meeting, and he wrote on 10th April 1985: —
"I would therefore like to propose that we do meet together with a representative from each of the Broadwater Farm Tenants' and Youth Associations. I would also be accompanied by Neale Coleman, the Broadwater Farm Neighbourhood Officer, and an officer from the police sub-committee research unit."
Chief Superintendent Couch replied on the 9th May 1985 expressing "reservations" about the number of people proposed: —

"If you feel that such numbers are required to meet police, then I doubt if we are starting off on the right foot. I would like to know what you require of the police before I meet what appears to me to be a vetting group."

THE POLICE AND THE COMMUNITY

3.48 The negative result of this exchange of correspondence was that police officers never attended the Broadwater Farm Panel before the 6th October disturbances. They never had the chance to discuss, in the valuable open forum which the panel provided, any of the policing problems which began to emerge during the summer of 1985. Councillor Grant views this as a tragedy: —

"I would suggest to the Inquiry that if the police had come onto the Broadwater Farm Panel from as early as January 1985 when we had invited them to, then I believe that we would have not had those disturbances on 6th October on Broadwater Farm. Because if the police had any problem with regard to the estate, they would have been able to put it down in front of the panel, we would have discussed it properly, it would have been reported on. The Youth Association was represented there, and the Tenants' Association, and the matter could have been resolved."

We certainly agree that another valuable opportunity had been lost because of the attitude of the police. We are glad to record that Tottenham's new senior officer, Chief Superintendent Alan Stainsby attended the Broadwater Farm Panel meeting of 15th April 1986 and submitted a written report on crime figures and arrests on the estate.

3.49 The next chapter in this history of failed opportunities between the police and the council concerned the Haringey Community and Police Consultative Group. The proposal made by Lord Scarman for a statutory consultative scheme had been implemented by section 106 of the Police and Criminal Evidence Act 1984, which provided: —

"Arrangements shall be made in each police area for obtaining the views of people in that area about matters concerning the policing of the area and for obtaining their co-operation with the police in preventing crime in the area."

In London, it was the duty of the Commissioner to make the arrangements in accordance with guidance issued by the Home Secretary. The Commissioner was obliged to consult with the council of each London borough as to the arrangements that would be appropriate for the borough.

3.50 On 27th February 1985 Commander Dickinson wrote to Mr Limb asking for a discussion about these arrangements "with the leader and yourself". On 2nd April 1985 Councillor Narendra Makanji, chair of the police sub-committee, replied to Commander Dickinson. He observed that membership of the existing sub-

committee broadly coincided with the recommendations contained in the Home Office guidance. He concluded: —
"We believe that the terms of reference of the council's police sub-committee provide an appropriate basis for this area's consultation arrangements and accordingly invite the Metropolitan Police Y District to enter into an arrangement for consultation on the basis of these existing terms of reference."

3.51 We think that in writing this letter the council was itself indulging in obstructive tactics. It must have been quite apparent to them that Commander Dickinson could not possibly agree to enter into consultative arrangements on the basis of the police sub-committee's terms of reference, when the Home Office guidance stressed the importance of such arrangements being independent of local authority structures. The reply from Commander Dickinson was swift and inevitable: —
"I am not able to discuss consultative arrangements on this basis further."

3.52 Neither side had left any further room for movement. The next communication about the consultative group was from D.A.C Richards on 24th May 1985 when he invited the council to attend an exploratory meeting at which a good section of community repesentatives would be present. The council considered that it had not been properly consulted, and did not attend this meeting, or any other meetings of the Haringey Community and Police Consultative Group which was subsequently formed. We will return later to consider this state of affairs.

THE SUMMER OF 1985
3.53 Morale on the Broadwater Farm was high. In the 3rd June edition, *"Broadwater Review"*, the Youth Association magazine of community news, led off with an article headed: "Plan for new jobs." Other articles reflected the spirit of a community on the move: —

"SERVICES FOR TURKISH SPEAKING RESIDENTS."

"ASIAN ACTIVITIES AT THE MOTHERS' PROJECT."

"MINISTER TO VISIT."

THE POLICE AND THE COMMUNITY

"DISABLED PEOPLE START TO ORGANISE."

"HAIRDRESSING SALON OPENED."

The fourth annual festival was announced for August, with "the one and only Junior Delgardo" and many other talents. The pool team and the junior football team had done well in their leagues. The Mothers' Project announced a crowded programme of events.

3.54 In July the Youth Association organised a trip for its members to Jamaica. The Youth Association had raised the funds for this trip through fund-raising events, and no council money was involved. Four councillors and Mr and Mrs Limb were invited on the trip by the Youth Association, at their own expense. Mr Limb explained the purposes of the trip:—
> "One, it was to mark the enormous progress that the Youth Association had made. It was a sort of reward to itself for all the efforts that it had made over the last three or four years to arrive at that stage. And secondly, and as a really marvellous example of the stage it had arrived at, it was going to Jamaica to help a Youth Association over there called West Park to raise its sights and to do some actual work for it."

This was a valuable international exchange. The youths from Broadwater Farm built a fence around the West Park club in Clarendon, and repaired the access road. Even more, they learned about Jamaica, where many of their parents had been born. There is to be a return visit by the West Park club in August 1986.

The main party returned at the end of August. Dolly Kiffin stayed on in Jamaica until 23rd September.

3.55 Before the Jamaica party left, a number of youths from outside the estate had begun to congregate on Broadwater Farm. Norton McLean, Principal Youth Officer for Haringey explained one of the reasons why, in his view, so many youths were attracted there:—
> "One of the major points is that there were subsidised meals. And there were large groups of unemployed young people that, if they can go somewhere where you can get a good cheap West Indian meal for about £1.60 which, in other places, you would pay £5 to £6 for, quite clearly that's an attraction."

The youths were not accepted inside the Youth Association building, and they used to hang around the Tangmere precinct, kicking footballs, and sometimes riding motor bikes around the precinct.

3.56 While the party was away in Jamaica, a new set of strangers arrived — drug traffickers. They came in expensive cars and parked along Willan Road. They had been pushed out of their former patches in Stoke Newington and Hackney after a police operation. They were selling drugs in little square packets. They were remarkably conspicuous in their activity:—
"It was horrible. You couldn't walk without someone propositioning you to buy drugs. Even if your mother walked under there, they would ask your mother if she wanted to buy drugs. It was not nice. They were out there day and night making a noise, driving their cars up and down. It was really horrible." (Joanne George, community worker).
"I was confronted with an individual walking up the steps with fists spread out with a joint sticking through each gap in the fingers." (Mike Bates, Youth and Community Service Officer).

3.57 The officers of the Youth Association wanted the police to get the pushers off the estate. Rupert Downing, the other Social Services community worker on the estate, remembers one of the meetings with Supt. Stacey at the Youth Association in August 1985:—
"It was a completely unanimous policy that the police should be identifying the vehicles that were being used, and that there was no reason once they had identified the vehicles for those vehicles not to be apprehended off the estate prior to them coming on and causing us all the hassle."
Supt. Stacey's view was that there was a vacuum in the community because the leaders were away in Jamaica. Those present replied: "What leaders? We are all working together here."

3.58 In September, when Roy Limb returned, he spoke to Chief Superintendent Couch. He was told of the large numbers of strangers on Broadwater Farm, and accusations of drugs being sold. There had been some incidents involving things thrown at policemen. There had been parties late at night at the Social Club. Mr Couch said that he was in a dilemma whether to send in considerable numbers of police, or "try and keep it calm and hope that normality would be restored in due course." The conclusion reached by both men was:-
"That it would be better for us to avoid a major confrontation until

THE POLICE AND THE COMMUNITY

the leaders returned and hope that they could control things."

By the leaders, Roy Limb was referring to Dolly Kiffin and to Clasford Sterling, who was also away. Chief Superintendent Couch made the same point in an interview with *"World in Action"* in October 1986:-

"There were two ways I could deal with it. One was through the community representatives. Regretfully both of them, as you may well know, had gone on holiday and I had no-one to talk to."

3.59 We believe that this was, with the best of intentions, a misjudgement. it was not the case that there was "no-one to talk to". There were other officers at the Youth Association in the absence of Dolly Kiffin and Clasford Sterling. There were many people with whom the drug trafficking problem could and should have been discussed, and action taken. If, as was the case, there was general agreement that the police ought to act, an operation could have been mounted which had the Youth Association's consent. As one of those workers, Millard Scott told us: "There is not going to be no riot for drug pushers".

3.60 The inaction of the police leadership through August and September had the further consequence of infuriating the team of home beat officers. To them it was the final proof of the lunacy of "community policing". Cliff Ford, a sweeper on the estate, was approached by one of the beat officers:—

"He came up to me and said 'Are you a member of the Tenants' Association? Could you get your Tenants' Association to write a letter to our Superintendent, because we want to come in and sort this estate out.'"

Woman Sergeant Gillian Meynell in her report leaked to the press, records that on one occasion, at the request of Mr Couch, the home beat team collected 50 of the empty drug packets and brought them back to the station:—

"Mr Couch said 'Oh how many have you got?' I said 50. He said 'Oh just throw them out.' Why we bothered, I do not know. Needless to say morale plummeted once again."

The *Police* magazine recorded later that constables were being stopped by members of the public and asked why police were unable to control the drug taking on the estate. It is a sad irony that the same question at the same time was being asked by the Youth Association of Superintendent Stacey. If the Youth Association and the home beat officers had known each other, they would have found much to agree about.

3.61 The pages of the *Police Magazine* for October 1985 suggest that in addition to the selling of drugs there were frequent attacks by people on the estate against the patrolling home beat officers. In the light of this we have examined very closely the Richards report. D.A.C. Richards has listed a large number of incidents, some only supported by rumour, suggesting that violence was being prepard during the weeks prior to 6th October. There is one incident, and one incident only, of an attack upon the police. On 11th September, the day after the Handsworth disturbances, two home beat officers were attacked with missiles by a gang of Black youths, and one was struck on the head and injured. We deplore this attack, but if there were others, D.A.C. Richards would surely have recorded them in his report.

3.62 On 23rd September Dolly Kiffin returned. She immediately noticed a "an enormous amount of cars, and strange faces that I have never seen in my life". Within hours she was meeting with Superintendent Stacey. He told her about the drug traffickers. He said that they were coming from Brixton, Stoke Newington and Finsbury Park. Dolly Kiffin asked him what he was going to do about it. He replied that the police were waiting for her to call them in. Dolly Kiffin described her reaction:—

> "I jumped off my chair. I said you are waiting on me, Dolly Kiffin, to call you in and use the law? You get paid as the police and you work as an officer, and you are waiting for me to call you in? That means you are putting my back against the wall, so that if there is anything, you can say that Dolly Kiffin called you in and publish that. And then what happens? I get a knife in my back or shot in my back, with these strange people? No, I am not going to call you in."

Neale Coleman was also present at one of the discussions with Dolly Kiffin during that week. He agreed that the police appeared to be trying to put the responsibility onto the Youth Association:—

> "And I think their feeling and Mrs Kiffin's feeling at the time was that this was not her responsibility. Her view was clear that this was undesirable, and that action should be taken, but that it was not for her or for anyone else in the Youth Association to give authority for this. It was felt that if there were undesirable or criminal elements involved, that was a matter for the police."

THE POLICE AND THE COMMUNITY

3.63 We think that there was another serious misjudgement here about the nature of community policing. It should not be a question of abdicating responsibility for policing decisions to community leaders, particularly in a matter so dangerous as drug trafficking. Rather, there should have been close communication about the nature of the operation which the police would have had to mount, in order that responsible people in the community could understand it and support it. This did not happen. It seems that there well may have been conflicting views between the Scotland Yard Drug Squad and the local force as to the nature of the operation required. As to this, we are lacking evidence from the police which might enable us to understand what, if anything, was being planned against the drug traffickers. But that does not excuse the mishandling of the situation which continued after Dolly Kiffin's return.

3.64 On Saturday 28th September Mrs. Cherry Groce was shot and seriously injured in Brixton, and there were disturbances in the streets. It must have been appreciated by police in Tottenham that the shooting of a mother in her home by a police officer would cause feelings of outrage in their community as well. Following on the Handsworth disturbances three weeks earlier it was a time for particularly sensitive policing and close liaison with community representatives.

3.65 On Tuesday 1st October the police took action without any such consultation. Black people in cars were stopped and searched as they went in and out of the estate. The relevance of this operation to the drug trafficking problems is far from clear. Nick Wright of the Police Research Unit, having had discussions both with local police and Scotland Yard officers, told us that this stop and search operation was unconnected to any drugs surveillance, and that the police themselves said that they were looking for stolen property. He believes that the Drugs Squad officers were annoyed that a careful operation which they were mounting, which depended upon a degree of subtlety and discretion, was being disrupted by this crude stop-and-search. Whatever its purpose, the operation was called off after only a day, having achieved nothing except further resentment. As Mr Limb said:—

"The day of action was a disaster. The police ended up picking people up who were just entering and leaving the estate. It was the old routine all over again. It had no effect except to wind up all of the young people on Broadwater Farm."

The home beat officers were angry as well. In the words of *Police* magazine, they believed that "The smack of firm policing suddenly descended on Broadwater Farm", only for the operation to be called off before it had hardly begun.

RUMOURS OF RIOT – TRUE OR FALSE?
3.66 The Richards report states that in the week immediately preceeding 6th October there were:—

"Persistent rumours that there were plans afoot for a major disturbance and looting, Wood Green Shopping City being identified as the prime target. It is emphasised that these were only rumours, but there were a number of occurrences which tended to indicate that there may have been some substance in them."

Later the report states that "it is a matter of conjecture what would have occurred had Mrs Jarrett not died." Sergeant Meynell in her leaked report states explicitly that she and her team had warned Chief Superintendent Couch of the possibility of a riot at a meeting with him four days before:—

"He balked at the idea of rioting on the estate, saying they would not damage their own property. We told him that we had received information that they would riot there and that it would be that weekend."

3.67 Rumours there undoubtedly were. They started after the Handsworth disturbances on 10th September, and they intensified after the shooting of Mrs Groce and the subsequent disturbances on 28th September. Arthur Lawrence, a West Indian community leader, heard it from the manager of an off licence ("There is going to be a riot in Wood Green"). Russell Simper, the estate supervisor heard it from his children from school ("trouble at the High Road or Wood Green"). Residents close to the estate heard it in the local shops ("something would happen at the weekend, at Wood Green or Broadwater Farm"). Mrs Kemp, who worked for British Telecom, heard that staff at Wood Green were being allowed to go home early. Dolly Kiffin was twice told by police officers that there was going to be a riot, by Superintendent Stacey on 23rd September, and by Inspector Gee at a reception at the Civic Centre on 4th October ("there is going to be a riot tomorrow").

3.68 What foundation of fact did these rumours have? We have

THE POLICE AND THE COMMUNITY

closely examined the eleven "occurrences" listed in the Richards report. Six of them are pure hearsay: "unconfirmed reports", "information was received". In the course of our Inquiry we met people who had given "information" to the police. We interviewed one person who lived in a high tower block who believed that things were going on which she could not possibly have seen. She was making assumptions rather than visual observations, as many people do. We do not therefore place any weight upon "unconfirmed reports". On the contrary, they were themselves part of the rumour, and a small example from the pages of *Police* magazine indicates how unwise it is to rely on them. During September 1985, an arsonist went about burning cars, seven in all. He was finally caught and found to be a White youth with a mental illness. But the police diary records:—
"Attended scene of arson on car. It appears Black youths from off the estate did this."

3.69 The other five occurrences recorded in the Richards report are:—

(1) The daubing with graffiti of the Asian-owned supermarket on the Tangmere precinct on 20th September. It is alleged in the Richards report "that the perpetrators of this offence are believed to be known to a council officer" — an allegation much resented by Neale Coleman, the Neighbourhood Officer , who witnessed the daubing by a single Black man who was a stranger to him and telephoned Chief Superintendent Couch while it was actually going on. As Mr Coleman says, and we agree:—
"I take it rather ill, having done that, and as far as I know the police having done nothing whatsoever about it, that it should then be suggested that a council officer had in some way not co-operated about the matter."

(2) The shooting of a man in the Social Club on 22nd September — an offence for which a man has been charged. It was in relation to this incident that an officer had made an entry in his diary, later printed in *Police* magazine, which revealed his attitude of mind:—
"As predicted, trouble last night at the IC3 (i.e Black) party. One IC3 shot twice and police car damaged. (At least it's one of them!)"

(3) The robbery of a post office in Mount Pleasant Road near to the estate by masked Black youths on 1st October.

THE BROADWATER FARM INQUIRY REPORT

(4) The finding of a petrol bomb in a drain under one of the walkways on 2nd October.

(5) Reports on 4th October that postmen delivering mail to the estate were being subjected to harassment. The Post Office have been good enough to supply us a list of all incidents in N.17 during 1985, from which it appears that there were three unsuccessful attempts to get at postal vans around the estate, on 4th September, 5th September, and 2nd October.

3.70 Only the fourth of these incidents can fairly be said to have any relevance to the issue whether people on the Broadwater Farm Estate were preparing to riot prior to 6th October 1985. And that reference to a single petrol bomb is itself significant, in view of other rumours that were going about concerning petrol bombs. Cliff Ford, a sweeper on the estate, said that the police were going around collecting every little bottle they could find. He himself was asked by Sergeant Meynell to hand in any bottles, as they might be petrol bombs. But as he said to us:—

"I just saw bottles scattered in normal litter, and normal litter could be quite a lot of bottles. I can't keep running up to a policeman with every little thing bottle I find."

In the light of that, the finding of one petrol bomb on 2nd October, the day after the police operations, hardly suggests preparations for mass riot.

3.71 We have carefully examined the evidence presented in the Richards report. It was undoubtedly true that there were tensions between the police and members of the community in the week before 6th October. The police were fully entitled to take precautions. We recognise that police officers are exposed to physical dangers which the rest of us do not face. Difficult decisions have to be made in order to reduce the risks to their safety. However on the evidence before us, the tensions were in fact under control.

There had been rumours of riots every summer since 1981. But there was in fact no riot after Handsworth, or after the shooting of Mrs Groce, or after the stop-and-search operation. During that operation, Youth Association workers told us that they were actively speaking to their members, telling them to keep calm and not be provoked. There was, as we have seen, little basis of hard fact for the rumour that was going round. We do not believe that a riot was being planned by members of the Broadwater Farm community.

Chapter 4
THE DEATH OF MRS JARRETT

INTRODUCTION
4.1 Mrs Cynthia Jarrett was born in June 1937 in Clarendon, Jamaica, and came to England in 1958 to join her husband. Mr and Mrs Jarrett lived in Tottenham for some 25 years, during which time they raised a family of five children. The family never lived on Broadwater Farm, but when the children were young they lived in Mount Pleasant Road and had many friends on the estate. Mrs Jarrett worked for National Plastics in Walthamstow for 11 years before being made redundant in 1983. She was grandmother to ten children, and often looked after the children of neighbours and friends. Her daughter Patricia remembers her as "loving and kind to everybody". Mr Jarrett says with great affection: "Cynthia was very understandable and a lover of kids." She was a deeply religious woman who attended the local Catholic church. She bore no ill-will towards the police.

4.2 The death of Mrs Jarrett was the subject of an inquest which lasted for seven days from 27th November to 4th December 1985. The police officers who were involved in the search of her house, and members of her family who were there, gave evidence and were represented by barristers. Many other witnesses were called. The Coroner gave a full summing up to the jury, instructing them as to the different verdicts which were open to them, depending on what view they took of the evidence. The jury of 12 people delivered a verdict of accidental death. This meant, following the Coroner's direction, that they considered that Detective Constable Randall, while searching Mrs Jarrett's home, had given her a push, but not deliberately, causing her to fall and contributing to her death through hypertensive heart disease.

4.3 We accept this verdict. It was the judgement of 12 citizens made at the end of a fairly conducted inquest, and we do not question it. Nor have we attempted to conduct a re-run of the inquest evidence; that would neither have been possible nor useful. Instead we have obtained the fullest possible notes of the inquest proceedings, and of the later court proceedings in which Floyd Jarrett was acquitted of assault. In this chapter we summarise the evidence given to the inquest and to the court, adding our own comments where appropriate, and we comment on the statement made by the Police Complaints Authority (PCA) at the end of their investigation of the circumstances surrounding Mrs Jarrett's death.

4.4 In obtaining material about the inquest we have had generous help from members of the Jarrett family and their solicitor. They had applied to the Coroner for a transcript of the inquest proceedings, which they were ready to put at our disposal. Regrettably, such a transcript has not been forthcoming from the Coroner's Court. It seems that shorthand notes were made by a shorthand writer whose fees were paid by the Metropolitan Police: transcripts cannot be made available to the Coroner without the consent of the police which has not been forthcoming. An official tape recording was also made, but no transcript from that could be completed in the time available to us. Accordingly we have relied on full notes which were taken both by Dave Leadbetter, who was there as a representative of the Inquest organisation, and by Tracey Blom, a barrister. They represent a very full though not verbatim record.

THE ARREST OF FLOYD JARRETT
4.5 Floyd Jarrett has been an active member of the Broadwater Farm Youth Association for many years. He had been on the trip to Jamaica. He lived in Enfield, having moved away from 25 Thorpe Road about six months before. The events of 5th October 1985 begin with the arrest of Floyd Jarrett, and the circumstances of that arrest are important. For the police, the suspicion which was said to attach to Floyd justified the decision to search his mother's home. For the family, the whole sequence of events beginning with the arrest of Floyd, was part of their complaint to the PCA.

4.6 Just before 1.00 pm on Saturday 5th October, Floyd Jarrett was driving with a friend along Roseberry Avenue, Tottenham, when he was stopped by uniformed police officers. The reason given later for

THE DEATH OF MRS JARRETT

the stop was that one officer (PC Casey) had noticed that the car had an out-of-date tax disc, showing the expiry date 31st August 1985. PC Casey had radioed to officers in another police car (Sergeant Parsons and PC Allan) who had carried out the stop. PC Allan filled out a form which required the driver to report to a police station with his driving and insurance certificate. The incident would normally have ended there.

4.7 PC Casey then decided to connect to the Police National Computer to make a check upon the car number and the name of the driver. He was asked at the Magistrates Court why he had done this. Stephen Solley, counsel for Floyd Jarrett, asked him: "Would you have checked me out if I had been driving with a tax disc five weeks out of date?" The officer said no. Mr Solley asked if he could give any reason, other than that he was a Black man driving a flashy-looking car (a BMW Coupe). He could give no reason.

4.8 The computer check revealed that there was no trace of the car number UGX5OF, the number on the plates. But PC Casey observed that the number on the tax disc was different – WGX5OF – and he put a check through the computer on this number. This did check out with a BMW car with the right chassis number – the record showing that it had been sold a year before. Therefore it was not listed as a stolen car. Floyd Jarrett was waiting by the car while these steps were taken; he was not asked any questions about how he obtained the car. He explained that the number plates had always been like that, and it was apparent that they were very old and had not been recently fitted. On the basis of this information, PC Casey decided to arrest Floyd Jarrett for suspected theft of the motor vehicle.

4.9 At this point Floyd Jarrett made a run across the road. He was chased by the three officers and soon caught. The officers claimed that when they caught up with him, he struck two blows with his fist, the second of which hit PC Casey in the face. However, an independent witness, architect Ralph Harris, had witnessed the whole incident. He had seen the three officers run across the road and jump at Floyd Jarrett from behind. He had seen no punch to an officer's face, aimed or otherwise.

4.10 Floyd Jarrett was charged with assaulting PC Casey. On 13th

THE BROADWATER FARM INQUIRY REPORT

December 1985 he appeared at the Magistrates Court and was acquitted of the charge. The magistrates made an award of £350 costs against the police, which indicated their belief that the charge should have never been brought. In the course of the hearing the whole sequence of events leading to the arrest was closely examined. For example, the police officers had alleged that the engine number inside the car looked as if it might have been filed down, and that the chassis plate looked slightly curved. So the car was brought to court, and all present were able to see that neither the engine number nor the chassis plate had been tampered with in any way. Mr Solley in his closing speech to the magistrates said that this incident was a striking demonstration of the importance of our civil liberties and that a careless and prejudiced use of police powers had in this case set off a chain of events which had led to terrible consequences. The magistrates by their verdict appear to have agreed. The charge itself was a classic example of a "knock-on" charge such as we referred to earlier (3.5), where the arrested person is charged, not with anything relating to the supposed reason for his arrest, but for an incident alleged – in this case falsely – to have occurred as a result of the contact with the police.

4.11 At 1.25 pm on 5th October Floyd Jarrett arrived at the police station. He had given a false name and address. He said at the trial that he had failed his driving test and ought not to have been driving without L plates. But within a few hours his true identity had been discovered. There was an invoice in the car in the name of Mr Jarrett, and the police were able to check that name against a photograph which was on file at St. Ann's Police Station and which proved that the man in their custody was Floyd Jarrett, of 25 Thorpe Road, N.15. Sergeant Parsons and PC Casey returned to Tottenham police station with this information at 3.30 pm.

4.12 At that point there were no grounds for holding Floyd Jarrett any longer and he should have been released. There was no evidence whatever that the car was stolen; indeed the invoice showed that it had been in Mr Jarrett's possession since at least May, and the computer information showed that its last registered owner had sold it. The officer even checked to discover whether any crimes were known to have been committed by people using a blue BMW, but the answer was negative. The sequence of events involving Floyd Jarrett and the police should have ended.

THE DEATH OF MRS JARRETT

THE DECISION TO SEARCH THE HOUSE.
4.13   At this point Detective Constable Michael Randall intervened in the case. DC Randall is a C.I.D officer, then aged 24. He had been based at Stoke Newington police station for some time, and had then moved to Tottenham. He was an officer against whom two complaints had been made in the summer of 1985, relating to his conduct of searches in the homes of Black people. The barrister appearing for the police at the inquest informed the Coroner that in one case there were no formal disciplinary proceedings but DC Randall had received "words of advice". In the other case the complainant was awaiting trial, so the complaint was still pending. The barrister said that he had received this information from Inspector Clarke, who was duty officer at Tottenham police station on 5th October.

4.14   DC Randall was officially off duty but had come into the police station at 4.15 pm to do paper work on a number of forthcoming Crown Court trials. According to his evidence, he heard about Floyd Jarrett being in custody, and went to his cell at 4.50 pm and Floyd Jarrett recognised him. Floyd Jarrett told us that he had never met DC Randall at all. The official custody record states not that Floyd Jarrett recognised DC Randall, but the opposite. He then took the decision that the Jarrett home should be searched. It was his decision, and it was approved by the duty officer, Inspector Clarke. He also decided that he should go on the search himself.

4.15   DC Randall claimed that "from dealing with many of the youths around the Tottenham area" he knew that Floyd Jarrett "was heavily involved in handling stolen goods". He had heard "other rumours from reliable sources" that he was "a major handler". It is impossible for us to know the exact nature and source of DC Randall's information; or to assess whether DC Randall had exaggerated the information which he had, in order to justify (after the event) the decision to search. His attitude to house searches, and to the evidence needed to justify one, can be gathered from an answer which he gave:—
   "I believe that PC Casey had sufficient grounds from the time Floyd was arrested. He had given fake particulars. It looked as if the car plates might have been fakes."
We do not agree that suspicion about a car should justify the serious step of invading the home. It would be a speculation, instead of concretely based suspicion that there were stolen goods to be found in the home.

4.16 There are other worrying features about the search. The pro forma warrant for a search for stolen goods contains a space for the description of the goods to be inserted. The instruction on the warrant says: "Specify stolen goods". Yet on the warrant drawn up for 25 Thorpe Road, all that has been inserted are the words: "Diverse Goods". It would appear that the officers were very unsure about what they were looking for.

4.17 Secondly, when the search did take place it was conducted in a cursory manner, as if all that was intended was a speculative visit. There was one locked room in the house, which was in fact Patricia Jarrett's bedroom. She normally kept it locked because her brother used to borrow her tapes. No attempt was made to enter it. Sergeant Parsons said that he could see "from the reflection in the brass light switch" that it was not a store room. The Coroner intervened:—

Coroner: "In my experience the best way to keep you out would be to have a locked door!"

Parsons: "It depends on the search. This was intended, sir, to be a low key search, a search of someone's home. We didn't knock things down. We conducted a search of what we could see. We were satisfied that it was not a room full of stock."

Coroner: "This is the most ridiculous thing I've ever heard!"

4.18 All the evidence points to this being a speculative search which should never have taken place. If Floyd Jarrett was seriously suspected of being a "major handler", then a proper investigation should have been mounted on the basis of specific information if and when it was known. If, however, there were only vague rumours about him, then the search was unjustified, and it did not become justified because he was in police custody.

THE WARRANT
4.19 DC Randall said that the search warrant was typed by PC Casey at 4.50 pm and that PC Casey left around 5.00 pm to go to the home of a magistrate. PC Casey said that he and PC Allan had left around 5.00; that the warrant was signed by the magistrate Mr Gardiner at about 5.15 pm and that he returned to the police station about 5.30 pm. The magistrate lived in St. Paul's Road, about five minutes drive from the police station.

4.20 Inspector Clarke gave evidence of a quite different time scale. He said that he had authorised the search warrant at 3.45 pm; that PC Casey had shown him the typed warrant at 4.15 pm; and that PC Casey had left the police station to go to the magistrate at 4.50 pm and returned at 5.15 pm. He said that he had then seen the warrant and saw that it had been signed. He was challenged at the inquest about an earlier statement which he had made to the Essex police in which he said that he "agreed to issue the search warrant at 5.00 pm". In answer he said: "In police work times are not very significant". This is a curious statement for a police inspector to make.

4.21 Under the Police and Criminal Evidence Act, which although not in force was being given a "trial run" at Tottenham police station at this time, there is a requirement for a custody record to be kept in relation to everyone detained at a police station, in which all matters relating to the case must be recorded. From 2.00 pm to 7.00 pm on 5th October the officer responsible for keeping that record was Sergeant Bowell. The first two lines of the second page of the custody record read as follows:—

"5.10.85. 5.15 pm. Search warrant obtained, declined to accompany police (signed) B132".

The date is in Sergeant Bowell's handwriting, but the time and the rest of the entry are in the handwriting of Sergeant Parsons. Sergeant Parsons had said in evidence that he had made the entry at 5.15 pm after PC Casey had returned with the signed warrant.

4.22 The Essex police, who had been investigating the circumstances of Mrs Jarrett's death under the supervision of the Police Complaints Authority, went to the magistrate on 7th October and took a statement from him. He said that he had signed the warrant for the search at 25 Thorpe Road between 6 pm and 6.30 pm. Assistant Chief Constable Simpson, who was in charge of the investigation, told his officers to go back to the magistrate and re-interview him. In his second interview on 8th October, Mr Gardiner said that he thought the time was between 5.30 pm and 6.15 pm. The magistrate gave evidence at the inquest, and said that he thought that he signed the warrant at about 5.45 pm. We have no notes of his evidence, but we understand that in cross examination he was extremely vague. A statement was also taken from the magistrate's mother, who said she put the arrival of the police at between 5 o'clock and 5.30 pm, because the cups of tea, which they usually take between 4.30 and 5

THE BROADWATER FARM INQUIRY REPORT

pm were still on the table. She was not called to give evidence at the inquest.

4.23 The search of 25 Thorpe Road began, according to the police, at 5.45 pm, although the family maintain that it was just before 5 o'clock. The officers left Thorpe Road at about 6.20 pm when the ambulance had gone. Did the officers then rush in a panic to the magistrate, knowing that they had no signed warrant and that the search had ended in tragedy? Or did they, as they claim, have a properly signed warrant before they went to 25 Thorpe Road?

4.24 The visit to the magistrate's house took two to three minutes (according to the officers) or about ten minutes (according to the magistrate). The range of possible times for the signing of the warrant, according to the evidence is:—

Approx. 5.00 pm	Inspector Clarke (said that PC Casey had left the station about 4.50 pm).
Approx. 5.05 pm	Sergeant Parsons (made entry at 5.15 pm).
Approx. 5.05 pm	PC Allan (said they arrived at the magistrate's house at 5.00-5.15 pm).
Approx. 5.10 pm	DC Randall (said PC Casey left at about 5.00 pm).
Approx. 5.15 pm	PC Casey (evidence to the inquest).
5.30-6.15 pm	Mr Gardiner's second statement to the Essex police.
Approx. 5.45 pm	Mr Gardiner (evidence to the inquest).
6.00-6.30 pm	Mr Gardiner (first statement made to the Essex police).

4.25 There are a number of points which support the argument that no warrant was signed there until after the search was over:—

(1) The time which the magistrate gave when first asked about this matter two days after the event, as against the confused times given by the officers.

(2) The entry in the custody record, which the Coroner had described as "peculiar". Every other entry in the record was made by Sergeant Bowell; this one alone was made by Sergeant Parsons. Sergeant Bowell himself, who was on duty as the custody officer, said in evidence that he had never seen the signed warrant.

(3) The fact that the usual practice of telephoning the magistrate before going around to his house was not followed. This was even more strange because Mr Gardiner was not normally called on to issue warrants out of court hours. The magistrate normally used had suffered a bereavement. PC Allan told the inquest that the name and address of Mr Gardiner were only given to himself and PC Casey by radio while they were in the car; and DC Randall said that it was he who had suggested the magistrate's name. All this suggests a hasty operation rather than one which had been properly arranged from the police station.

(4) PC Casey alone went into the magistrate's house. PC Allan, who was a probationary officer 14 weeks out of training school, stayed in the car. It would have been normal for PC Allan to accompany PC Casey in order to learn the procedure. But not, perhaps, if the search had already taken place, and the magistrate was being deceived.

(5) After returning to the police station DC Randall made an entry in the "premises searched record". He filled up everything except for one line — the name of the magistrate who granted the warrant. This was left blank. At the inquest it was put to him that this was because no warrant had by then been obtained. His reply was:—
"No. I did have the warrant in front of me. I cannot remember why I missed it out. I was going down the page filling the form in."

It seems to us extraordinary that DC Randall, who had himself suggested the magistrate's name, did not fill it in — unless there was still some uncertainty as to whether he had in fact signed the warrant.

(6) Finally, as we shall see, Patricia Jarrett stated clearly that no warrant was shown to her by any of the officers who came to her house.

4.26 On the other hand, the police would argue that there was no reason for them not to obtain a search warrant before carrying out the search, and that people are frequently vague and inaccurate about times. While we are unable to make a definite finding on this issue, there was at least a strong case against the officers that they carried out the search without a signed warrant. We return later to consider how the Police Complaints Authority dealt with this aspect of the case.

THE SEARCH

4.27 The police officers involved thought that the search might not be straightforward. Inspector Clarke said to PC Casey at a briefing meeting held before the officers left, that he hoped that "the search would not start any riots". A district support unit and an area car were provided to stand by in case there should be any trouble. The controller at the police station, PC Fletcher, said to the inquest that he had been asked by DC Randall to keep his radio open because he was going to search "a coloured family", and if there was any trouble he would want urgent back-up. In the circumstances, and given the rumours of trouble which the police were well aware of, it is strange that there was no liaison with more senior officers, or with the community liaison officer, about this search. The Chief Executive Roy Limb was angered by this failure to recognise the sensitive implications of Floyd Jarrett's arrest:—

"Floyd Jarrett was arrested about 1.00 pm on a Saturday. DC Randall knew that he was a founder member of the Broadwater Farm Youth Association. Everybody knows Floyd Jarrett. Yet he was held in custody for about four hours, and neither Couch nor any of the senior officers appeared to know anything about this. Here was a vital thing that happened and it didn't get to the senior policeman, so the matter could be handled in a sensitive way. That is one of the really worst features for me of the events."

When asked about this, Inspector Clarke said that "he did not consult Superintendent Stacey because of the distance from where we had expected trouble". DC Randall said that he "didn't think community liaison came into it".

4.28 The four officers — DC Randall, Sergeant Parsons, PC Casey, and PC Allan — arrived at 25 Thorpe Road at around 5.45 pm. Sergeant Parsons was the senior officer in rank, but it is clear that DC Randall effectively took charge of the operation. He said to the others as they approached the door: "I'll do the talking". It is a quiet street. Across the road Mr Adams was sitting on his roof doing repairs. He saw the arrival of the police, and was curious. He saw them stop on the path as if discussing their tactics.

4.29 The officers had taken Floyd Jarrett's keys along with them. They had not booked the keys out with the custody officer Sergeant Bowell, who confirmed that this should have been done. They used the keys to enter 25 Thorpe Road. There seems little doubt that they did not knock at the door. Mr Adams did not hear any knock and nor did Patricia Jarrett inside the house. The officers claim that they knocked three times, but none of them remembered the distinctive horseshoe knocker on the door. DC Randall, who said that he did the knocking, said that the knocker was a lever on the letter-box.

4.30 Inside the house were Mrs Jarrett, Patricia Jarrett, with a grandchild of two and a neighbour's baby. Patricia Jarrett heard her mother say "Lord, Lord, there's some police in the house". When asked how they got in, Sergeant Parsons said that the front door had been left open. Mrs Jarrett and Patricia Jarrett knew that to be untrue; they would never leave the door open with young children in the house. Sergeant Parsons admitted to the inquest that he had told this untruth, "in order not to aggravate the situation". In our view the whole account of this entry into a private house – the use of the keys, the failure to knock, the lie about the open door – reveals a casual indifference on the part of the officers and constituted a shocking violation of the privacy of the Jarrett's home.

4.31 The house is on two floors. On the ground floor at the front was Mrs Jarrett's bedroom: half way back, a room which used to be Floyd's room; and at the back a dining room, with a kitchen attached. On the first floor at the front was a lounge; towards the back a locked room which was Patricia Jarrett's room; and at the back Michael Jarrett's room. On this floor there was also a bathroom. The officers after entering started to move through the various rooms. Patricia Jarrett told the inquest that she asked if they had a warrant, and was shown nothing. But DC Randall and PC Casey claimed that she had at one point taken the warrant and read every word out aloud – even the words "to each and all the constables of the Metropolitan Police Force" at the top of the warrant. The new law requires that a copy of the warrant be left with the householder, but even though the new law was having a trial run, this was not done. The officers said that they did not know about this requirement.

4.32 Patricia Jarrett said in evidence that the officers searched Floyd's old room. Then they searched Mrs Jarrett's room; Mrs Jarrett asked why they were searching it, as she only had her personal possessions there. (At one stage the officers tried to deny that her room was searched – until PC Allan admitted that he had searched it). They searched the lounge upstairs, and the laundry in the bathroom. They searched Michael's bedroom, but made no effort to get into the locked room. Patricia then described what happened when DC Randall moved towards the dining room:—

"He went into the dining room. My mother had put Jerome into the armchair and was standing in the doorway. He took his left arm, pushed her out of the way. She fell with one arm in the armchair and the rest of her body towards the armchair going towards the kitchen. I tried to help her up. When I had managed to get her to her feet DC Randall had come back into the dining room and passed over and went to the sideboard. I helped my mother to the chair. She was gasping for breath and gasping quite heavily. She asked me to phone for the emergency doctor as she was not feeling well. I took the telephone book and called the emergency answering service. I spoke to a woman who said that there was not a doctor available so I should dial 999 immediately and explain the symptoms of my mother. I did this and they told me there would be an ambulance."

The electronically timed record at the exchange showed that Patricia Jarrett's 999 call was made at 5.55 pm. It took two minutes for her to be connected, and the ambulance service received her call at 5.57 pm.

4.33 Patricia Jarrett described the push again in detail:—
"I saw Randall take his left arm and put it around my mother's shoulder and part of his body pushed her and she fell with her left arm out, breaking the small table."

Patricia's account continued as follows: Mrs Jarrett was sitting at the dining room table. After Patricia telephoned the ambulance, her mother asked for her tablets on top of the fridge in the kitchen. DC Randall was still in the dining room. He had been looking in the drawers of the sideboard, and while Patricia was telephoning for an ambulance he was looking at the hi-fi and the television. Patricia gave tablets and some water to her mother, who asked for some underclothes to be packed. She went into the garden to collect some clothes from the line. When she came back she noticed that her mother's breathing had become laboured. She asked her: "What's the matter mum?" She then heard a voice in the passage which she recognised as her brother Michael's. Michael asked the officers why they were there, and asked his mother if she felt all right. He asked one of the officers if he had a warrant and received no reply. DC

THE DEATH OF MRS JARRETT

Randall then left the dining room and went upstairs. He had not shown any concern, but simply continued with the search. Michael followed him upstairs, where they were looking into the loft of the house.

4.34   Patricia's evidence continued:—
"The officer left the dining room and went upstairs. My mother was breathing hard. She tumbled sidewards out of the dining room chair, lying on her side. I rushed over and started talking to her. I then saw a uniformed officer and my brother Michael standing at the bottom of the stairs. Michael said Floyd does not live here, and he wanted them to leave the house. I then showed the officer out. We made it quite clear to them that Floyd did not live there, we felt it was in our rights to ask them to leave. They did so. Michael and I rushed back into the dining room. I knelt down at my mother's side. Michael rushed out of the house. I put my ear to her mouth to see if I could feel any breath. I felt for her pulse but did not feel any pulse. I blocked her nose, opened her mouth and gave mouth to mouth resuscitation. Nothing was happening. She looked up at me, her eyes keeled over, her head slumped back and she was completely still. I ran from the house screaming into the street."

4.35   Michael Jarrett had left the house in order to see if a nurse who lived at number 12 was at home. She was not, but Michael used the phone there to ring for an ambulance. His 999 call was electronically timed at 6.00 pm. He was connected to the ambulance service at 6.01 pm. As they waited for the ambulance to arrive the police remained outside. Inspector Clarke arrived, having been alerted by a message from DC Randall. DC Randall said that he had first-aid experience, and that the family should let him come in and help. Michael Jarrett persuaded Patricia to let DC Randall in. For a time he tried mouth to mouth resuscitation, and an airway device was brought in from one of the police cars. But when a mirror was put to Mrs Jarrett's mouth, there was no mist on the glass. At 6.11 pm the ambulance arrived, and Mrs Jarrett was lifted into it. The ambulance left at 6.20 pm and reached North Middlesex Hospital at 6.35 pm where it was certified that Mrs Jarrett was dead on arrival.

4.36   At the inquest, the four officers gave an account which conflicted with that of Patricia in major respects. The main thrust of their evidence was that Patricia Jarrett had been abusive almost from the start, shouting and swearing obscenities at the officers; that Michael Jarrett had joined in the abuse after he arrived; and that there had been no contact of any kind, accidental or deliberate, between DC Randall and Mrs Jarrett. The case put by the barrister representing the four police officers at the inquest was that Mrs Jarrett suffered stress:—

"Not by misbehaviour on the part of the police, but by the anti-police attitude of the children."

4.37 At the inquest this central allegation effectively fell to the ground. It was contradicted by evidence from Inspector Clarke that he received a message at 5.55 pm from DC Randall, made after he had searched Floyd Jarrett's former room, that "we are in the house and the search is under way. There are no problems". As a result of this message, Inspector Clarke radioed the area car and told it to go away. It was contradicted by Mr Adams, who heard no sounds of any shouting from inside the house. It was contradicted by the evidence of the electronicially timed calls showing that Patricia Jarrett was on the phone seeking assistance for about two minutes. DC Randall claims not to have seen this. He said only that Patricia tapped out a number, slammed the telephone down and went on swearing. It was contradicted by further evidence from Mr Adams, who heard DC Randall making another radio call after being told to leave the house. He heard DC Randall say these words:—

"The search was quiet but I must warn you .... the lady of the house has collapsed."

4.38 At one point, while PC Allan was giving evidence, the Coroner made a telling intervention. PC Allan had said that he had not seen Patricia Jarrett pick up the phone or make a call, but she was just shouting and swearing. Counsel representing the Jarrett family then told the officer of the evidence of the electronically timed calls, and the Coroner said:—

"It is quite obvious that their statements are contrary to the facts. Members of the Jury, the purpose of learned Counsel's questions, which he is fully entitled to ask, is to go to the credit of the police officers. It may not bear directly on the death but I am allowing it because it is important for you to be able to assess the truthfulness of the witness."

THE DEATH OF MRS JARRETT

THE MEDICAL EVIDENCE
4.39 Mrs Jarrett, who was 48 years old, was suffering from a very severe heart disease. She had had treatment for high blood pressure, but her family had no idea of her heart condition. Evidence about the cause of her death was given to the inquest by a leading heart specialist, Dr Somerville. He said that as a result of the disease, death might have been triggered off by physical activity or an emotional upset. There would be a sudden increase in the heart rate, accompanied by an alteration of the rhythm of the heartbeat. This would reduce the effectiveness of the heart and could lead to the lungs becoming water-logged. The strain, whether physical or emotional, would release adrenalin, and this would cause the acceleration of the heart rate. Once that train of events had been precipitated, it would be impossible to halt.

4.40 Dr Somerville was questioned at length as to the severity of the emotional or physical upset which would be needed to set these fatal events in motion. It was pointed out that Mrs Jarrett had led a normal and active life, and had survived a number of family difficulties including troubles that some of her children had had with the police. Dr Somerville agreed that if the police officers had simply gone into one room and then left, it was unlikely that death would have been caused. He said that the sudden arrival of the police in her hallway would be likely to cause pumping of adrenalin. But a push by the police followed by a fall would have been "an important precipitating factor" on top of the emotional stress aroused by the arrival of the police. The Coroner summed up the medical evidence to the jury in this way:—

> "If there were this continuous emotional stress, Dr Somerville has reminded us that a fall or push would make an important contribution to continuing stress. It would, indeed, be an important contributory factor in the chain of events. This is because the humiliation and indignity consequent on a push or fall would be an added precipitating factor in a heart already under strain from emotion.
>
> "Mrs Jarrett could have died at home, or while she was out. Dr Somerville said that she was a candidate for death at any time. Obviously we must accept that, but, ladies and gentlemen of the jury, she didn't die at any time, she died then."

THE VERDICT OF THE JURY

4.41 In an inquest, the parties who are represented have no opportunity to address the jury about the verdict which they would wish the jury to return. The only guidance they get is from the Coroner. The Coroner in this case, Dr David Paul, told the jury that four verdicts were open to them: —

(1) *Unlawful killing.* To bring in such a verdict, the jury would have to be sure that the police officers were either intentionally or recklessly threatening harm or causing harm which caused Mrs Jarrett's death: or that they were deliberately doing something (in this case pushing) that all reasonable people would realise would subject a person to a risk of being harmed, and which did in fact cause death. The Coroner told the jury that if they were satisfied that Mrs Jarrett was pushed so that she fell, they would be entitled on the basis of Dr Somerville's evidence to find that the fall caused the death.

(2) If the jury was satisfied that there was a push, but were not sure that the push was a deliberate act, but was merely a consequence of someone going through a narrow place and brushing Mrs Jarrett aside, the proper verdict would be *accidental death.*

(3) If the jury were sure that there was no fall, but that the fatal chain of events was started solely by the emotional stress surrounding the search, then the proper verdict would be that death occurred from *natural causes.*

(4) Finally, if the jury were not sure that they could return one of these three verdicts, then they would be entitled to return an *open verdict.*

4.42 The jury returned an unanimous verdict of *accidental death.* The Jarrett family said in a statement through their solicitor: —

> "The verdict of the jury is a vindication of our complaint against the police officers who arrived at our house on 5th October. Our mother died as a result of a push by a detective during a careless and callous search by four police officers who during the inquest had been forced to admit to lying, to numerous breaches of their code of conduct and to total inconsistency between the ambulance records and their fabricated story. We expect that apart from any other action, the officers concerned will be severely disciplined."

THE DEATH OF MRS JARRETT

4.43 This was a case which demonstrated the value of inquest proceedings in throwing light on the circumstances of a tragic and controversial death. The Jarrett family were well represented by barristers and by a solicitor who, since legal aid is not available for inquest proceedings, gave their services without a fee. The evidence of all the witnesses – the family, the police, and other witnesses – was fully tested in cross-examination. The Coroner, according to many who were present, conducted the proceedings fairly and impartially. The jury were given a range of verdicts which fitted the various possible theories of the cause of death. The evidence had raised a number of serious questions about the propriety of police actions on 5th October. The verdict not only underlined these questions, but showed also that the jury believed that DC Randall at least had been lying in a central aspect of his evidence. We must now compare the investigation made at the inquest with the investigation made into the same matters under the supervision of the Police Complaints Authority.

THE POLICE COMPLAINTS AUTHORITY
4.44 The Police Complaints Authority began to function in January 1985. It was a new body set up by the Police and Criminal Evidence Act 1984. Its letterhead proclaims that it is "the Independent Police Complaints Authority – the public's impartial representative in the investigation of complaints against the police". Under the law it does not investigate complaints itself; it supervises the investigation of complaints, the investigation itself being carried out by police officers. Normally the P.C.A becomes involved because of a complaint; but there is an exceptional procedure whereby a chief officer of police may refer a matter to the P.C.A because of its gravity, even though there has not been a complaint, if the matter appears to indicate that a police officer may have committed a criminal offence or an offence against discipline. This was the power which was invoked on the evening of 5th October 1985. It is significant that the Commissioner, in invoking this power, must have considered that the officers involved may have committed a criminal offence or an offence against discipline, but did not even so suspend those officers from duty. We return to this question of suspension in the next chapter.

4.45 The investigation was carried out by Assistant Chief Constable Simpson of the Essex police. In correspondence with Bernard Carnell, solicitor for the Jarrett family, he sought to clarify the extent of the complaints which they wished to raise. Mr Carnell made it clear that the family were complaining not only about events inside the home — the push of DC Randall against Mrs Jarrett, the insensitive behaviour of the four officers, and their failure to produce a warrant — but also about the whole basis upon which the decision to carry out the search was made, the means by which the officers gained access to the house, and the entire sequence of events that caused the officers to stop and detain Floyd Jarrett in the first place.

4.46 The "independent" status of this investigation came under severe attack during the inquest itself. Patricia Jarrett and other members of the Jarrett family had provided signed statements to the Essex police in confidence for the purpose of the investigation. But during the course of Patricia Jarrett's evidence at the inquest, the barrister representing the four officers began to suggest that something said by her in her evidence was at variance in her statement to the Essex police. It became apparent that this barrister had received copies of these confidential statements. The barristers acting for the Jarrett family protested at this breach of confidence and secured, as a matter of fairness, that the statement made by the four officers should be disclosed to them. It transpired that A.C.C. Simpson of the Essex police had passed the statements to the Commissioner, without consulting the P.C.A. and without imposing any limitations upon their use by the Commissioner. The P.C.A. issued a press statement stating that they were disturbed to learn that the statement had been used by the Metropolitan Police without their consent.

4.47 The reason given for the handing over of the statements was that the Commissioner as the disciplinary authority, was entitled to see them. That is no doubt the case at the end of an investigation, but this investigation was still in progress. We are most concerned, both that the statements were given to the Commissioner at that stage, and that the Commissioner saw fit to supply them to the solicitor who represented those very officers whose conduct was being investigated.

4.48 When an investigation has been completed, the investigating officer submits a report to the P.C.A. The P.C.A. must make a statement as to whether the investigation was conducted to their satisfaction, and the case is then considered by the chief officer of police for the area, who decides whether or not to refer the case to the Director of Public Prosecutions for criminal charges, or whether to prefer disciplinary charges. The P.C.A. also has the duty to consider the question of criminal or disciplinary charges, and they have the power to direct that the case be referred to the Director of Public Prosecutions, and to recommend to the Chief Officer of Police (or if he is unwilling, direct him), to prefer specified disciplinary charges. They are precluded from publishing any information which they have received except in the form of a summary statement.

4.49 On 14th April 1986, four months after the end of the inquest, the P.C.A. published a news release and attached to it their summary statement about the investigation into the death of Mrs Jarrett. But the news release stated that no criminal charges had been preferred by the Director of Public Prosecutions, and no disciplinary charges were recommended by the Metropolitan Police. It stated that the P.C.A. agreed with that recommendation. They said that the investigation conducted by Assistant Chief Constable Simpson had been comprehensive and "a model of speed and thoroughness", The summary statement of the P.C.A. is for the most part a recital of the different versions of the offence given by the witnesses at the inquest. But there are two passages where the P.C.A. appear to give their own interpretation of the material which was before them. The first passage concerns their comment on the inquest verdict:—

"The jury tended to accept neither party's version completely but implied, in accordance with directions given by the Coroner, that DC Randall did not push Mrs Jarrett but in all probability inadvertently brushed past her causing her to lose her balance."

4.50 This was a serious misreading of the jury's verdict. It is incorrect to say that the jury "tended to accept neither party's version completely". On the essential issue of whether DC Randall pushed Mrs Jarrett, they accepted Patricia Jarrett's evidence and rejected that of DC Randall, who totally denied that he had any kind of physical contact with Mrs Jarrett. On the further question, was the push deliberate or unintentional, the jury decided that they could not be sure that it was intentional. This was not a rejection of Patricia Jarrett's evidence. Patricia Jarrett could only tell the jury what she saw DC Randall do; whether what he did was deliberate was a matter for the jury. Further, the words "inadvertently brushed past" made much too light of the action for which, on the jury's verdict, DC Randall was responsible. An officer carrying out a search has a duty

THE BROADWATER FARM INQUIRY REPORT

to treat members of the household being searched with care. A pushing or brushing aside of a large woman standing in a doorway even if it was not intentional, was an act of carelessness and grave discourtesy, and as such, in our view, a serious departure from the standards which the public are entitled to expect from police officers.

4.51 Secondly, the P.C.A. reviewed the evidence relating to the search warrant and the time of the visit to the magistrate, and concluded: —

"The police officers claim they were in Thorpe Road from 17.45 until just after 18.20, when the ambulance left and this is corroborated by evidence given by an ambulance officer. It would have been very difficult for the police officers to leave Thorpe Road at 18.20, return to Tottenham Police Station, type out the warrant and then go to Mr Gardiner's house by 18.30 and get the warrant signed, remembering that 18.30 is the latest time by which Mr Gardiner is prepared to admit signing the warrant."

We are to assume that on the basis of this reasoning the P.C.A. are satisfied that a warrant was duly obtained. We do not find it convincing. In the first place, the officers may well have typed up a warrant before leaving the police station, but had decided for some reason to get it signed later on. Secondly, there was time after 6.20 pm for the officers to rush at speed to the magistrate's house. Thirdly, and perhaps most important, this reasoning does not confront the basic problem that the magistrate, when first asked about the time on 7th October, estimated it to be between 6 and 6.30 pm, — a full hour after the police officers claimed to have visited him.

4.52 We are bound to say that the P.C.A., in agreeing that there should be no disciplinary charges preferred against any of the officers, have failed lamentably to grapple with the real issues raised by the events of the 5th October. Let us recall what the evidence of the inquest and the Magistrates Court hearing revealed: —

(1) That the officers who first stopped Floyd Jarrett made computer checks on his car, apparently for no other reason than he was a young Black man.

(2) That they arrested him and took him into custody on a suspicion that his car was stolen which had little if any reasonable basis.

(3) That they made a charge against him of assault which was found to be false.

(4) That they embarked upon a search of his family's home which

appears on the evidence to have been entirely speculative.
(5) That a number of features in the evidence indicated strongly that the search was carried out without having obtained a warrant signed by a magistrate.
(6) That the officers took Floyd Jarrett's keys out of his property without the authorisation of the custody officer.
(7) That they used those keys to enter 25 Thorpe Road without having alerted the occupants by knocking on the door.
(8) That one of the officers lied to the occupants of the house in saying he found the door open.
(9) That distress was caused to Mrs Jarrett both by the sudden intrusion of the officers and by a quite unnecessary search of her bedroom.
(10) That one of the officers conducted himself so carelessly as to push past Mrs Jarrett as she stood in the doorway and cause her to fall.
(11) That this push and fall, coupled perhaps with other upsetting features of the search caused her death before it would naturally have occurred.
(12) That after Mrs Jarrett fell and was clearly unwell the officer present expressed no concern but merely continued his search.
(13) That after the event the officers told lies about the behaviour of the Jarrett family and covered up their own misconduct.

4.53 The offences for which police officers may be disciplined are contained in the Discipline Code, which is part of the Police (Discipline) Regulations 1985. It includes the following offences:—

- Abuse of authority, "which offence is committed where a member of a police force treats any person with whom he may be brought into contact in the execution of his duty in an oppressive manner and, without prejudice to the foregoing, in particular where he:—
    - (a) without good and sufficient cause conducts a search, or requires a person to submit to any test or procedure, or makes an arrest; or
    - (b) uses any unnecessary violence towards any prisoner or any other person with whom he may be brought into contact in the execution of his duty, or improperly threatens any such person with violence; or
    - (c) is abusive or uncivil to any member of the public."
- Discreditable conduct, "which offence is committed where a member of a police force acts in a disorderly manner or any manner

prejudicial to discipline or reasonably likely to bring discredit on the reputation of the force or of the police service."
● Racially discriminating behaviour, "which offence is committed (without prejudice to the commission of any other offence) where a member of a police force:—
   (a) while on duty, on the grounds of another person's colour, race, nationality or ethnic or national origins, acts towards that other person in any such way as is mentioned in abuse of authority (above); or
   (b) in any other way, on any of those grounds, treats improperly a person with whom he may be brought into contact while on duty."
● Neglect of duty, "which offence is committed where a member of a police force, without good and sufficient cause:—
   (a) neglects or omits to attend to or carry out with due promptitude and diligence anything which it is his duty as a member of a police force to attend to or carry out, or
   (b) fails properly to account for, or to make a prompt and true return of, any money or property received by him in the course of his duty."
● Falsehood or prevarication, "which offence is committed where a member of a police force knowingly or through neglect makes any false, misleading or inaccurate oral or written statement or entry in any record or document made, kept or required for police purposes."
● Being an accessory to a disciplinary offence, "which offence is committed where a member of a police force incites, connives at or is knowingly an accessory to any offence against discipline."

4.54 In our opinion the P.C.A. failed to act as an independent or impartial authority in two major respects. First, it disregarded the verdict of the jury. There had been two conflicting cases argued at the inquest on behalf of the family and the police officers. The jury had found against the officers on the central question of the push, and by implication cast severe doubt on all the other claims of the officers which were in dispute. By recommending no action, the P.C.A. appeared to put itself above the jury. Secondly, the P.C.A. specifically failed to exercise its powers to recommend, and if necessary direct, that disciplinary charges be preferred. The 13 matters raised above, if proved, would constitute one or more of the offences in the Disciplinary Code. Given these failures in one of the

THE DEATH OF MRS JARRETT

P.C.A.'s first major investigations, it is not surprising if confidence in the new machinery is low.

THE EVENING OF 5TH OCTOBER

4.55 At 7 o'clock, Floyd Jarrett was released. He told us that an officer told him, on the way out of the police station, that his mother had had a stroke. He did not even know that there had been a search of his mother's home. He went to the hospital and then later on to Broadwater Farm. Martha Osamor was telephoned, and she went with Floyd and Dolly Kiffin to 25 Thorpe Road. Many community leaders called at the home during the evening in an immediate reaction of sympathy and respect.

4.56 Chief Superintendent Stainsby, who was acting as chief officer at Tottenham Police Station as Chief Superintendent Couch was away on that day, called at 25 Thorpe Road and expressed sympathy to the family. He told them that an independent investigation would be carried out by an officer from another force. Martha Osamor described the meeting: –

"The family were still very, very angry and a lot of questions were asked. Some of the questions were: How did they get into the house? He said he doesn't know. Did they have a warrant? He said he doesn't know. Where are they are now, are they still working? He doesn't know. He is going to find out."

It was also confirmed at the inquest that Patricia Jarrett on that evening was saying to Chief Superintendent Stainsby that her mother had been pushed by DC Randall.

4.57 It is all the more surprising that on the evening of 5th October the following statement was issued by the Metropolitan Police:—

"Mrs Jarrett was initially very co-operative. But, towards the end of the search, another of her sons arrived home and began strongly objecting to the presence of the police. She collapsed and the officers were physically shoved out of the house. Eventually they persuaded the occupants to let them back in, and one of the officers trained in first aid, administered mouth to mouth resuscitation without success."

This account is clearly designed to put the officers in the best possible light and the Jarrett family in the worst. Far from maintaining a neutral position while investigations continued, the higher authorities of the Metropolitan Police took a partisan position from the outset.

They appeared to pre-empt and influence the "independent" investigation before it had even begun. The statement led directly to a report in the *Mail on Sunday* on the 6th October which appeared to put the police story beyond doubt:—

> "Scotland Yard confirmed that 49-year-old Mrs Cynthia Jarrett became ill after she was in a struggle with officers who visited her home following the arrest of her son."

We consider that it was quite wrong for an official statement to be put out which stated the police view alone of an event which was known to be disputed and which was under investigation by another force.

4.58 Late that night after midnight, members of the Jarrett family and a number of friends went down to Tottenham Police Station to demand more information. They again saw Chief Superintendent Stainsby. After a lot of pressure he went away and produced a copy of the warrant. Mr Jarrett could see at once that it was not a warrant which could have been taken on the search, because it was a clean, uncreased piece of paper. But the original warrant was not produced, and they could obtain no more answers. Martha Osamor said of the visit:—

> "For them to behave in such an insensitive way, for him to keep repeating to us what he has already said, meant that a lot of people who were there felt they were treating us as if we hadn't got any sense at all."

4.59 While they were inside the police station they heard the sound of smashing glass. People in a small demonstration outside had thrown some stones at the police station windows. The Jarrett family and the community leaders present were able to persuade them to stop and go home. George Martin, of the West Indian Leadership Council, was one of those there. Before he left he said these words to the Chief Superintendent:—

> "This is no longer a family matter. It's gone beyond that. It has now become a community matter, and I think that it is important that somebody of some importance makes a statement."

Chapter 5
OCTOBER 6 – WHAT HAPPENED?

REACTIONS TO THE TRAGEDY
5.1 The news of Mrs Jarrett's death spread quickly. Some learned about it during the night at a party, some the next morning. People were stunned: –
> "Just hearing the news on the radio about Mrs Jarrett, it made something just turn over inside of me."

> "On the Sunday morning I picked up this newspaper and I read it. And while I was sitting there...my hands were shaking with the paper, because I personally know Mrs Jarrett and I know all of her family because I've been to school with them."

The younger people reacted to what they had heard in the light of their own experience, and they thought of their own mothers. Stafford Scott spoke for the feeling of many: –
> "Because it has happened before – police officers have taken away people's keys and entered their homes without alerting the people inside – it was easy for people to believe it had happened in this instance. Because people have seen police manhandling members of their families whilst raiding, it was easy to believe in this instance. So what was actually taking place was a lot of emotional transferral. They wasn't thinking just in terms of Floyd Jarrett's mother died today, they were thinking in terms that it could very easily have been my mother. So people were feeling very sickened by what had happened. People were very upset."

Youth worker Harry Adams saw the death against the shooting of Stephen Waldorf and the subsequent acquittal of the police officers, and the shooting of the child John Shorthouse in Birmingham: –
> "If they could stand by and watch them damage White people in that way, what they could get away with with us? People watched that and watched it very carefully. Now when Mrs Jarrett died, that was the end. As far as we were concerned they had overstepped the mark – not overstepped it, they had run it completely out of existence."

THE BROADWATER FARM INQUIRY REPORT

Millard Scott put it quite simply: —
"There is no way we can accept the death of a Black mother within our community."

5.2 During the morning there was a lot of telephoning between community leaders and the police. Roy Limb had heard the news from Dolly Kiffin at about eight o'clock: —
"I thought about it that Sunday morning and then rang Couch and said 'There is enormous tension within the community now. We must explain to people properly what happened. You've got to tell us what happened', in my own mind hoping and praying that there was a rational explanation for what had taken place."
At the same time the senior youth officer Mike Bates was instructing Stafford Scott and other youth workers to go down and help keep things calm.

5.3 The police arranged a meeting which started at 12.45 pm at Tottenham Police Station. D.A.C. Richards was in the chair, with Chief Superintendent Couch and another senior officer. There were two councillors, Ernie Large and Andreas Mikkides; Roy Limb, the Chief Executive; Eric Clarke, chair of the Community and Police Consultative Group; Chris Kavallares, chair of the Haringey Community Relations Council (HCRC); Jeff Crawford, senior Community Relations Officer of the HCRC; Hyacinth Moody, chair of the HCRC Police Liaison Committee; Dolly Kiffin; and Floyd and Michael Jarrett, who came after Dolly Kiffin insisted that she would not attend the meeting unless members of the Jarrett family were there.

5.4 In the words of Ernie Large, D.A.C. Richards was "totally in charge" at the meeting. In answer to all questions, all he would say was that there was going to be an inquiry under the supervision of the Police Complaints Authority; that the Chief Constable of Essex would look into the matters raised; and that he could not comment further. Because of his experience as a magistrate, Ernie Large concentrated on the question of the warrant, but got no answers: —
"Down came the curtain that it was subject to an inquiry, there was nothing they could say, therefore it was all a one-way traffic. Which annoyed me. If you want to defuse a situation, you have to defuse it by being open".

5.5 There were demands from all the people from the community for the suspension of the officers who had been involved in the search of Mrs Jarrett's home. Roy Limb was very clear about the reaction of D.A.C. Richards: —

> "Richards' answer to that was that the matter was now out of his hands. They had already put it in the hands of the Police Complaints Authority. I was rather surprised by that and said so. But that was what they insisted upon, that the matter was in the hands of the Police Complaints Authority and therefore they couldn't say anything about it."

This was an incorrect answer. The suspension of police officers pending inquiries is a matter of internal discipline for the senior police officer to decide. Later on in a letter to Roy Limb, the deputy chair of the Police Complaints Authority, Roland Moyle, confirmed: —

> "The question of suspending police officers is outside the powers of the Police Complaints Authority. Suspension is a matter for the Metropolitan Police."

The Police (Discipline) Regulations lay down the legal position:

> "Where a report, allegation or complaint is received from which it appears that a member of a police force may have committed a disciplinary or criminal offence, the chief officer concerned may suspend that member from membership of the force and from his office as constable, whether or not the matter had been investigated."

5.6 We find it extraordinary that an officer of D.A.C. Richards' high rank was not able to give correct information about a matter which was of intense concern to those present. Many witnesses have stressed to us that the suspension of the four officers was the one action which the police could have taken which would have given some assurance to the Black community that the circumstances of Mrs Jarrett's death were being taken seriously. We agree. Suspension from duty is a common practice in many walks of life when something serious has happened and there are disputed allegations to be investigated. Suspension would have implied neither guilt or innocence. The death of a woman during a police search of her home was just such a case. The failure to suspend was short sighted and insensitive. The community leaders left the police station at 1.50 pm in a sombre mood. Roy Limb said: —

> "All I can say is I was extremely sad when I left there and very

concerned, because we had heard nothing that could help us to go and defuse the tension that was there in the community."

5.7 As they left, a demonstration was gathering outside the police station. It grew to over a hundred people and lasted for about one and half hours. There was angry shouting at the police officers who were present. Some people lay in the road. One stone was thrown through the police station window but otherwise there was no violence. The police response was restrained and sensible. They blocked off the High Road in both directions to give room for the demonstration. They policed the demonstration with a thin line of officers in ordinary uniform, with special units well out of sight. They stood while the crowd shouted angrily and made intimidating gestures, without reacting or making arrests. Chief Superintendent Couch described the scene to a meeting of the Community and Police Consultative Group which we attended: —

"I and nine officers stood for one and a half hours taking all that they could give us. We wanted to let them vent their feelings."

Nick Wright of the Police Research Unit paid tribute to both the Chief Superintendent and his officers: —

"Couch is perhaps the most sophisticated politician amongst the police locally. He understood the necessity of dealing with it in those terms. He wasn't the only one. His subordinates right down to the local PCs understood that they had to deal with it on the streets there. It wasn't just him but his officers were in amongst the crowd, unarmed, not equipped with riot gear, talking to people. They didn't arrest anybody, they didn't get angry, they just stood their ground and argued the point and it gradually went down. I don't think that could happen without effective leadership."

5.8 A meeting of Black community leaders had been arranged for the afternoon at the West Indian Centre in Clarendon Road. People at the demonstration protested about this. They said they did not know the West Indian Centre and did not believe that it would be an adequate place to hold a meeting. They believed that there should be a meeting on the Broadwater Farm Estate. They thought — rightly as it turned out — that many people would come to the Youth Association because of Floyd Jarrett's close involvement with it. They wanted those who were prominent in the Black community to come down and tell them exactly what the position was and assure them that there would be no cover-up of how Mrs Jarrett had died. So the community representatives who had been at the police station were asked to come on from the West Indian Centre to the Youth Association at any time after 4 pm for a second meeting. At around 3.30 pm, as the demonstration was getting a bit ragged and the Youth Association workers feared that there might be violence, they took action to avoid it. They advised people to leave the police station and come back for the meeting on the estate.

5.9 The meeting at the West Indian Centre started about two o'clock. There was an audience of about 40 people. On the platform were Martha Osamor, chair of the Haringey Independent Policing Committee; William Trant, an officer of the West Indian Standing Conference; Councillor Bernie Grant, and Councillor Steve Banerji, chair of the police sub-committee. Councillor Banerji noticed that there was "a significant absence of Black youth at the meeting"; but the older people in the audience gave accounts of their own experiences at the hands of the police. Nick Wright wrote in his report that "the most striking thing was the deep anger of the audience". There were calls for the suspension of the police officers, and a resolution was passed containing four demands: —
(1) A full public inquiry into Cynthia Jarrett's death;
(2) The resignation of D.A.C. Richards;
(3) The withholding of the Metropolitan Police precept by the council;
(4) For the Jarrett family's account of their mother's death to be accepted.

Dolly Kiffin came in during the meeting to report on the demonstration and the feelings of the people there. She then went on to the Youth Association. Other people followed to the Youth Association after the meeting at the West Indian Centre ended. They were George Martin, Vernon Moore and Arthur Lawrence, all members of the West Indian Leadership Council; Martha Osamor, Roy Limb, Councillor Grant and Councillor Sharon Lawrence. They reached the Youth Association at various times between 5.30 and 6.00 pm.

5.10 People had been gathering at the Youth Association during the afternoon. Eventually there were about 70 people there of all ages, including a number of older parents. Stafford Scott described to us the bewilderment and confusion he observed during the period before councillors and others came from the other meeting: —

"There were no plans. People were terribly upset — this was something totally new to the community. We as professional community and youth workers weren't sure how to handle the situation, much less the ordinary members of our Youth Association or ordinary members of the community. People were bewildered — there was no clear decision on what to do next. People wanted to see the big shots of the community, and they wanted to hear exactly what was being said so that they could come to some kind of decision. But because of the nature of what happened, emotions were running high, people were feeling bad, but they were feeling sad at the same time. There were no clear cut decisions being taken either way. A lot of people wanted to return to the police station to protest, a lot of people thought it would be a waste of time, a lot of people thought it would lead to trouble."

5.11 There were two community reactions taking place during the afternoon which though separate were not in conflict. The established representatives of the Black community, mainly from the older generation, were meeting in an ordered way to express their grief and anger through a formal resolution. Others, mainly but not entirely young people, were gathering at the Youth Association and were wanting to express that grief and anger through an immediate and active protest. Martha Osamor described the interaction between the older and younger people: —

"By this time, remember it's almost 24 hours now, there hasn't been any kind of answer to any of the questions. No move on the part of the police to calm things down or help us to calm things down. So we got to the meeting and the youths were still very angry. So what they said to me was that we've come to the stage now where I have to go. They said they are not going to stop me from meetings, from passing resolutions and so on, but at the same time they don't want me to stop them from going back to picket the police station, because they want the answers".

5.12 Dolly Kiffin had gone upstairs to her office and did not take part in the meeting. The Youth Association workers tried to get a formal meeting structure going, with Martha Osamor in the chair, but as she told us, she could not play a chair's role: —

"It's difficult to say who chaired it. What I wanted to do was for me to speak to them, then introduce Bernie from the council to say that the council has agreed things like this Inquiry, and other things that we were demanding for them to do. But they didn't even let me finish or let Bernie start."

Councillor Grant spoke of the intensity of the anger in the room:—
"The fact that they didn't allow me to speak seemed to indicate to me that if I had spoken it wouldn't have made any difference at all. People were really hyped up. I have never seen anything like it. People were very, very threatening. They were very aggressive."

Mrs Scott, the mother of Millard, Stafford and Roger Scott, recalled what happened in vivid language:—
"And Bernie was mentioning marching to Downing Street and the House of Commons, but the voice of the children went over Bernie, and he couldn't talk. And because Bernie wasn't able to talk there, I shouted at them and asked them to listen to what Bernie had to say. But they think Bernie was more White minded. That was the opinion of most of them, that Bernie wasn't going to give them the right."

5.13 Mrs Scott spoke strongly for the proposal to go back to the police station:—
"And I said to them, 'let's go back to the police station today, and whatever they are going to do let them do it out there'. I said, 'when we get there we'll sit in the road and we'll stop every car that comes down. So let them take us up off the road and do what they like, because the next one can be me'."

George Martin was also content with the police station decision. We asked whether in view of the anger it would have been a peaceful demonstration. He replied that there were enough older people that were respected by the youths to make sure of that. "I don't think they would have created any problems while we were there."

5.14 The decision to go again to the police station reflected the established custom in the Black community, which had been expressed on many occasions in the past, that when they believe that the police have been responsible for an outrage, it is to the police station that people must go to express their feelings and to demand information. Stafford Scott described the reasons:—
"We knew that by going to the police station we wouldn't achieve anything. The police would not suddenly say OK, we did wrong, you can all go home. But we wanted the police to see that this community was going to stand together, that this community would not accept the death of one of its older members, a law abiding

older member at that. And yes, we would like to stop traffic, we would like to cause enough inconvenience that television cameras are down there, so what we are feeling is actually being made known to the public."

5.15 Around 6.30 to 6.45 pm the meeting broke up and people began slowly to move towards the police station. There was not to be a march. Groups were just going to make their way there. If they had reached the police station, there would have needed to be a further example of sensitivity on the part of the police for a confrontation to have been avoided. It would have been the duty of the police to have done everything possible to have enabled that demonstration to have passed off without disorder. But in the event those who resolved to go back to the police station got no further than the edge of the estate.

THE DEPLOYMENT OF THE POLICE
5.16 We described earlier how the Tottenham police were saying well before 5th October that a riot was likely in their area. Their precautions intensified after the shooting of Mrs Groce at the Brixton disturbances. We have read the reports of Mr Kennedy, the Fire Officer in charge of operations for North London. In a report written after the Brixton disturbances, he said:—
"It should be known that every day since 28th September, the brigade had been advised by the police that civil disturbances had been expected in both North and South London areas, with Brixton, Balham, Lewisham, Tottenham, Harlesden and Hackney as possible sources where trouble on a large scale could be expected."
In his report on the Broadwater Farm events Mr Kennedy said:—
"Due to closer liaison with the police in all divisions since the Brixton civil disturbance the previous weekend, the duty officer in the J Division had been informed on 5th October 1985 by the police that trouble was expected that weekend in the areas of Tottenham High Street and Wood Green."
He set up a "forward control point" on 5th October at the New River Sports Ground in White Hart Lane in order to be accessible to both areas.

5.17 It is clear from these reports that the police were generally expecting riots in areas with large Black populations in the week following Brixton, and were specifically targeting the Tottenham/

OCTOBER 6 – WHAT HAPPENED?

Wood Green area for the weekend of 5th/6th October, before the death of Mrs Jarrett. Dolly Kiffin recalls going shopping on the morning of 5th October in Wood Green and Bruce Grove and seeing "a whole heap of police cars and vans".

5.18 Since the police were expecting riots in the Tottenham area they would also have had the Broadwater Farm Estate in the forefront of their minds. It was revealed in the *Police Magazine* that there had for many months been in existence a document entitled *"Contingency Plans for the Control of Disorder on the Broadwater Farm Estate – Tottenham"*. A visitor to Tottenham police station had observed that in four or five parts of the police station there were pinned up maps of Broadwater Farm, which stood out as the only maps apart from the map of the district.

5.19 So there was already a keen state of readiness on 5th October. By the morning of 6th October, the police leadership would have been well aware of the reaction of the community to the death of Mrs Jarrett. According to the Richards report, the reserve manpower for the area was increased for Sunday to 200 officers in each of two eight hour shifts, made up of some coach serials and some district support units in transits. One of their bases was a feeding centre in Northumberland Park, half a mile north of the estate. In the early afternoon they would have heard of the demonstration at Tottenham Police Station. We have already given credit for the policing of that demonstration, and the fact that the reserve units were not called out to confront it. But as the Richards report states:–

> "Police officers who were present had differing conceptions of the intention of the demonstrators. Some thought that the threats that had been made were more rhetoric arising from a release of anger and tension; others were quite convinced that there would be attacks on police and/or serious disorders later in the day."

As the day shift (10.00 am – 6.00 pm) waited through the day, the atmosphere must have been charged with anticipation of trouble.

5.20 At 3.15 pm on 6th October two of the Broadwater Farm home beat officers were visiting an address in The Avenue when bottles and missiles were thrown at them. The Richards report says that a crowd of Black youths were responsible. A witness whom we interviewed saw the two officers retreating "under the attack of two coloured youths, who threw bottles and missiles at the police". One officer, PC

Caton, was struck in the back and suffered a severe injury to his spleen. Information about the attack must have been passed back to the waiting officers. They must also have been aware that the people who had been at the demonstration outside the police station had gone into the Broadwater Farm Estate for the groups leaving the police station would surely have been observed and followed. Indeed the police received calls between 3.15 and 4.15, according to the Richards report, that up to a 100 youths, some of them wearing masks, were running through the estate banging on doors. We have had no direct evidence about this. But whether true or not, it confirms that the attention of the police was centred on Broadwater Farm.

5.21 Then for two hours, while the meeting was going on in the Youth Association, nothing happened. According to the Richards report this was also the period of change over of the police shifts at the Northumberland Park "feeding centre". The report says:—
> "It was necessary, in order to provide all day coverage to have a 10.00 am to 6.00 pm shift and a 4.00 pm to midnight shift, each of 200 men, the two hour overlap being required for briefing, feeding and changeover purposes."

5.22 Because the police have not participated in the Inquiry, we do not know what was said at the briefing of the new shifts. We do know from the Richards report that at around 6.30 pm there was an order that only protected district support unit vehicles should answer calls to the Broadwater Farm Estate. The report states that this was ordered because of the attack on PC Caton, and because of a second attack at 6.30 in The Avenue, when two Black youths on a motor cycle had smashed a bottle into the driver's window of a police car. We do not know what other instructions were given to the large force of police that was assembled to deal with the situation that had developed through the day. It was obvious by the end of the afternoon that Black youths had gathered on the estate in large numbers and that the situation was still very tense. Some plans must have been made to deal with possible disorder on the estate.

THE OUTBREAK
5.23 After about 6.45 pm some people left quite promptly from the Youth Association after the meeting. Mrs Scott wanted to take her young daughter home and go on from there to the police station. She walked up Willan Road and onto The Avenue, where she saw two big

transit vans coming up "full with officers in uniform with riot gear". They passed the head of Willan Road and continued down The Avenue. Then she saw a third van. She looked back and saw the third van turn down Willan Road:—

"So I thought: 'Oh my God, they gone down there and those children are there'. But I still didn't think there was going to be anything."

She went on her way to Bruce Grove. Martha Osamor was very tired and drove home to have a rest. She too saw the three transit vans driving down The Avenue. At the time that she left the youths from the meeting had not begun to come up Willan Road.

5.24 A woman who lives at the junction of Willan Road and The Avenue left home at about two minutes to seven to go to the shop on the corner of The Avenue and Mount Pleasant Road. As she came back, she saw two minibuses with metal grills come past and turn into the estate. About three cars which were coming out of the estate made U-turns and followed the police vans back in. Soon afterwards she heard a sound as if bottles were being smashed.

5.25 The view from inside the estate was given to us by Arthur Lawrence and George Martin, who with Vernon Moore, were representatives of the West Indian Leadership Council. They were being driven by Vernon Moore out along Willan Road from Tangmere. They were just reaching the bend in Willan Road when the first clash occurred. About ten youths, the first group to come from the meeting, were walking up towards the Willan Road exit. Arthur Lawrence recalls seeing one police transit van which had reached a point in the road by the day nursery. The youths went up and knocked on the van with their hands. They had no weapons. The van reversed back and the youths ran after it. At that moment two other police transit vans approached from The Avenue.

5.26 George Martin also described the first contact between the group of youths and the lead van:—

"They rushed out in front of the vans, attempted to stop them coming any further and shouted out that they are coming. Obviously the other youths that were behind us heard and chased up to pass us, to make sure that it didn't proceed any further. They banged the van to make sure that the van didn't come down there."

He too saw no weapons used. He said that the three vans came down one after the other in line, but we think, looking at the evidence both from those outside and those inside, that one van came down first and two others followed shortly afterwards.

5.27 Joanne George saw the scene when the vans had reversed back and reached the junction of Willan Road with The Avenue. She was being driven back in a mini-cab from the Bruce Grove area. As she reached Willan Road, two of the police vans were reversing out. A group of about ten youths ran down from the direction of Stapleford and threw some bottles at them. She had her young children with her, and ordered the driver to go straight on and away from the estate.

5.28 A woman living in Rochford, with a good view over Willan Road, saw three or four youths going up the hill. Then a police van came half way down the hill. She believed that it reversed into the driveway near the day nursery and turned around to go up the hill again. Then other police vans came down. Soon the whole area was swarming with police and youths.

5.29 Stafford Scott had stayed behind to help lock up the Youth Association, and caught up the main group as it moved up the hill towards the exit. He could see vans at the junction, and one or two missiles thrown. He went with a large group towards Mount Pleasant Road. The officers were getting out of their vans at the junction of Mount Pleasant Road and The Avenue. By the time he reached the junction, officers in riot uniform were already out of their vans, hitting people with truncheons and telling them to get back into the estate. He was pushed back. He spoke of the fury in the voices of the police: –
> "There was cries of 'wait until we get in there and get you, you coons, you don't come out until we tell you, get back in there, you bastards, get back in there'. So the whole group got pushed back into the estate. The only people who may not have been pushed back were a few of the older ones. Most of the people ran down – this was a very frightening moment, people had just seen police officers jumping out of vans and attacking them with truncheons, people pushed back into the estate with no apparent reason. A lot of people said 'no, don't go back, why should we go back?' So a lot of people wanted to resist the police pushing us down the hill. A lot of people were not interested in resisting, they decided to run back down the hill. It was a general state of confusion. There were

young girls there with young children and then a lot of screaming, a lot of shouting."

5.30 At a little before 7.00 pm Cliff Ford heard a shout and looked out of his window on the 12th floor of Northolt block. He saw a group of lads running up Willan Road and off the estate. Within a few minutes "the group seem to be running back", and he saw the Willan Road exit "sealed off by the police".

5.31 Arthur Lawrence and George Martin saw the three vans return to the junction and move down towards Mount Pleasant Road. Mr Moore then drove his car across the junction and stopped a short way across in Marsden Road. George Martin and Arthur Lawrence got out while Vernon Moore went to park his car further away. By the time they had returned to the junction, The Avenue was completely blocked by police in riot gear, out of their vans, at the Mount Pleasant Road junction. The youths were on the corner of Willan Road and The Avenue. Some of the youths then began to turn over cars, and missiles were thrown at the line of police. Two cars were turned over and burned close to the junction. They attempted to turn over another car but were stopped by George Martin and his colleagues. Soon after a wall at the corner of Willan Road and The Avenue was knocked down and dismantled for ammunition to throw at the police line. The fighting had started.

5.32 Nick Wright of the Police Research Unit had been, with his colleague Debbie Wild, observing the movement of police vehicles in Tottenham High Road. From about 6.00 pm to 6.30 pm he had seen a build-up of police traffic in both directions, with district support vans and big green buses. At a certain point towards 7.00 pm it became clear that something serious was going on, because police vehicles were coming from both directions and turning into Bruce Grove towards Lordship Lane. They were clearly in a hurry:—

"There was one incident where two big green police coaches were detained at the red traffic lights at the junction of Tottenham High Road and Bruce Grove. They were so anxious to go up Bruce Grove and Lordship Lane that they jumped out of their vehicle and banged on the roof of a car that was waiting at a red traffic light, and told the car to move so that they can jump the lights."

The time of this observation would correspond with the time of first contact between the group of youths and the police van on Willan Road.

5.32 The Richards report states that at 6.40 pm there were two district support units of local officers in the vicinity of the estate. 999 calls were made at 6.49 pm and 6.53 pm, saying that police were needed in The Avenue. The report continues: —

> "A D.S.U. (Y 32) went to the scene to investigate but shortly after their arrival, at 7.05 pm, they were subjected to a violent attack by a large group of Black youths, who threw bricks and petrol bombs at their vehicle and struck at the bodywork with machetes. The ferocity of this attack was such, that had the officers not been in a protected vehicle, they would almost certainly have been killed or seriously injured."

The report adds that Y 32 then withdrew to a safe location in order to put on protective equipment, and the Wood Green control room began to mobilise the men who were immediately available. The report continues with a paragraph which we will have to examine with great care: —

> "Units began to arrive at the scene from 7.10 pm onwards. They found that a barricade of blazing vehicles had been erected at all four vehicular entrances to the estate, (Gloucester Road, Willan Road, Griffin Road and Adams Road) and at each location they came under missile and petrol bomb fire as they approached."

5.33 This report conflicts with the evidence which we have received in a number of very important respects: —

(1) The evidence is that the first van came into the estate and down Willan Road as far as the day nursery. The Richards report does not state this, saying only that the van was called to The Avenue, and went to "the scene".

(2) The report mentions only one district support unit van. But the evidence is that three vans were on the scene in the initial stages and came down Willan Road into the estate. They would contain a total of over 30 officers.

(3) The evidence before us is that the initial contact between the lead van and the initial group of youths was through the youths banging with their hands against the vans; that they did not use bricks or petrol bombs or machetes; that missiles were not thrown until the vans had reached The Avenue and officers began to block the road; and that bricks began to be thrown at that point by some of the youths who obtained them by demolishing the wall.

(4) The evidence is that, while cars were over-turned and set alight in The Avenue, that happened after the officers from the vans had

OCTOBER 6 – WHAT HAPPENED?

blocked The Avenue, and not before.

(5) The evidence from many witnesses is that the police officers in the vans were already in riot gear and did not withdraw to any location in order to put on their equipment.

(6) The precise number of youths is difficult to determine. The evidence is that the initial clash with the lead van involved a small number of youths, around ten. Others followed behind them to the junction, but of these many ran back when the police blocked the road. The numbers involved in any actions against the police in this initial phase were small.

5.34 How then do we conclude that the disturbances began? By the evening of 6th October, police community relations at Broadwater Farm had reached a very low point indeed. The youths leaving the estate were extremely angry. They not only knew that a Black woman had died in the course of a police raid; they were also sure that senior officers had not taken this death at all seriously. They were leaving the estate to demonstrate their feelings outside the base of local police power. They are confronted by three police vans with riot protection containing police in riot gear. They express their anger by banging on the side of the lead van with their hands. The police in the vans know that young people have been assembling on the estate. They are aware that their colleagues have been attacked twice during the afternoon. They react to the banging on the side of the van by immediately calling for assistance. The nature of the call is indicated by the claim in the Richards report that "they would have almost certainly have been killed". As a consequence the police response is massive. It takes the form of officers in riot gear coming out of their vans, stopping the youths from going further and pushing them back into the estate. For many of the youths this blocking of their free movement at such a time is intolerable. They react to it by using any means which are available.

5.35 Yet in the afternoon a different method of policing had been used. The same youths had stood and expressed their anger for 90 minutes in front of the police station. Here, the police had accepted that it was necessary to allow this to take place. We have no doubt that the youths were just as angry at this time as later on when they were leaving the estate. But in the afternoon there had been no disturbance. Why was the response different in the evening? We have already identified two very different approaches to policing in this area. We have noted the disagreement of many officers with the approach of Chief Superintendent Couch. In the afternoon, his strategy of policing was followed. In the evening, the strategy deployed was one of massive force.

THE FIGHTING SPREADS
5.36 The view of Cliff Ford from his twelfth floor flat in Northolt covered both Willan Road to the south and Griffin Road to the east. Four or five minutes after he had seen people running down from Willan Road, he saw police at Griffin Road:—
 "I saw them all arrive there and go straight across the road and block it."
When he saw them arrive nothing was happening at Griffin Road, and no barricades had been built.

5.37 A woman whom we interviewed had seen the confrontation at Willan Road and decided to leave the estate with a friend by the Griffin Road exit where nothing was happening:—
 "At the point of getting to Griffin Road, about eight lines of police came around the corner in formation, trotting, with all their riot shields, and as they swooped round the corner and filled up the road, my friend and I had to squeeze by on the pavement. Abuse was shouted at me, like 'Black slag'."
She too was clear that there were no disturbances at Griffin Road at that point.

5.38 It seems that some of the police officers who arrived at the Griffin Road entrance actually came down Griffin Road and under the Rochford block. Stafford Scott, after coming down from the Willan Road junction, says that he saw police officers emerging from Rochford, and that a crowd rushed toward them and forced them to retreat back to Griffin Road. Leonardo Leon, who lives in Rochford, with views from different rooms in his flat facing both south to Willan Road and north towards Griffin Road, saw people moving up towards Willan Road and then suddenly running back. He could see police officers blocking the road, bricks being thrown, and a car set alight. Then he heard shouting underneath Rochford. He went to the window on the north side of his flat. He then saw people pushing cars up, towards Griffin Road towards police lines at the mouth of Griffin Road.

OCTOBER 6 – WHAT HAPPENED?

5.39 Nick Wright and Debbie Wilde had hurried towards Broadwater Farm after seeing the rush of police vehicles in that direction. They cut through the back streets to the Adams Road entrance, just to the north of Griffin Road. Nick Wright said that as they arrived, various police units were also arriving, a short shield unit and then a long shield unit arriving in a green bus. They deployed across Adams Road. There were some people in the estate on Adams Road, shouting and arguing, but there was no fighting and no barricades. Soon after that missiles started to be thrown and a vehicle was pushed up and set alight.

5.40 The only other entrance for vehicles onto the estate is at Gloucester Road. A resident with a view over the Gloucester Road entrance smelt burning outside, at about 7 pm, and when he looked out saw three or four vans burning on the entrance road near the edge of the estate. But he could see no activity going on there at all. Indeed Gloucester Road remained quiet for the greater part of the evening, and there was never the same pattern of missiles being thrown at lines of police officers, as was the case at the other three exits. We did not have evidence as to how the three vans at the Gloucester Road entrance got set on fire.

5.41 We can now examine again the statement made in the Richards report that the units arriving on the scene "found that barricades of blazing vehicles had been erected at all four vehicular entrances to the estate, and at each location they came under missile and petrol bomb fire as they approached." D.A.C. Richards relies on this allegation that barricades were erected before the arrival of police, as being proof that this was part of a pre-arranged plan, rather than a spontaneous reaction to police surrounding the estate. The evidence which we have heard shows that this is not correct so far as Willan Road, Griffin Road, and Adams Road are concerned. At Willan Road no cars were burnt until after a large number of police officers were in position across The Avenue and pushing people back towards the estate. At Griffin Road the evidence of Cliff Ford, who saw the police arrive, is very clear, and supported by other sources. As for Adams Road we had direct evidence from Nick Wright, confirmed by Debbie Wilde, and based on notes which they made at the time. They are very clear that on the arrival of the first police officers, which they witnessed, there were no burning cars. Only at Gloucester Road is the picture unclear.

THE BROADWATER FARM INQUIRY REPORT

5.42 The speed with which the entrances were blocked by the police was remarkable. In the absence of direct police evidence we do not know with certainty what messages were passed over the radio to the many police units in the vicinity. The most likely explanation is there was a call for urgent assistance to prevent a crowd of youths from leaving the estate. Whether it was a pre-arranged plan, or an immediate response from the units on the spot, the fact is that the exits were blocked. When they were, the youth on the estate felt even more the sense of being trapped and under siege. It was in those circumstances that they began to push cars toward the police lines and set them alight. It was then that the fighting at Griffin Road and Adams Road, which was the fiercest in the whole area, began.

THE ACTIONS OF THE CROWD
5.43 The fiercest encounters were at Griffin Road and Adams Road, and they took on a pattern which continued for many hours from soon after 7.00 pm to about 10.30 pm. From the side of those on the estate, there were constant volleys of dangerous missiles. Slabs of pavement were broken up and thrown. When the available slabs from nearby were used up, young people were seen rushing through the estate carrying missiles in various containers. A shopping trolley, a milk crate, and a large communal rubbish bin were all mentioned to us as being used. At a later stage, tins stolen from the supermarket became a common form of ammunition.

5.44 Many petrol bombs were thrown. On the clear evidence that we have, they were crudely and hurriedly made on the spot, not carefully prepared beforehand. Leonardo Leon, looking from the Rochford block over the Griffin Road area, saw:—
> "People with bottles, then some people syphoning off fuel from cars, three or four people laughing and putting cloth inside. There was a white cloth, a large piece, and they were tearing it apart and then putting it into the bottles, and throwing it. But of ten bottles they threw, one of them would actually light up and land in the road. All the others would just be nothing."

Michael Keith, a research assistant at St Katherine's College, Oxford, had been preparing a history of rioting. He went to Tottenham after hearing of the death of Mrs Jarrett. He witnessed the disturbances both from outside and inside the estate, and later in the surrounding streets and the High Road. He saw how easy it was to make petrol bombs while he was watching the action in the streets outside the estate:—

"Two people, both Black, started shouting orders at the others: 'we need more ammunition'. Immediately five or six responded by running round the houses gathering up empty milk bottles, while four others turned over a car for petrol. In less than five minutes I counted more than 50 petrol bombs completed."

5.45 We conclude that it was entirely possible for many petrol bombs to have been assembled within a short time. In a large estate there were many milk bottles ready to hand which could be quickly gathered. People were seen to fill them on the spot. We have no evidence whatever that they were prepared beforehand. In the light of this we have considered with care reports of the statement made on behalf of the prosecution on the 12th June 1986 at the Old Bailey that "petrol bombs were prepared in advance and stored". On all the evidence, we consider this to be both unproven and unlikely.

5.46 A great number of cars were burned. 47 wrecked vehicles were later removed from the estate by the council's contractor. Many of these were in the Griffin and Adams road area. Mr and Mrs Kemp, watching from their flat in the Rochford block, counted at least eight or nine in Griffin Road. As one burned out, another was set on fire. A mini-bus was pushed out from one of the schools and burned. A rubbish skip in Adams Road was also set on fire.

5.47 One building on the corner of Adams Road at its closest point to the edge of the estate was burned out. Families living in the maisonettes in the building were evacuated. They were not injured, but they must have suffered a terrible experience. We have no evidence as to how that house caught fire. It was situated beside the centre of the action in Adams Road, by the area of road where cars were set on fire. The Richards report states that the house was set on fire "as the result of the actions of the rioters in petrol bombing the cars outside".

5.48 Many of those involved in the actions against the police wore masks or scarves to disguise themselves. But several of the people who we interviewed who lived in flats overlooking Griffin Road were sure that there were many strangers among them, both Black and White. Leonardo Leon gave a vivid picture of four strangers who played a prominent part:—

"It was like when you look at ants, you see how ants move and you identify which ones are the soldiers and which ones are the workers. Because you see them from high. Now what I saw was three or four people moving and giving signs to each other with their hands. They were people in bomber jackets with trainers and jeans. I cannot say absolutely for sure if they were White, but I think they were White. And they were moving like a group. You could see they were White by their hands."

One other woman, a retired White woman whom we interviewed, who was watching from Hawkinge block, was also struck by a group of four White men: —

"There were these four White young men that I would call the thug type, they came from under Lympne, and they had on their heads these hoods."

She described how she could see they were White from their hands, and from the fair hair of one who took his hood off. They had petrol bombs in their hands. She continued: —

" I can't describe the hatred that I felt on that night, that I still feel, for those four Whites that I saw . They were outsiders doing it to our estate."

5.49 However from the general pattern of the evidence, it is impossible to say that people were being "organised" or "led". Some people were more active than others. Some threw missiles, some shouted, some just watched. Michael Keith had the strong impression that all were united in their anger against the police. He said this on the question of "organisation": —

"Most of the people were united by a sense of anger which regularly escalated to fury. In this situation a dramatic cast, representative of any cross-section of society was clearly evident. Here were the people who were 'all mouth', loudest in the cries of abuse, standing furthest away from the police lines, throwing the occasional brick from the safe distance of a 100 yards or more. Others were more committed, outdoing one another in their attacks on police, going as close as 30, 20 or ten yards away from police lines before throwing brick, bomb or baked bean can. Many more spent most of the time giving moral support, joking with each other, but no less committed in occasional forays against the rows of riot shields. Amidst all these characters, there inevitably emerge those who try and impose some order upon confused actions. In this sense organisation was extemporised."

OCTOBER 6 – WHAT HAPPENED?

There was evidence that some people had whistles, and one person had a bell, which fitted this pattern of "extemporised organisation". Arthur Lawrence of the West Indian Leadership Council, who with his colleagues walked around both inside and outside the estate, gave similar evidence of people supporting each other in a loosely organised way:—

"When people thought that their lines were a bit thin, then they went to reinforce the lines, running from one point to another. There were no generals."

5.50 Two of the schools next to the estate to the north of Adams Road were damaged and property was stolen. The Moselle School had extensive damage to glass and doors and the loss of seven computers, a television and other equipment, and a large photocopier. We have no evidence as to who removed such bulky items. Both the William C. Harvey School and the Broadwater Farm Junior School had damage to windows and doors, and some equipment stolen. On the Tangmere block, as we shall describe in more detail, the supermarket and newsagent's shop were broken open, looted and burned, and one flat was ransacked. Many of the lights on the estate were broken. That, plus the burning of cars, was the extent of property damage, and there were no attacks on residents of the estate.

5.51 The actions which we have described so far all concern the Griffin Road/Adams Road area. At Willan Road, after the police had blocked off The Avenue, the action had started with the throwing of bricks from the demolished garden wall. A local resident was struck by how young they were. She saw "kids of 12 and 13" and no older men though generally people spoke of young people of a variety of ages taking part. Arthur Lawrence spoke of about 30 youths being involved at Willan Road. People who lived in the Avenue were coming out and trying to move their cars, and it seems that surprisingly little damage was done to cars in The Avenue area. After a time, the brick throwing eased off and the police were able to block the top of Willan Road, where they were preventing people from entering and leaving the estate. Nick Wright observed a "second confrontation" at Willan Road at about 8.45 pm, which worried the police because they thought that they had secured that area. In general there was no sustained attack after the initial confrontation; rather there were intermittent forays.

THE ACTIONS OF THE POLICE

5.52 For hour after hour at Griffin Road and Adams Road the police stood in their lines across the road, behind their long perspex shields, passively fending off the missiles which came at them. From time to time they would advance a short distance, 40 or 50 yards, and then retreat again. Occasionally the short shield squads made what one witness called "half hearted sorties" towards the estate; but the difficulty was that the space was too confined for the short shield officers to be covered by long shield units. The short shield units are intended to be "snatch squads" who make arrests, but on this occasion hardly any arrests were made. We understand from police sources that on one occasion a small unit did succeed in getting into the estate and staying there for about half an hour, but it had no support and eventually was forced to retreat. The officers beat on their shields in unison and gave voice to a cry that was described as "the gorilla chant of the football terraces", "oooh oooh noises", "a zulu war cry". The evidence which we heard from many onlookers fully confirmed the statements made in the *Police Magazine* in October 1985 that officers were "required to crouch behind static lines of long shields to become Aunt Sallys of the petrol bombers".

5.53 We have no doubt that for the officers who were required to stand in this way the experience was terrifying. Directly opposite the Griffin Road and Adams Road corners were the elevated balconies of the Rochford and Martlesham blocks; and although most of the missiles came from ground level, some also were hurled from above. Fire extinguishers began to run short, and according to a journalist close to the police lines the officers were told not to use fire extinguishers to put out petrol bomb fires, but only if a person was burnt. Some officers became more confident at their success in batting down the missiles with their shields, and some hurled missiles back into the crowd. But any confidence turned back to fear when, as we shall describe, it became known that gun shots had been fired. Howard Simmons, the council's head of community affairs, described the officers behind the lines along Mount Pleasant Road:—

> "A considerable number of police were stood down. They were standing around looking shaken, looking exhausted. Some of the police were lying on the pavement, stacking their shields up in people's front gardens. There was an immense emotional feel amongst the police in that area."

OCTOBER 6 – WHAT HAPPENED?

5.54 At Willan Road, where the police had more of the upper hand, much more aggression and abuse was directed at Black people, many of whom were trying to get in or out of the estate. It was there that Steve Platt, reporting for *New Society*, overheard some disgusting racial abuse:—

"A Black couple trying to leave the area via Willan Road were turned back at the police lines, to a chorus of the monkey noises used to abuse Black footballers by racists at soccer matches. 'Fuck off niggers' yelled one of the policemen 'Go and live in the zoo.' 'You can burn that down.' 'Get back in your rat hole, vermin,' echoed another. 'We'll be in to get you soon enough'."

Other witnesses spoke of similar shouts. A woman resident in The Avenue spoke of police "riling up the kids" with cries of "you wogs, you vermin". Whatever the circumstances, racist abuse of this nature is wholly unacceptable in a force which even under pressure should be disciplined and impartial.

5.55 At the Gloucester Road entrance the situation was far more calm and controlled. The officer in charge at Gloucester Road was Chief Superintendent Couch. In contrast to the other entrances many people were able to get in and out through Gloucester Road without being stopped or harassed. Many of the officers there were not in riot gear. Arthur Lawrence and his colleagues from the West Indian Leadership Council made their way to Gloucester Road around 7.45 pm, and spoke to Chief Superintendent Couch. He said that he was glad to see them and asked them to do something to help calm the situation. They went down The Avenue towards Willan Road, where they saw a police van moving towards the crowd at the junction. They went back to Chief Superintendent Couch and asked him to withdraw the van as it was aggravating the situation. Chief Superintendent Couch agreed. They went back and the same thing happened – two vans were moving into the crowd. This time Chief Superintendent Couch said that he couldn't give them instructions, as they were not under his control. Chief Superintendent Couch continued to ask help from the community leaders by asking them to try to ensure that no houses were set on fire. Arthur Lawrence's group did in fact secure an undertaking from the crowd at Willan Road that no property would be set on fire.

5.56 The evidence of Mr Lawrence and his colleagues, and the lack of confrontation at Gloucester Road, indicates clearly to us that there was sensible leadership in that location which could act flexibly to minimise the trouble. Unfortunately it appears that the police leadership at the other locations was not of the same quality, and at Griffin Road and Adams Road appeared not to be in control of the situation at all. Howard Simmons walked down Mount Pleasant Road between about 8.30 – to 9.00 pm identifying himself as a senior council official and trying to find someone in command. The junior officers whom he spoke to were in a state of confusion and had no idea where the control point was. He said: –

> "My view on the night was that the chain of command and communication between police was virtually non-existent. The police themselves did not know what was going on. I was staggered to find them standing shoulder to shoulder about ten deep in receipt of all these missiles, but clearly they were going to sustain substantial injuries. God knows what their senior officers thought they were doing."

5.57 The junior officers believed that they could and should have gone into the estate with maximum force and subdued it. They said so in the pages of the October 1985 *Police Magazine*. They were saying so on the night. A journalist heard an officer who had served with the Royal Ulster Constabulary in Belfast say that they should have used plastic bullets to disperse the crowd and then move into the estate for "search and seize".

5.58 We are in a state of some uncertainty as to who, if anyone, took overall charge of the night's operations. The Richards report states that there were four senior officers – Couch, Sinclair, French, and Rowe – who took command at each of the four main locations. Two hours later Chief Superintendent Jeffers took over at Griffin Road. Above them there were high ranking officers at the district headquarters at Wood Green, the area headquarters at Chigwell, and the Metropolitan headquarters at Scotland Yard. According to a report in *The Job* magazine, traffic on the police radio wavelengths was seriously overloaded, so that clear commands could not be issued and implemented. This information was confirmed from fire brigade sources, for their operations too were affected. According to their report, they had a senior officer in the Wood Green Police control room who experienced considerable difficulty because no facilities were provided for a brigade radio to be installed, and so he was out of touch for much of the time with the brigade's involvement. At the

OCTOBER 6 – WHAT HAPPENED?

time of finalising this report we had not had sight of the report of the Metropolitan Police's internal review of the disturbances, which may provide, if published, more information about the chain of command on the night. Our view on the evidence available is of confusion, which was likely to lead to unnecessary danger to officers in front lines, and to minimise the chances of scaling down the confrontation.

5.59 It is difficult without police evidence to determine the total numbers of police officers involved on 6th October. Lord Gifford asked for this information in a parliamentary question, and received this reply from Lord Glenarthur: –

> "I understand from the Commissioner that the number of officers deployed at the Broadwater Farm Estate on 6th October 1985 varied as the disturbances developed. At 10 o'clock pm, some three hours after the riot began, about 600 police officers, drawn from all areas of the Metropolitan Police district, were deployed in the vicinity of the Broadwater Farm estate."

The answer is incomplete, and we are not told whether the time chosen of 10 pm was the time when the maximum number of officers was deployed. Further information is available from the report of the Commissioner for 1985, in which it is stated that "nearly 2000 officers were available for deployment within four hours of the outbreak of violence". As to the numbers injured, Lord Glenarthur in another parliamentary answer said that 71 officers required treatment in hospital, of whom 17 were detained for longer than 24 hours.

'LAKES OF PETROL'

5.60 The Richards report contains two references to lakes or floods of petrol. In seeking to justify the police strategy of "containment", the report states: –

> "Any concerted effort to advance into the body of the estate (in which lakes of petrol were seen) could well have resulted in death or serious injury to police and/or members of the public."

Later in the context of dealing with the anti-police character of the attacks, the report states that: –

> "Subsequent inquiries reveal allegations that some basement garage areas on the estate had been flooded with petrol, for the alleged purpose of use in the event of an incursion by police."

Predictably these references became banner headlines when the report was leaked to the press.

5.61 At the meeting of the Community and Police Consultative Group on 13th March 1986, which was attended by members of our panel, D.A.C. Richards was asked directly by Councillor Mitchell whether there were any lakes of petrol. In answer D.A.C. Richards said that people had had plastic bags of petrol and two litre bottles which were lobbed to the police lines. The police were confronted by sheets of petrol which came about from these bags bursting in the basement area. There was evidence of a police officer who finished up in a deep puddle of petrol. A civilian witness had said that petrol was poured down the stairs to the garage area. Some petrol was set alight and the flames shot towards police officers. Councillor Mitchell asked him whether he had therefore withdrawn his allegation about lakes of petrol. D.A.C. Richards said that he had corrected statements in the press. There had been a misunderstanding. The allegations of floods of petrol were made after the event. A further statement was made by D.A.C. Richards in a letter to the *Police Review* on January 24th 1986, which mentions evidence of a police constable about the plastic bags, and continued:—

> "He saw an expanse of petrol which he estimated was equivalent to a car's full tank of petrol. He then sustained serious injury and fell to the ground in what he once more thought to be water. However his footwear and clothing were saturated with petrol."

5.62 We have concluded that there have been two quite separate allegations made about petrol which, whether deliberately or not, have become confused. On one hand, there was undoubtedly a quantity of petrol on the ground and in various places, particularly around Griffin Road and Adams Road, because of the actions of members of the crowd in throwing petrol bombs and possibly other petrol filled missiles, many of which did not ignite when landing. The fire brigade report contains a contemporary record from Adams Road at 9.20 pm saying "copious amounts of petrol spread on the road unignited at this time". These quantities which D.A.C. Richards more accurately referred to as "puddles", clearly represented a danger of injury if they were to ignite.

5.63 On the other hand the use of the word "lakes" was clearly calculated to convey the impression that whole expanses of the basement car-parks were awash with petrol which had been spilled deliberately by people in the estate in order to be ignited and burn up police officers if they came into the estate. If this were true, it would have been a horrific plan. But it was not true, and D.A.C. Richards in his reply to Councillor Mitchell appears to accept that. As members of the council's Building Design Service have observed to us, there are no "basement garage areas". The under-deck parking spaces could not have been turned into "lakes of petrol" without the construction of additional walls and the blocking of rainwater gullies. The reference in the report to "lakes" was therefore grossly misleading.

GUN SHOTS AND FIRE ARMS
5.64 The Richards report states that at 7.55 pm an officer deployed at Griffin Road sustained a bullet hole in his shield, and shortly afterwards a police officer was found to have been struck in the body by a bullet. The report states that following this, at least one shotgun was fired in Griffin Road and several officers and two BBC cameramen sustained pellet wounds, fortunately none serious; and that one officer experienced in the use of firearms said that he heard a shotgun fired more than 30 times in the Griffin Road area. Seven people whom we interviewed in our door-to-door inquiries had heard gun shots, in each case two to three shots. Those who gave a time put it between 9 and 10.30 pm. Two people said that the shots came from the Rochford area. A journalist whom we interviewed was behind the lines at Griffin Road at about 9.30 when he heard a gunshot sound and saw that a BBC cameraman had fallen. He had "pepper shot" across his face and upper body and his chest was bleeding. He noticed also that a riot shield had been peppered with shot. There is no doubt at all that a shotgun was fired, but we do not accept the suggestion of 30 shots made in the Richards report. The number of people hit would suggest a very low number of shots. We have no direct evidence of the bullet shot, but we have no reason to dispute the facts given in the Richards report. A riot shield pierced by a bullet was shown to the press, and it was reported that surgeons had removed a bullet from the stomach of the police officer.

5.65 The Richards report states that officers from D11 Branch, the force's firearms unit, were alerted soon after 8.00pm and sent to Tottenham to stand by. It states that at 9.45 pm the Commissioner authorised the use of baton rounds (plastic bullets) and/ or CS gas as a last resort, and that the officers equipped with these weapons arrived at Griffin Road at about 10.20 pm. In the event, the baton rounds and CS gas were never used. Howard Simmons saw a section of police armed with plastic bullet launchers march past him and stand behind the cordon. He thought the time was about 9.45 pm. In an interview on the *TV Eye* programme four nights later, Chief Superintendent Couch said that he had been authorised to use baton round and CS gas but he had been concerned for the public; and that if he had used the ultimate weapons, the bridge would have been more difficult to build. However, the Richards report suggests that the reason why they were not used was because "the severity of the attack had lessened considerably" by the time that the team arrived.

5.66 There were also police marksmen on the scene. The police had been given access to one of the houses in Mount Pleasant Road which backed onto the estate, and were looking through windows at the back. They had set up an infra-red night sight, and an officer looking through the sight claimed to have identified someone on a balcony in the Rochford block. He said to a senior officer: "We could take him out." The senior officer replied: "No, there is no question of that, we are not doing that". There was a heated exchange between the two officers.

THE SHOPS ON TANGMERE
5.67 On the Tangmere precinct there was a supermarket and a newsagent's shop, side by side. At about 9.30 pm Arthur Lawrence and his colleagues went into the estate by the Gloucester Road entrance. Superintendent Dick Stacey had seen them at the Gloucester Road entrance and had told them that he believed there was looting on the Tangmere precinct. He asked them to go and see if this was the case. Mr Lawrence and his colleagues felt that it was the police's duty to investigate looting. Even so, they went into the estate. One of the remarkable features of the evening is the way in which Arthur Lawrence, George Martin, and Vernon Moore, and (for the earlier part) one other man, went about the scene throughout the whole evening and night, apart from one short break for a snack, quietly helping to calm things if they could. We have seen how they helped Chief Superintendent Couch on The Avenue. Later on "four well dressed Black gentleman" – obviously the same group – were seen by Mr and Mrs Kemp to be talking quietly to people at Griffin Road. And later in the night on Tangmere, as we shall see, their actions almost certainly saved many lives.

5.68 When they reached the precinct, they saw that both the newsagent's and the supermarket had been broken into. People, Black and White, were "running in and out of the supermarket with bags of goodies". They spoke to seven or eight of them, and told them it was not right to do that. There was a child of eight or nine with a carrier bag. There was "this little White kid with two carrier bags" saying to his mother "Mum, what shall I do with this?". There was another White boy with a suitcase full of groceries who said that he didn't live on the estate, but in Downhills Park:—

"When he spoke I discovered he was an Irish boy and he said that it's the first time he has had so much food in six months because he's unemployed."

Others looted the shops for ammunition such as cans and bottles to throw at the police.

5.69 Arthur Lawrence and his colleagues went over to the Griffin Road area and observed the scene there for a while. They came back to Tangmere around 10.00 pm and saw smoke and a few flames coming from the newsagent. It was a small fire, and they thought that somebody tried to put it out. Unfortunately they did not stay on the precinct, but went back over to Griffin Road, and then out of the estate by the Willan Road exit. They were very hungry and went to the High Road for something to eat. They came back to the estate between about 11.30 pm and 12 pm by the Gloucester Road entrance. The period during which they had been away had seen the tragedy of PC Keith Blakelock's death. He had been sent into the estate with other officers to protect the fire brigade as they put out the fire in the Tangmere shop. As stated earlier, we can make no comment about this tragic episode because of the sub judice rule.

5.70 By this time Roy Limb and Dolly Kiffin had returned to the estate. They had left after the Youth Association meeting in order to attend a reception for Mike Henry, the Jamaican Minister of Culture, who had been visiting Haringey. They had hurried back from the reception when they had learned of the intensity of the disturbances. Arthur Lawrence and his colleagues spent some time escorting Roy Limb onto the estate and later off again. Arthur Lawrence, George Martin, and Vernon Moore remained around the Tangmere precinct. It was by now after 1 am. The precinct was full of water from the previous actions of the fire brigade, and a fire hose was still there.

THE BROADWATER FARM INQUIRY REPORT

5.71 Suddenly George Martin saw a frightening sight:—
"There were three White youths and they were going in and out of the supermarket and the tobacconist's shop, catching the place fire. I see fire start to come up from one end of it. I keep chasing back and forward to this fire. I say to them, you are catching this place afire. They were doing it with matches. Eventually the one in the tobacconist's became the largest fire."
Dolly Kiffin was in her office inside the Youth Association. Through the window, which looks over the precinct, she too saw the fire started:—
"I saw three men, one blonde, a fattish one, and the next one, he threw something in the paper shop, it came red, and then bang — the fire was raging."

5.72 We accept the evidence of George Martin and Dolly Kiffin that this fire was deliberately started by three White youths. Mr Martin in particular was very clear about his observations. Other witnessess including Arthur Lawrence saw the White youths — one witness described them as "three White skinheads" — but did not actually see them start the fire. The possible implications of this evidence are frightening. There were, as the fire brigade confirmed in their report, exposed gas pipes in the newsagent's shop, which is presumably why it caught fire again after the previous fire had been doused. Who were these three White youths? Why were they doing this? Had they been responsible for the earlier fire in the shop? It is worth noting that journalist David Whitfield saw a group of White youths in The Avenue at around 1.00 am who may be the same group. They stood out as being a group that were not making common cause with Black youths. He told us:—
"What was interesting was that there were Black and White young people on the streets together. At one stage I'd seen a bunch of White youths and I was a bit nervous because I didn't know whether they were facists. But what was clear was that there were a lot of Blacks and Whites on the streets together mixed in with no animosity. Apart from these boys who — didn't look too pleasant."

5.73 Dolly Kiffin ran out with fire extinguishers from the Youth Association, and Arthur Lawrence and George Martin tried in vain to put the fire out. They went back to Gloucester Road and asked the fire officer to turn the hose back on. But it was twisted and there was no pressure. The fire was burning fiercely with flames coming out of the top and smoke spreading upstairs. George Martin and a youth went upstairs and knocked on the doors upstairs to get people out, but nobody came. By now there was a large group of 30 or 40 youths around the precinct, and George Martin argued with them to get the fire brigade in, and eventually they agreed. The three men — Arthur Lawrence, George Martin, and Vernon Moore — went back to the fire officer and told him that the fire was getting out of hand. The fireman asked: "Can you guarantee our safety?" There were several trips backwards and forward between the fire officer and the youths on Tangmere, and George Martin was finally able to say: "We can guarantee that they won't interfere with you". The fire officers assured the community leaders that only they and no police would come onto Tangmere. George Martin gave this account of the arrival of the firemen:—

"I then went upstairs and I said to all the youths who were literally trying to put out the fire to move away and go over the far side and wait. And I managed to get them all over there and then I shout to the fire officer to come upstairs. Then myself, Mr Lawrence and Mr Moore stand between the fire officers and where the youths were standing."

5.74 Eventually, after more trips in and out with hoses, the fire was put out, except for the gas pipe that remained alight but safe. We pay the highest tribute to George Martin, Arthur Lawrence and Vernon Moore for this action which they took; and also to the fire officers and the senior officers of police who responded to the negotiations in the knowledge of what had happened to PC Blakelock on the occasion of the earlier fire. The fire had reached a stage of intense danger. Sheila Ramdin lives below the newsagent. The room where her children were asleep was filling up with smoke when she went in and got them out. As she said to us:—

"If the fire brigade never come, the whole of Tangmere would have just caught alight."

THE ENTRY OF THE POLICE
5.75 Long before the episode of the second fire, the conflict had been dying away. Sometime before 11.00 pm a police helicopter had arrived overhead, shining a strong beam of light, and causing youths to take cover to avoid identification. After 11.00 pm it began to rain. Roy Limb had persuaded Chief Superintendent Couch that the news of the officer's death ought to be communicated to the youths inside.

When George Martin and Arthur Lawrence escorted him on to the estate, it was to give Dolly Kiffin that message, and she passed it on. For all these reasons the fighting ended, but the ranks of police remained for many hours at the entrances to the estate.

5.76 There were a number of incidents off the estate in the latter part of the evening. Michael Keith had left the estate around 10.30 to 11 pm and witnessed severe attacks on the police line in Mount Pleasant Road from Wimborne Road. A garden wall along Wimborne Road was rocked and demolished for further ammunition to throw at the police. A car was turned over and an unsuccessful attempt made to light it. Michael Keith counted over 200 people, the majority involved in verbal abuse, a minority doing the brunt of the attacking. For over an hour police officers moved backwards and forwards against this crowd and eventually forced them away from the estate through the surrounding residential streets. They finally reached Bruce Grove and the High Road, for a further half hour the police were seen to be clearing people from the High Road in a fairly violent way, causing injury to at least two bystanders.

5.77 At 4.30 am a massive number of police in riot gear entered the estate. The estate was by now completely quiet; many of those who had taken part would have been able to leave across the Lordship Recreation Ground, which was never sealed off by the police. A great number of the officers came up the steps onto the precinct of Tangmere. Arthur Lawrence, George Martin, Vernon Moore, Dolly Kiffen and about six youths were in the Youth Association premises, some of them taking a nap. They saw the officers arrive, with the Community Liaison Officer Superintendent Stacey in front. George Martin described what he then saw:—

"I was standing at the door of the Youth Association, and we saw the police as they came upstairs, and they went towards the supermarket, and I saw one of them hitting something. I was trying to see but it was in darkness. He had a shield and he had a baton. He was hitting this thing, down like this. Eventually when I managed to look, he picked this thing up and chained it against the door. Then I realised it was a young chap."

Arthur Lawrence saw two youths being beaten. He said that the police had found them inside the shop, and beat them "with truncheons and kicks and that sort of thing".

OCTOBER 6 – WHAT HAPPENED?

5.78 The officers came up to the glass door of the Youth Association, and asked Arthur Lawrence to open up. He had not got the keys, and one of the youths went upstairs to get them from Dolly Kiffin. Before she came down, the officers smashed through the glass with their truncheons. The community leaders were surrounded by officers in riot gear armed with plastic bullet launchers. Arthur Lawrence said: –

"By that time I was having 10,000 butterflies, because I thought my number had been called, because things were being pointed at us."

George Martin told us, "at that time I thought we had had it, quite honestly". Vernon Moore told us that an officer shook a truncheon in his face. There was a youth in the building, and the officers took him out onto the precinct. Authur Lawrence described what he then saw: –

"They kicked and punched and threw him on the floor and stamped on him, kneed him. Then they hung his head over the balcony."

The officers then spread out and took positions, occupying the whole estate.

CONCLUSION
5.79 It will be apparent from this chapter that during the evening of 6th October there were many people involved in many different kinds of action. Some were trying to use their position as community leaders to be intermediaries with the authorities, as far as they were able to be. Some were looking on, and we have heard many stories of residents coming out on to the balconies and chatting to the youths who were more directly involved. Some threw missiles of various descriptions, and set cars on fire. Some, for reasons which may have been entirely separate and personal to themselves, broke into the schools and stole equipment. Some looted the shops for ammunition; others looted simply to steal food. Some were prepared to commit arson which endangered life. Some were prepared to endanger life by shooting.

5.80 Some of the actions done that night were shocking and inexcusable. But many of the actions were not condemned by many witnesses. They said that the youths were defending themselves against officers who had first interfered with their right to walk to the police station, and then threatened to enter the estate and attack them in force. Sheila Ramdin, chair of the Resident's Association,

was one of those who put this view: —
> "They weren't looking to start any riot, they didn't want trouble. It just happened. It was just in self-defence, they had to defend themselves and they tried to defend the Farm."

Michael Hutchinson-Reis put it in similar terms: —
> "They had nothing to gain from what they did. The motivation was something else. And that motivation quite clearly in my mind was that they saw themselves defending their community, they saw themselves under threat, they saw themselves threatened physically, and they defended themselves. And that understanding of the motivation of those arrested, when you actually follow through the implications, that's got serious consequences not just for social workers but for this society as a whole."

This issue of "reasonable self defence" may be raised at the forthcoming trials. We must therefore avoid making judgements about the legality of particular kinds of action, which may be the subject of argument before a jury. The purpose of this chapter has been to describe, as fully as possible upon the evidence which we have gathered, what happened on 6th October at Broadwater Farm.

We return in Chapter 8 to discuss why it happened and how to stop it happening again.

Chapter 6
THE AFTERMATH

THE FIRST WEEK

6.1 On 7th October the police remained on and around the estate in force. In the evening the Police Research Unit staff noted around 200 officers on the estate, the majority dressed in riot overalls and carrying shields; two coaches full of police parked in Adams Road; another coach at the junction of Mount Pleasant Road and The Avenue; and ten transit vans parked in The Avenue. In the whole Tottenham and Wood Green area, they calculated that nearly 1,500 officers were deployed. The focus of attention on the estate was the Youth Association. Outside there were police officers spread all over the precinct and balconies of Tangmere. Inside people gathered, talking about the night before, unsure what was going to happen now. Councillor Andrew Mitchell tried to act as a mediator between the youth and the police. He met D.A.C. Richards, who said that he would only agree to reduce the level of policing if the council would agree to let the police have a flat or an office on the estate. He also said that it would help if the Youth Association could be shut for the night. The council refused to offer accommodation, and the officers of the Youth Association reacted with considerable hostility to both of the requests which the police had made. Councillor Mitchell remained on the estate until 1.00 am pleading with the police to step back from their positions close up to the Youth Association doors, which eventually they did. We think that Councillor Mitchell showed considerable moral courage in his actions on that day. Although he failed to achieve any concrete agreement (which in the circumstances was not surprising), by staying around and being in touch with both sides he helped to ensure that there was no further flare-up in the course of that day and night.

6.2 The estate was also swarming with journalists and broadcasters. The events of the night had been reported in the morning papers,

THE BROADWATER FARM INQUIRY REPORT

which featured pictures of the rioting and headlines about the death of the policeman. On Monday the journalists' job was to discover the background to what had happened. Their efforts, as printed in the papers of 8th October, make sorry reading. A frequent theme was that the whole event was organised by left wing agitators:—

"Street fighting experts trained in Moscow and Libya were behind Britain's worst violence." *(Daily Express)*

"The Tottenham riot was ignited by well prepared outsiders." *(Daily Mirror)*

The responsiblity for this theme must be taken by the Commissioner Sir Kenneth Newman, who at a press conference on 7th October said;—

"Groups of trotskyists and anarchists had been identified as orchestrating the disturbances in Tottenham and in Brixton a week earlier. They are both Black and White and come from within and outside London, operating in areas of ethnic concentration."

It was highly irresponsible for the Commissioner to make this statement at a time when the investigations into the Tottenham disturbances had scarcely begun. As it turned out, within ten days, the police had completely discounted this theory. The London *Standard* reported on 17th October:—

"No evidence of agitation before the riot by politically inspired groups had been found by police. A Scotland Yard spokesman said: 'We don't believe outside agitators were responsible for what happened in Tottenham'."

But many more people must have read the original headlines than read the later retraction. Prejudices were fed, and distress and anxiety caused, by a statement which should never have been made.

6.3 A second theme was the picture of Broadwater Farm as a hellish place of criminal activity and racial hatred:—

"A daily war being waged against White families by the younger members of a burgeoning Black community who occupy virtually all the flats in the 12 blocks of grey, stained concrete that make up the divided zone." *(Daily Mail, 8th October)*

"The local name for the 12 blocks of flats there is Alcatraz, and if you are poor and White, old and ill, it's a vicious and frightening prison. White people there do feel they are living in an alien and terrifying land and nobody will even listen to them, let alone help them." *(Daily Mail, 9th October)*

THE AFTERMATH

"They sit there, these gaunt tower blocks, like citadels of disillusion. They are scruffy. They are battered. They smell." (*Daily Mirror*, under the headline "Living hell".)

An Asian man whom we interviewed described the attitude of reporters who spoke to him on the Monday:—

"When the newspapers interviewed me the next day, they wanted me to say it was Black against White. When I said it wasn't, they didn't really want to know anything. It didn't make headlines."

Cliff Ford, an estate sweeper and active Tenants' Association member, tried to exercise a right of reply:—

"I wrote to the *Daily Mail* myself and said, 'what about the Christmas dinners, the social things that the Youth Association does?' They didn't want to know about that, they never published that at all."

An article in the *Times* headed **"THE ESTATE THAT DOLLY KIFFIN RESCUED FROM NIGHTMARE"** stands out as being a serious effort to describe the achievements of the Broadwater Farm community. Neale Coleman, Neighbourhood Officer, spoke of the "considerable anger" among residents about the reports in most of the newspapers, and added that the television and radio tended to be more responsible.

6.4   The racist theme which appears in some of the reports which we have quoted — White people being hated and terrorised by Black — was reinforced by headlines about "hyenas", "butchers", and "monsters". It became personalised in a particularly unpleasant way around Councillor Bernie Grant. A report in the *Sun* of 9th October, under the headline **"DON'T CALL ME BARMY BERNIE"**, describes Councillor Grant as "peeling a banana and juggling with an orange". An unnamed Labour councillor is quoted in the report as saying that:—

"Bernie Grant is like the leader of a Black tribe — always looking for battles and shaking his spear. He sees all Whites as his enemy."

This kind of reporting had nothing to do with criticism of Councillor Grant's statements, which we analyse below. The crude images of Councillor Grant as being a madman from the jungle were inexcusable, and they were to continue for months.

6.5   One theme which did not feature prominently in the newspapers was any serious analysis of how Mrs Jarrett's home came to be searched or what happened there, nor any of the wider issues about policing in Tottenham. On 7th October a number of newspapers had printed the two conflicting versions of the circumstances of her death. By 8th October virtually all the press coverage centred on the hatred and the violence of rioters towards the police. There was little attempt made to understand why it was (apart from the "agitators" theory) that so much hatred was felt. Exceptions were the *Guardian* and the *Morning Star*, who on 8th October both printed detailed reports about the raid on the Jarrett home.

6.6 On 7th October Councillor Bernie Grant spoke at a press conference. He gave the press a number of details about the raid on Mrs Jarrett's home. He was asked if he condemned the violence of the riots and replied:—

"I find it difficult to condemn anybody for what happened after the death of an innocent woman."

In answer to questions about the murder of PC Blakelock, he said:—

"I don't know anything about it...maybe it was a policeman who stabbed another policeman. I don't know the circumstances of it and I do not wish to get involved in it."

On the following day, 8th October, there was an open air meeting going on outside Tottenham Town Hall. Councillor Grant was visiting the Town Hall on other business, and was asked to come over and say a few words. He took the megaphone and, according to a press report, which he accepted as being accurate, he said:—

"The reason Sir Kenneth Newman is threatening the use of rubber bullets is because on Sunday night the police got a bloody good hiding. The police will not accept that Black youths can successfully organise themselves and outsmart them and outmanoeuvre them."

He again repeated that he was not going to condemn the actions of the youth on Sunday night.

6.7 We questioned Councillor Grant closely about these statements. He made a distinction between them. He regretted that he had made the remark that the policeman may have been killed by another policeman. He had been trying to make the point that the death was still being investigated and one should not jump to conclusions. He told us that it was "a bit of ridiculous thing to say, in retrospect". He commented that he must have spoken half a million words during that period, and the press had pulled out and concentrated on two or three statements.

6.8 Councillor Grant did not withdraw his remarks about the police getting a good hiding and being outmanoeuvred. He explained that he had been putting forward the view not only of the young people, but of a substantial section of the community. We asked him whether he agreed with that view. He replied that factually the youths did outmanoeuvre the police. There then followed a question and answer session which we think right to set out in full. Lord Gifford referred to Councillor Grant's speech of the 14th October calling for reconciliation, and continued:—

> **Lord Gifford:** "Is it really consistent with a desire for reconciliation to make statements which, whether factually true or not, give the strong impression of taking sides with the youth against the police and supporting them in a battle of two sides?"
>
> **Councillor Grant:** "Well yes, I would think so, because I think we have to understand that the young people are at the bottom of the social pile; that all the forces were ranged against them at the particular period. I think that it's part of the job of a political leader to assess the situation and face various sections of the community. If I had condemned the young people, as well as the whole of the press, media, Government and so on, I think that today we would have the situation that has occurred in other places in the country, in Liverpool and in Handsworth. When Neil Kinnock came to Broadwater Farm, he made one important observation. He said he had been to other places after disturbances, and on Broadwater Farm he found that the spirit of the young people was very strong, that people weren't demoralised. In all the other cases, in Handsworth and everywhere else, all the people were demoralised. And I think that the reason that they were not demoralised was that I did not come out and condemn them like everybody wanted. So they felt Haringey and the rest of the council and the Labour Party stood behind them in this particular situation. They felt that they were not condemned totally by society. This tenuous thread that we set up between us and the youths is now beginning to develop, and now we are able to wean the youths away from acts of violence into political action. For example, in the election they voted for the first time."

6.9 We consider that this was a cogent answer which deserves careful attention. Councillor Grant was clearly aware on 7th October of the need to maintain a relationship between the Black community, particularly the youths, and the established political structures which he represented. He himself, it is clear, did not believe in the use of violence against the police, and was shocked by both of the deaths which had occurred. But he understood the background of injustice, and had himself experienced, at the meeting at the Youth Association on 6th October, the bitter rejection of many of those present of conventional political methods.

6.10 Instead of avoiding the problem by distancing himself from Black youths, he tried honestly to articulate their position. In doing so he walked a tightrope, for as an elected leader he represented others also. The words quoted above were not well chosen and should not have been said. He knew as a political leader that the press would seize on an ill-considered phrase; and in this case they did, leading to the impression that Councillor Grant revelled in the defeat of the police. However, we are impressed with the honesty and courage which Councillor Grant showed in trying to articulate the grievances which had led to the disturbances, and in particular the death of Mrs Jarrett, rather than evading the issue with bland statements.

6.11 Councillor Grant gave his considered views to a special meeting of the council on 14th October 1985. He expressed his wholehearted personal sympathy to the families of Mrs Jarrett and PC Blakelock. He explained why he had spoken as he had, and accepted that "some things could have been better said". He appealed to the police to show respect for the young people of Haringey, and asked for a rethink of how Tottenham is policed. He said that the Labour group had stepped back from withholding the police precept. He then continued:—

"Next I want to speak to the young people of Tottenham. I said earlier that I had spoken the truth last week about their situation and their attitudes. Now I want to speak my mind to them. I want to say that some things are wrong. Drug trafficking is wrong. Thieving is wrong. Attacks on old people are wrong. Many of them have spent a lifetime fighting oppression also.

"And I want to say to the young people: violence offers no solution to your problems. You can't fight hatred with hatred. You can't fight fear with fear. You can't fight violence with violence. The state's response will always escalate. Next time rubber bullets and CS gas will be used. The time after that, the army will be brought in.

"The only way forward is through political action. I believe that the

THE AFTERMATH

line I have taken over the last week has opened up at least the possibility of drawing young people into a dialogue about peaceful political solutions to your problems. If we could achieve that, it would be a great step forward. So I appeal to you: step back from the violence and allow the council to speak for you."

The whole of this speech was applauded by a large public from the Broadwater Farm community. The evidence which we have received indicates that they wished to heed Councillor Grant's words. The high voting turnout — 55% at the local election — also indicates a willingness to use political channels. It may well be right that Councillor Grant's actions helped to contribute to social unity and constructive change.

6.12 On Broadwater Farm in the week following the disturbances, there was a real emergency. Postmen made no deliveries on the estate on 7th October, 10th October, 11th October and 12th October. The reason recorded in the Post Office report was "police advice". Joanne George was told by the Chief Postmaster that postmen did try to deliver letters, but the police told them not to, because it would hamper their inquiries. Giro cheques, on which so many people depended for their income, had been sent back to the Department of Health and Social Security, leaving many people with no money at all. Emergency supplies of food were distributed twice during that week — first on Monday, to pensioners and other vulnerable people who could not get to the shops outside the estate, and again on Friday because the Giro cheques had not arrived. The agencies which had been set up on the estate over the years proved their value — council staff from the Neighbourhood Office worked with Youth Association workers to cope with the needs and problems of many residents. This collaboration provided essential supplies to people whose situation would otherwise have been desperate.

6.13 The physical damage and mess was cleared up with remarkable speed. There were pavements to be repaired, burnt cars to be removed, rubble and glass to be cleared away and the shops to be boarded up. But by the end of the second day, only the burnt scorch marks on the roadway and smoke on the pillars of the blocks remained. The Broadwater Farm Junior and Infant schools were opened on 8th October, and the more damaged special schools by the following Monday. The Head of the Junior School – appreciating that children would have experienced the events and perhaps been disturbed by them, encouraged them to speak and write about them. He told us:—

"In their writing they expressed fear and fright from the noise, the explosions and the police, but some of them quite enjoyed the event."

The owners of cars which had been destroyed were left without compensation for their loss. Their claims under the Riot Damages Act were refused; the Act provides compensation for damage to premises through riots, but was passed in 1886 before the age of the motor vehicle.

THE ARRESTS AND SEARCHES
6.14 On Thursday 10th October came the first arrests by the squad of officers assigned to the murder investigation. By the end of November, there had been 141 arrests; by the end of May there had been 359. 18% of those arrested were juveniles, 9% were women. The great majority lived on or were closely connected with Broadwater Farm. 271 homes on the estate — over a quarter of the whole estate — were searched by the police. In 18 cases the doors were smashed in with sledgehammers and had to be replaced. By the end of May, 162 people had been charged with offences alleged to have been committed on 6th October, including six charged with murder and riot, seven with riot, 56 with affray and three with explosives (petrol bomb) charges. According to government statistics 71% of those arrested were Black, and 25% were White.

6.15 It is important to set the legal context in which these arrests were made. The police team had reason to believe that hundreds of people had done acts which (subject to any legal defences) were crimes under the law. They had taken a huge number of photographs on the night. From 13th October they had been conducting house-to-house inquiries around the whole estate, recording a range of information from place of birth to knowledge of neighbours and of the night's events. It would not have been surprising if they had identified a number of people who could reasonably be suspected of having committed offences. If so, the law allowed them to arrest such people and search their homes. The law also allowed the police to question suspects, subject to certain safeguards. If from legitimate questioning they obtained information which led to reasonable suspicion of others, they were entitled to arrest them also.

THE AFTERMATH

6.16 The investigation has undoubtedly caused and continues to cause great fear, suffering and outrage, particularly for those arrested and charged and their families. Is this the inevitable result of a legitimate criminal investigation? Or have the police in carrying out the investigation abused their legal powers? A representative of the Broadwater Farm Defence Campaign understood this key distinction when he said: −
"In a way it is accepted that they are going to be arrested for what has happened, but I feel that in many cases they are not so much worried about being arrested, but about the way they are arrested."

6.17 In dealing with this issue the Inquiry faces certain limitations. Nearly all the people who have been charged are still awaiting trial; they and their solicitors have not been able to give evidence to us about their cases. The justification of the investigating team for some of their actions − breaking doors, detention over days, refusing access to solicitors − is not known, and may become clearer during the coming trials. Even those who have been released without charge continue to be fearful, and few have given evidence to us. Many people's experiences have been relayed at second hand by other witnesses. Accordingly, in reviewing the evidence about the police investigation we have described the position at law (this itself is complex because the law changed on 1st January 1986); set out the allegations made in general terms; and raised certain questions. In most cases we have not made definite findings. But the questions, and the answers which must eventually be given at the end of the trial, are of central importance to the integrity of the police investigations.

6.18 On 1st January 1986 the main provisions of the Police and Criminal Evidence Act 1984 relating to police powers of arrest, search, detention and questioning, came into force. As well as the Act, there were Codes of Practice, in particular codes relating to the searching of premises and the seizure of property, and to the detention, treatment and questioning of persons by police officers. We will refer to the Act and the Codes of Practice as "the new law". Before the new law came into force, there were a number of legal controls over police investigations, such as the Judges' Rules; but in general these controls ("the old law") were less clearly defined.

6.19 A further complication was that in the period from July to December 1985, the police at Tottenham Police Station were conducting a "trial run" of the new Act. We understand this to mean, in theory at least, that police officers had been told to use the procedures and safeguards of the new law as far as they were legally able to. Many have alleged to us that in practice, the extended police powers of the new law were operated, but its safeguards were not.

6.20 The smashing down of the front door is the most horrific intrusion imaginable into the privacy of the home. It was done to 18 homes on Broadwater Farm, a shattering experience for the occupants, and a cause of great fear to many others. Joanne George said:—
> "You would go to bed and you would just lie there and you would think, are they going to come and kick my door, what's going to happen to my children? Wherever you went that's all you heard — am I next? If your friend's house got raided and arrested, are they coming for me? It was that horrible fear that you lived with day by day, knowing that they could come and kick down your door and come and drag you off and hold you for hours."

6.21 The smashing of doors was carried out by a large squad including armed officers. Rupert Downing described a scene early one Sunday morning, after he had slept overnight in a flat on the estate:—
> "There was this huge noise and the whole block was rocking. I went out of the front door of the flat to find out what was going on, to be confronted by an officer with a very large high-powered rifle standing immediately outside the flat. He looked very surprised to see this White geezer with a brief-case coming out of the flat. I went downstairs to the precinct to find about 50 police officers hammering in the door of the Fruit and Veg Co-op."

Rupert Downing knew that the police had already searched the Co-op several times with the full co-operation of the workers. He asked the officers why they did not contact the Co-op, but got no answer. He overheard a plain clothes officer say to another, "We are going to have to be a bit more careful."

6.22 D.A.C. Richards, interviewed on the *Diverse Reports* programme in October 1986, said:—
> "Policemen would not force their way into flats if there were any other means of getting into the flat. We have to gain entry into the premises and because they are well fortified the only way we can get into the premises is by way of sledgehammers or fairly hefty

equipment. If we had the keys to get into the premises it would be very much easier."

Later in the same programme, D.A.C. Richards sought to justify the methods used by reference to the scale of the crimes committed:—

"I wonder if we can get the Broadwater Farm in its true perspective. We are investigating a most horrific murder – a policeman stabbed to death. We witnessed at the Broadwater Farm the most ferocious, the most vicious riots ever seen on the mainland. It is therefore in the very nature of things if we are seeking murderers and gunmen, that on occasion, we will have to take what some people will see as dramatic action, reactive measures."

6.23 The statement that the premises were "well fortified" was misleading. It suggested people making a barricade of their doors. In fact, as D.A.C. Richards must have known, the doors were "fortified" by the council, on the advice of crime prevention officers, as a protection against burglars. If there is any proper justification for the smashing down of so many doors, it could only be in the context of the use of firearms during the disturbances. A reasonable belief that the smashing down of a door was necessary to protect police officers from being shot, would in theory justify such force. But in reality, how would the heavy and continuous smashing of a door protect the lives of police officers? Would it not rather alert the alleged "gunman" to their presence outside his door? Did the investigating team who smashed these 18 doors consider seriously what outrage they were inflicting? Did they balance that against the supposed risks to their officers? Or were they acting in this way simply to intimidate not just the occupants of the particular flats, but the estate as a whole?

6.24 Vivid evidence was given to us about the arrival of the arresting team on 17th October at the home of Mrs Scott, who lives in a house in Tottenham (not on the estate):—

"While I was ironing I heard the gate open and two persons talk so I thought somebody was coming to the door and I look, I didn't see anybody. Then I saw something rush across the window and I saw one pointing up. I went over and look and I saw one pointing to my bedroom, on at the gate with his hand on the trigger like this, pointing straight to the front door, one next door pointing like this. I heard my daughter scream, the youngest one. She was partly dressed in the bathroom and there were three pointing the guns at her in the bathroom. And others surround the place."

THE BROADWATER FARM INQUIRY REPORT

Mrs Scott said that there were seven officers who entered the house with guns, and others over in the gardens behind her house. One of the officers produced a piece of paper which he said was a warrant to search the house for firearms. Mrs Scott described what was taken from the house:—

"My husband was going to Jamaica and we went out shopping in Finefare. All my food has the stamp on it for Finefare and we brought a lot of tinned meats and flour, sugar, rice and all — everything possible to send home, and they took everything just the same. And photographs. There were six in Roger's room. They took all his complete clothes, his complete wardrobe. I remember one count 17 pairs of jeans. They took suits, they took everything. They broke my trunk, they took out things I bought before Millard was born and you don't see those things now."

Mrs Scott said that some of the clothes had been returned but none of the food. She got no receipt for the goods which had been taken. She herself has been visiting hospital for her nerves ever since. It should be noted that none of her family were charged with any offence arising from 6th October; Stafford Scott was arrested on the same day, held for 36 hours, and released without any charge.

6.25 Bagfuls of personal possessions were removed from many homes, including complete wardrobes of clothes, contents of food cupboards, kitchen knives, television and stereo equipment, personal diaries and photographs. People needed emergency assistance from Social Security because they were literally without anything to wear. A lot of property has now been returned, but some remains in police hands, even though the owner has not been charged. Requests from solicitors have often been met with the excuse that the police are too busy. The law allows a police officer to seize and retain property if it is needed for evidence at a trial, or for forensic examination, or if it may be stolen. We can understand that the investigating officers would justify the retention of knives and clothes for traces of blood or matching with photographs. Taking food seems more difficult to justify, since the supermarket was looted mainly for ammunition, and labels could be checked on the spot without taking everything away. The questions which we have to ask are :— Was there a real belief that the property taken might provide evidence of an offence, or was property taken on mere speculation? Were personal papers and diaries taken because of their relevance to any crime, or to enable the police to build up and record on computer a

THE AFTERMATH

general network of intelligence about the residents of the estate, their habits of life and their friends? Were the searches and seizures normal for a serious inquiry, or were they also part of a process of intimidation?

DETENTION AND QUESTIONING

6.26 Those who were arrested were taken to one of a variety of police stations (14 in all were used) and held incommunicado. The one police station which was not used was Tottenham. Their relatives had no idea where they were. Sheila Ramdin, chair of the new Residents' Association, describes their distress:—

"I have had mothers coming to me screaming, crying. They don't know where their son is, someone has been picked up, they don't know what police station. We tried to phone around to find out where their son is. They might say, well he's in Chingford, and then we phone Chingford. Who told you he's at Chingford? It's not Chingford. It must be somewhere else. We don't know where he is. We haven't got him here."

In one case it took the workers at the day nursery a whole day to find out where a mother was, whose child was at the nursery. Debbie Wilde reported on the detention of a pregnant woman whose relatives were kept waiting all day to see her, despite promises that access would be given. There is no doubt that great suffering was caused through the mental anguish of not knowing where a relative was or what was happening to him or her.

6.27 The new law provides that a person arrested and held in a police station has the right to have one friend or relative told of the arrest and where the person is detained. Delay in allowing this right is only permitted when an officer of Superintendent rank has reasonable grounds for believing that this will lead to interference with evidence, or the alerting of other people, or will hinder the recovery of property. The old law gave a similar right, except that delay was permitted if it was necessary in the interests of the investigation or prevention of crime. What justification existed for the denial of the right in these cases? What evidence would have been interfered with, if relatives had been informed? What other people would have been alerted? How would the recovery of property have been hindered? We find it difficult to believe that these questions can be answered. However serious the investigation, it is not acceptable for police officers to hide suspects away in unknown places.

6.28 There was a uniform policy to forbid arrested people access to a solicitor. The new law provides that an arrested person has in theory the right to consult a solicitor privately at any time. But delay in granting this right may only be authorised by a Superintendent if there are reasonable grounds for believing that exercising it will lead to interference with evidence, or injury to other persons, or the alerting of other suspects, or will hinder the recovery of property. In any case, under the new law, the right must be granted after 36 hours. Yet in the months of 1985 when the new law was meant to be having a trial run, the 36 hour rule was not respected. The right of access to a solicitor under the old law was defined more loosely: a person had the right unless unreasonable delay or hindrance would be caused to the processes of investigation or the administration of justice. The Court of Appeal had clearly ruled that it was not permissible to deny the right because an investigating officer feared that a solicitor would inform the suspect of his or her rights. Yet in this investigation, the policy of refusing access to a solicitor was maintained on many occasions even after people had appeared in court, when they were remanded in police custody for further questioning. It is hard to avoid the conclusion that the investigating officers denied access to solicitors because they wished to hold suspects incommunicado for long periods and thus put maximum pressure upon them to make a confession.

6.29 On a few occasions the investigating officers went as far as saying that a suspect could not have access to his or her chosen solicitor, but only to a solicitor chosen by the police. The investigating officers claimed that there was "a conflict of interest" between that suspect and other clients of the same solicitor. An attempt was made to get a High Court order to prevent this, but the judge said that he had no jurisdiction to intervene. One of the solicitors involved, Gabriel Black, described this action by the police as "utterly outrageous", and we agree. It is no business whatsoever of the police to decide whether a solicitor has a conflict of interests. Another solicitor, Gwen Bart, said that the conduct of the police during this investigation was quite unlike anything that she had experienced before. We asked her in what way did she think that the police were abusing their legal powers:—
"Basically it's the attitude that they have had when they have arrested people. When you ring the station they take a long time to return calls, and sometimes they have not returned calls. They have declined to give a lot of information. They have interviewed some

THE AFTERMATH

of the suspects very late at night. I just feel as though they take it personally, ie 'one of us is dead and you are going to pay for it'."

Gabriel Black was concerned that when her clients' rights had been abused, there was no form of accountability or channel for complaint. In the past she had contacted Scotland Yard's Complaints Division, but in this investigation "it seemed that the whole way up the line was just a blank".

6.30 The time spent by suspects in detention and questioning at the police stations was considerable. It was common for people to be detained for two and three days without being charged. In the case of many who were charged, the charge would be for a minor offence, but the police would apply at the Magistrates Court for a remand into police custody for three days, so that they could continue questioning the defendant about "more serious offences". Andy Shallice, who was observing in Tottenham Magistrates Court on a research project for the Runnymede Trust, noted 30 such applications, of which 28 were granted, out of 100 Broadwater Farm cases which he witnessed.

6.31 Under the old law the police were obliged to bring an arrested person before a magistrates court "as soon as practicable". What was practicable would vary according to the time of arrest and the time of court sittings. The view of lawyers was that the law allowed for detention in a police station for 48 hours at the outside. Under the new law, the maximum period of detention without charge is 96 hours, but the police are obliged to obtain authorisation from a magistrates court in a private hearing for any detention after 36 hours. The power of the Magistrates Court to order a remand into police custody for three days existed both under the old law and the new, although in practice it had normally been employed when a defendant was willing to be detained in the police station; for example a defendant who was giving information to the police about other people. As noted above, the new law gives an absolute right of access to a solicitor after 36 hours, including during any period on remand in police custody, whereas the right to see a solicitor under the old law was much more vague.

6.32 Accordingly the police, by detaining people in the police station for up to three days in the first instance, were stretching their powers under the old law to the legal limit and beyond. By applying for remands into police custody, the police were obtaining legal authority for a further three days of questioning. By refusing access to solicitors during the whole of the questioning period, the police were taking advantage of the looseness of the old law, and (although they were meant to be carrying out a test run of the new Act) they were refusing to observe the provision of the new law which allows access as a right to a solicitor after 36 hours. Why were people being detained and questioned for such long periods? Was it in order to obtain true and voluntary information about serious criminal offences? Or was it to isolate and put pressure on vulnerable young people in order to obtain "confessions" from them? These are questions which are certain to be raised during the trial of particular defendants. We are only able to observe in general terms that the longer a person is detained incommunicado and interrogated, the greater the danger that a false confession will be made. That is the purpose of the safeguards in the new law, and we are disturbed that they were not respected during the course of this investigation.

6.33 The evidence relating to the treatment of juveniles was also most disturbing. 23 juveniles (ie young people under 17) were brought before the courts on charges arising from the disturbances, and the majority of these are still awaiting trial. Other juveniles were arrested and released without charge. Michael Hutchinson-Reis, one of the Broadwater Farm social work team and an experienced social worker, described the situation as he saw it:—

"A large part of our work after 6th October was actually tracking down where juveniles were being kept. It is a significant change in procedures that juveniles were being held for such long periods, quite often released without charge, and in many instances held incommunicado, when families, relatives, solicitors and social workers spent a lot of time actually trying to locate them."

The policy of refusing access to solicitors was applied also to juveniles. Michael Hutchinson-Reis described the problems which he faced in trying to help a juvenile who had admitted to having stolen three Mars bars on the night of 6th October:—

"That juvenile was questioned not so much about what he had stolen, which he admitted, but about his circumstances, his whereabouts, who he was with, what happened, for about three hours. Eventually at 9 o'clock on a Friday evening he was kept in the station. I made representations to the police about contact with relatives, solicitors and so on, and basically I was eased out of the police station in a way I have not usually had the experience of."

THE AFTERMATH

6.34 The written submission to us from the council's Social Services Department discloses other instances which give rise to intense concern as to whether the rights of juveniles were respected. It records that in some cases adults who were total strangers were brought in to witness interviews in police stations (since by law a "responsible adult" must be present when a juvenile is interviewed). It records that one boy was observed to appear in court wearing paper clothes, another barefoot, another wearing a pair of enormous men's trousers and large shirt, others looking tired, pale and unkempt.

6.35 Solicitor Gabriel Black told us of one case which she was free to talk about because no charges were pending against the boy concerned. The case was of a 15-year-old boy arrested as a suspect for murder and held in the police station for two-and-a-half days. The old law required that if a juvenile had to be detained overnight, arrangements had to be made with Social Services for him or her to be kept in their care. But in this case, the boy spent two nights in a locked police cell. His mother had been present during interviews with him and had found them oppressive and very threatening. She had asked the police for Ms Black to be present but they had refused. He was finally released at a police station miles away from Tottenham without any shoes on. We find it quite unacceptable for a young boy to be treated in that way.

6.36 Many allegations were made to us about the conditions of detention and the manner of questioning. Some concerned particular cases of actual maltreatment — deprivation of sleep, assaults and extreme threats. We cannot make findings about these allegations, since in most cases the alleged victims are awaiting trial and we did not hear directly from them. There was other evidence, some of it first hand, about the general pattern of questioning. People who were arrested were told that they were known to be involved in a serious crime — the murder or the rioting. The questioning went on and on. If people denied being involved, they were told that they must have seen who was involved, and names of particular suspects were put to them. If they claimed not to have seen anyone, they were asked about who was likely to have been involved. Panchita La Touche, Deputy Senior Playworker at the Broadwater Farm Play Scheme, described the experience as she saw it:—

"They said they had got strong evidence that I was out there. But I knew I was not out there. I just let them carry on with their games.

They were getting on my nerves, they were annoying me by telling me I was doing something and I knew I wasn't. Trying to get me to tell lies. The next morning they said they had strong evidence that I received bloodstained clothes from a suspect. I said no, that's not true, that's a lie. They said but you know that's the truth, just tell us that. They got on my nerves until they saw that there was nothing that they could do. To get me to tell a lie like that, that's what they wanted. Because they were trying to brainwash me, they were trying to get me to believe it. For me just to give up and say, well, oh yeah, it does go like that. "

6.37 We have to consider this evidence against the background of a serious murder investigation. It is lawful for police officers, if they have genuine grounds for suspecting people, to arrest and question them, putting their suspicions to them and pressing for an answer. But it is not lawful for the police to arrest people "on spec", without any genuine grounds for suspicion, and then try to induce them to implicate themselves or other people. And it is not lawful for the police to use such intense methods, to isolate people for so long, to put such pressure on them that they are confused and, in desperation, admit to things which they have not done.

6.38 Had the police genuine reason to suspect those whom they arrested? Or have they been fishing for information, using conditions of isolation and fear generated by an accusation of murder to extract unwilling and unreliable answers? Panchita La Touche was clearly a person who was able to defend her innocence. Others were more vulnerable. The story of Howard Kerr, reported in the *Daily Mirror* on 20th March 1986, reveals the danger. He was a youth of 17 who was detained for two and half days. He was not allowed to see a lawyer or relative. He at first claimed that he was in Windsor on the night of 6th October. Later he made a 50-page "confession" to taking part in the riots, naming 20 other "participants", describing a "factory of petrol bombs, and claiming to have seen the murder of the police officer. But later it was established from independent evidence that he was indeed in Windsor that evening, and the prosecution dropped all charges against him. Outside court he said:—

"I was frightened, so I told them what I thought they wanted to know."

From all the circumstances of the investigation, we fear that there must be many other young people who were so frightened that they similarly told the police what they thought they wanted to know.

6.39 Andy Shallice, researcher for the Runnymede Trust, gave evidence about the handling of the Broadwater Farm cases in the Magistrates Court. He said that there was a team of officers who presented the Broadwater Farm cases, who objected to bail in 95% of the cases. The most frequent reasons which they gave were that the defendant might commit further offences, or that defendants might be threatened and therefore should be kept in custody for their personal safety. He was concerned that in a number of cases the defence lawyers did not put much energy or effort into pressing for bail. He said that when a Broadwater Farm defendant appeared, it was apparent that the police "took over the cases and the organisation of the court room", particularly by arranging for a number of plain clothes officers to be standing around the court. We are unable to make comment upon individual decisions of the court, but we are concerned that there was not seen to be, in Andy Shallice's words, "a passive and equal atmosphere between defence and prosecution".

6.40 Andy Shallice gave us some particular information about the treatment of juveniles. He said: —
"In the first week after 6th October, four juveniles appeared in court, in the adult court at Tottenham. No reference was made by the Magistrates about the fact that now a juvenile court was essentially sitting. All those juveniles were charged on their own; they weren't charged with adult defendants over the age of 17. The public gallery wasn't cleared, the press were allowed to sit. In another five cases over the next weeks into the end of November, a total of nine juveniles appeared at Tottenham Court during the adult hearings and the public gallery wasn't cleared, and there was no attempt to reconvene the session into a juvenile court for that one hearing."
The law provides that no charge against a juvenile may be heard in an adult court, unless the juvenile is charged jointly with an adult. A juvenile court is not even permitted to sit in a court room which has been or will be used as an adult court within an hour before or after the sitting of the juvenile court. When a juvenile court is sitting, members of the public may not be present unless specially authorised by the court; the press may be present, but may not report the case in any way which might reveal the name or address of the juvenile. We

questioned Andy Shallice closely as to whether there were any adults jointly charged with the same offences at the time that the juveniles were brought into the adult court. He was certain that there were not. We are most concerned about the rights of juveniles which appear not to have been respected by the court.

BROADWATER FARM SINCE OCTOBER 1985
6.41 For three months a massive police presence remained on the estate. The Police Research Unit observed that every day around the estate there was a van filled with riot equipment; a mobile command centre; a mobile incident room; a tea van and mobile toilets; and a number of transit vans full of police. On 1st November their staff counted nine police support units at the entrances to the estate; on 6th November eight; on 13th November seven; and on 18th November thirteen. Every day there was a heavy deployment of uniformed officers patrolling the estate, especially on Tangmere, where they stood about the precinct and the many balconies over looking it. Reverend John Wheaton, Minister of the Miller Memorial Methodist Church, on the corner of The Avenue and Mount Pleasant Road, described the police presence at this time:—

"In the few weeks after the riot the police were in Mount Pleasant Road with their coaches, vans and real heavy force. It got oppressive after a while; you couldn't move without seeing a policeman in riot gear. One of their nasty habits, they have stopped it now, was when they parked their vans in Willan Road, Adams Road and Gloucester Road. One of the first things they would do — this went on for over a month after the riot had finished — was to take their riot shields out and line them up against the wall, which I found rather provocative."

He described also what happened when he visited the family of one of the youths charged with murder:—

"Immediately I approached the front door about four policemen would just appear from around the corner, and when I went out they would still be there. Very polite, but you knew you were being kept an eye on."

6.42 There was a decrease in the numbers after Christmas, and a further decrease after defendants on the murder charge had been committed for trial. The mobile command centre and other vehicles were removed; but there remained a level of patrolling which was far in excess of anything normally seen on an estate or in a residential

THE AFTERMATH

area. To this day, it is most unusual to make even a short visit to the estate without seeing two officers walking around, and a van full of officers is normally waiting in The Avenue near the Gloucester Road entrance. Lord Gifford asked a parliamentary question to attempt to discover the precise numbers involved. He asked:—

"What was the level of police manpower deployed on patrolling duties on and around the Broadwater Farm Estate, Tottenham, between 7th October 1985 and 27th March 1986?"

The answer which came back from Lord Glenarthur, Minister of State at the Home Office, was singularly uninformative:—

"I understand from the Commissioner that the level of police manpower deployed on the Broadwater Farm varied during the period in question according to operational demand. On 27th March, 15 officers were deployed on the estate at any one time through the 24 hour period."

The one figure given in this answer is significant. 15 officers deployed "at any one time" on an estate of 1,000 dwellings, nearly six months after the disturbances, represents a hugely expensive use of police resources. We record below, that we were informed that for every unit of officers on a shift, half will be on patrolling duty at any one time. Allowing for three shifts, the Minister's answer would indicate that up to 90 police officers were assigned to the estate every day.

6.43 The report of the Metropolitan Police Commissioner for 1985 includes a table headed "Public Order events which required the employment of more than 1,000 officers". We have studied it with care. There are the following entries which clearly relate to the policing of Broadwater Farm and the surrounding area:–

		Number of police
7th Oct	Aid requirements – central London reserve	1,409
8 & 9 Oct	Aid requirements – central London reserve	3,732
10–14 Oct	Aid requirements – central London reserve	9,165
15–18 Oct	Aid to 'Y' District (Tottenham)	3,044
19 & 20 Oct	Aid to 'Y' District (Tottenham)	1,522
21–27 Oct	Aid to 'Y' District (Tottenham)	3,213
28 Oct–4 Nov	Aid to 'Y' District (Tottenham)	3,744
5–11 Nov	Aid to 'Y' District (Tottenham)	3,744
12–18 Nov	Aid to 'Y' District (Tottenham)	3,104

19–25 Nov	Aid to 'Y' District (Tottenham)	1,736
26 Nov–2 Dec	Aid to 'Y' District (Tottenham)	1,715
3–9 Dec	Aid to 'Y' District (Tottenham)	1,715
10–16 Dec	Aid to 'Y' District (Tottenham)	1,051

These are extraordinary figures. There are only 12 other entries in this table for the whole of 1985 – major demonstrations, State visits and the London Marathon which have entries of between 1,000 and 2,000 officers, and the Notting Hill Carnival which has an entry of 7,259 officers. They show that in addition to the numbers of police observed on and around the estate, there were hundreds more, even thousands, held in reserve. In the period between 10th and 14th October when the first arrests were made, the number rose to an amazing 9,165. There are no entries which refer to the Brixton disturbances – apart from the Cherry Groce Support Campaign demonstration on 11th November (1,405 officers). The huge numbers of police assigned to Y District appear to us to be a measure of the serious over-reaction to the 6th October disturbances which continued for an excessive time.

6.44 The Richards report stated that high profile uniformed policing was necessary "to maintain the Queen's peace, reduce the fear of crime and enhance the quality of life for the residents". He listed four further considerations:–
(1) To afford protection to the patrolling uniformed officers.
(2) To give support to residents who have made statements to the police and felt under threat.
(3) To respond to the call of many who have articulated their need for a heavy police presence.
(4) To give support to C.I.D officers who are executing search warrants and making arrests.

6.45 On 5th November 1985, the Chief Executive wrote to D.A.C. Richards stating that the numbers of police officers on the estate and particularly on Tangmere were seen as "stressful and oppressive", and, as owners of the estate, asked the police to leave. Commander Richards replied that he would reduce the police presence "when I am satisfied that the likelihood of further breaches of the peace has receded". He reiterated his request for a police room to be allocated on the estate. There was further correspondence, and the council said that they were seriously considering instituting legal proceedings.

THE AFTERMATH

Finally, in what was discribed by Roy Limb as a "very responsible act", council members decided that to fight a legal battle with the police would be a bad move, which the community would not like to see, and that they should use every endeavour to secure a reduction to normal levels of policing without going to court.

6.46 The most recent public statement about the level of policing was made by Chief Superintendent Alan Stainsby, who took over as senior officer of the Tottenham Division in April 1986. Speaking to a meeting of the Community and Police Consultative Group on 15th May 1986, he said that at present there were 60 officers a day assigned to the estate, mostly from outside the division. There were three shifts of 20, of whom ten were on duty at any one time. They were not always patrolling, but often stayed in their transit vans keeping a watch out. He said there was no desire to intimidate residents. He said that he was taking steps to phase out the assistance from outside the division, and instead to set up a team of 16 Tottenham officers in two shifts from 8 a.m to 12 midnight, eight officers per shift. He hoped that after August this team would have taken over from the outside police officers, and at present the prospects looked good. However if there were further grounds for tension, the levels would have to be increased again. He recognised that this was "an extremely expensive form of policing", and hoped that in due course the team could be reduced to below 16 officers. He was asked directly about the idea of a mini-police station, and replied: —

"I can police Broadwater Farm with eight officers without a section house on the estate."

6.47 There were some people who were reassured by the large numbers of police in the early months, but many who found them intimidating and oppressive. Michael Hutchinson-Reis described it as:—

"A style and a school of policing that has more in common with the occupation of a foreign country by a colonising power."

Our own view is that the numbers of police officers on the estate in the months following 6th October were grossly excessive and did have the effect of intimidating many residents. We can fully understand the need to deploy large numbers of police officers in support of those who were making arrests or carrying out searches on particular occasions. But it was not necessary to cover the estate around the clock with police officers who were doing nothing except stand about or patrol. The position in law is that if a group of ordinary citizens had done what the police were doing, they would have been guilty of a nuisance to the residents on the estate, and in addition (after the council had asked them to leave) of a trespass. Police officers are only entitled to interfere with people's rights in such a way where there is a real and imminent possibility of a breach of the peace. In such cases they may take reasonable preventative measures. There have been no attacks on the police on Broadwater Farm since 6th October. We know of no evidence that further disturbances were likely, and we think that the measures taken far exceeded what was reasonable.

6.48 The position today is considerably better, and witnesses who had found the previous numbers of police officers most oppressive, found the present levels bearable. Our survey which was carried out after the significant reductions in the number of police, found that 35% of residents considered that the present levels were too high, 15% that they were too low, and 50% that they were about right. We return to this question of levels of policing in Chapter 8.

6.49 As well as their numbers, the actions and attitudes of officers on the estate have offended many people. Community worker Rupert Downing tried to intervene after a man had been arrested and a senior officer was shouting at the crowd who had gathered. He described the reaction of the officer when he pleaded with him to calm the situation:—
"He didn't quite physically attack me but he looked as though he wanted to, and he said something like 'you council worker bastards, you're responsible for the riot in the first place — you'd better watch it. We can nick you as well.'"

6.50 Many people fear that police officers patrolling the estate are affected by feelings of hatred and revenge towards Black people because of the death of PC Blakelock. The Middlesex Area Probation Service considered that this fear was justified. In their submission to us they wrote:—
"During the days following the disturbances certain numbers of our staff came into contact with several policemen and heard them talking of revenge and 'sorting out' the people on the estate. There is a real fear in the area, which is made worse by rumour and speculation, that a minority of police officers might exceed their

authority and take advantage of any future disorder to satisfy their sense of grievance."

But there was evidence that some police officers were not prepared to be swayed by the reputation of the estate. Russell Simper, the Estate Supervisor, told us of words which he had heard spoken by an officer from outside the Tottenham area:—

> "Well, I've got a different attitude towards the Farm to what I had when I first came. I expected to come and see a load of rogues, villains and vagabonds, but I find the majority of the people on this estate very nice people."

6.51 Hugh Sutherland, who is employed as a carpenter in the council's repairs unit on the estate, experienced provocation and racist abuse in a particularly ugly way, culminating in an arrest and charge. Police officers after the disturbances would follow him and his girlfriend, making monkey noises and making remarks like "climbed any good trees lately?". His Ford Capri car was frequently covered with stickers saying "I love the Met". He would peel them off and dispose of them. After some weeks of this, he was peeling off these stickers in the presence of a number of officers who were saying "What's the matter? Don't you love the Met then?". As he peeled stickers off the back window, he found that others had been stuck on the windscreen. He swore at the police and said that he would report them. On 16th December, a few days later, he was about his business on the estate when six or seven police officers came running towards him. They grabbed hold of him by the arms. One of them hit him in the face saying "Well Mr Fucking Mouthy Orange Capri, we've got you now, you cunt!" He was bundled into a police van, forced to lie down in the van, where officers kicked him and rested their feet on him. He had a badly cut and swollen face and bruised ribs for some weeks afterwards. He was charged with abusive behaviour, but the case was dismissed by the Magistrates Court. The case aroused considerable anger among Hugh Sutherland's fellow workers. Trade Unions organised a demonstration at the court and a one day strike, in which about 300 employees took part.

6.52 Having so many police officers on the estate and on call also leads to the danger of trivial incidents leading to large-scale confrontation. Michael Hutchinson-Reis was surrounded by five or six police officers when he went to collect a briefcase out of a colleague's car. Sheila Ramdin described an incident at the end of May, the day before she gave evidence, when she had seen two boys having a disagreement, and two patrolling officers went to see what was happening: —

"I just heard one of the police say 'do you need assistance?' and before you knew it there was about three vans downstairs, and 20 of them just came running upstairs, just standing there to see what was going on".

6.53 However, not everyone who acted cheekily was the object of such attention from the police. Ernie Large tested out his theory that it was Black people who were the targets of attention, on a day in October, when there were masses of police on the estate: —

"I drove round the estate a number of times minus a tax disc. I took out the tax disc and put a photo of my cat in place of it. I drove round there with the police in their dozens looking over the balcony, patrolling along the side. I also experimented by going in at Willan Road and coming out at Gloucester Road — backwards. A number of times. With all those attendant police, although I was looked at, I was never stopped once."

6.54 The events of 6th October and the subsequent police action have had deep and painful affects on the people of Broadwater Farm.

Social worker Michael Hutchinson-Reis summed up the situation in these terms: —

"In general terms the situation that many people are living in is so extreme and severe that the overall effect is to make people feel intimidated, fearful and very frightened. Certainly I myself have experienced the feeling that even though I am a social worker carrying an I.D card, I'm liable to arrest and detention and my family and friends won't know where I am. The realisation that that could happen to you at any moment is quite frightening."

He spoke about a young man who had committed suicide in April 1986 as being "a casualty of the situation in which Black communities and the people of Broadwater Farm in particular have to live." Mary John Baptiste, representing the Defence Campaign spoke of one woman who had developed a form of agoraphobia; she will not leave her house since the police raided it, and is terrified of her children leaving the house. Sheila Ramdin told us that the Mothers' Project were trying to form a family support group in order to provide support and counselling to both adults and children who had been psychologically affected.

THE AFTERMATH

6.55 We have heard disturbing stories about the effect of the police actions upon children. Community worker Joanne George, who has children aged four and five, said:—

"My children now believe that the police are going to get me. They say to me 'Oh mummy, don't let the police get you'. If they see a policeman they will want to run up and fight him — which is unbelievable. My child actually kicked a policeman in Tangmere — I was horrified, I had to run up and go and rescue my child."

Sheila Ramdin spoke of walking with a friend when two police officers came towards them. She described the reaction of her friend's four-year-old boy:—

"The boy was on the floor, he was just screaming, saying 'no Mummy I can see police'. He was really shaking. I had never seen anything like it."

She spoke also of her own child aged four, who was shaking with fear when there was a blackout on the estate and a fire engine came. He was crying "Mummy what's happening? Are they going to fight again?" Michael Hutchinson-Reis spoke of a child suffering an anxiety attack on 5th November, when fireworks and bonfires caused him to cling to his mother and scream with fear. Not everyone agreed that there had been psychological damage to children; Ronny Roach, senior worker at the play centre felt the children had not seen the riots as a real situation. But we remain very worried about the evidence on this point which we have heard.

6.56 After 6th October there was a rush of tenants asking for transfer requests. Many who were already on the transfer list came into the Neighbourhood Office, and about 90 to 100 new tenants made applications for transfers. The pressure eased off rapidly after the first two or three weeks. Some of those requesting transfers had clearly been urged to do so by younger relatives who were worried about their welfare. The Neighbourhood Officer, Neale Coleman said that a lot of people still did want to move, and had done before the disturbances: but the intense pressure on his office levelled off much more quickly than he had anticipated. We deal in the next chapter with the views that people have expressed about living on the estate.

6.57 In the minds of people outside the estate it carries an even more undesirable label than before. The experience of one woman whom we interviewed was :—

"Even when I go for a job, and they say where do you live, and I say Broadwater Farm, they look at you totally different."

Many other witnesses spoke of similar experiences when they told people where they lived. The post box in Gloucester Road was sealed up after 6th October and remains so to the present date. It has become more difficult than ever to obtain credit. Mail order firms, TV hire companies, and companies trading on hire purchase are reluctant to deal with people on the estate and in many cases have refused outright. Deposits of £100 are demanded for the connection of electricity or gas. Pat Ford complained to the Consumer Protection Service after Visionhire refused to offer slot TV rentals after the disturbances. The answer given by the company to the Consumer Protection Officer was:—

"It was considered unreasonable to ask our teleclub meter collectors to make calls on the estate as this could well lead to possible injuries to our staff who were known to be carrying reasonable large sums of money."

6.58 The community spirit, so buoyant in summer 1985, was far more subdued as the summer of 1986 began. The numbers taking part in community activities had gone down — particularly those such as the Mothers' Project which drew in people from outside the estate. One woman said to us that the community feeling was gone — it used to be "alive and happy with the music, but now it's so quiet". Cliff Ford felt that the atmosphere was "just beginning to come somewhere around normal, where you can see children playing around again, but it's only recently that that started to happen." Panchita La Touche felt that people trusted each other much less than before. Several people involved with the Youth Association spoke of a sense of despair about the future. Even so, they were continuing the day-to-day work of maintaining and extending services to their community. The old people never stopped coming to the Youth Association for their meals. The projects created over the last five years still continue. As we explain more fully in our recommendations in Chapter 9, it is more important than ever to give support to the initiatives of the Broadwater Farm community.

Chapter 7
WHO LIVES ON BROADWATER FARM –
– WHAT DO THEY THINK?

7.1 The Inquiry carried out a survey of the estate. We ensured that the stratified sample that we interviewed would be representative by drawing on a sample of 700 adults. In the 1981 Census there were 1063 households and some 1800 adults. Our sample was one adult from each of 700 households. This represents a sample size which is many times larger than necessary to ensure complete statistical representativeness. We took such a large sample for two reasons; firstly to ensure that we could fully defend the representative nature of the sample, and secondly so that we could break down the responses by age, gender and ethnicity, and still ensure that there were sufficient people within each category to provide a fully representative sample. Given the whole nature of statistical sampling we can be sure that these statistics represent the true picture of the residents of Broadwater Farm Estate in April/May 1986.

7.2 We commissioned a group of social scientists from Middlesex Polytechnic to carry out this survey for us. They had recently been involved in the Islington Crime Survey which had received some considerable acclaim both in the academic and popular press. They had experience of carrying out research in an area with diverse minority ethnic groups and analysing that data quickly. We drew up a questionnaire in conjunction with this group and within a few weeks of the Inquiry starting we were able to begin the field work.

7.3 We achieved a very high response rate of 75.2%. This means that some 527 individuals co-operated with the interviewers in providing us with information. This very high response rate compares most favourably with other surveys of London in recent years. We believe that this results from three major factors. Firstly the sample was drawn from a full enumeration of inhabited flats and houses on the estates. Rather than rely on the electoral register (which itself was being constructed at the time of the disturbances and would therefore almost certainly undercount) the research team carried out their own enumeration of the estate. This ensured that the sample was drawn from the full and real membership on the estate. Secondly, as much as possible, the interviewers were matched in gender and race to the interviewees. Thirdly, each of the interviewers had an identity card issued by the Inquiry Panel which guaranteed both their bona fide status and ensured the confidentiality of the replies.

7.4 We did not ask about the residents' experience of the disturbances. We do not believe that the survey method could provide such information. The survey does however settle a number of questions about what people on the estate think. Both the police and community leaders have made claims to be representing the estate — doing what "the community" want. Whilst it is clear that, as with any other locality, we can never talk of a unanimous opinion about anything, and it will always be possible for mischief-makers to find one or two people who will provide opinions that are those of only a small minority on any issue, we can say with some certainty and some accuracy what the majority of people think about a broad range of issues. That is why we can say in a way that no other organisations can, that these statistics represent, democratically, those who live on the Broadwater Farm Estate and what they think. In this Chapter of our report we cover only the most salient facts. We have asked Middlesex Polytechnic to provide a full report to Haringey Council later in 1986.

WHO LIVES THERE?
7.5 We wanted to know how long people had lived on the estate specifically to try and understand the extent of turnover and change. We stress that this will not tell us the change over in tenancies, since some individuals may have moved from one flat to another. We do however obtain a picture of the amount of movement.

How long have you lived on the estate? (all figures are percentages)

under 1 year	1–5	over 5 years
17	40	43

WHO LIVES ON BROADWATER FARM – WHAT DO THEY THINK?

There is some evidence of movement off the estate immediately after the disturbances so there may be some little over-exaggeration of new movement in these figures.

7.6 This means that over half the adults on the estate have moved since 1981. We chose that year because, as we explained in Chapter 3, it was in that year that the estate began to develop in a better direction. It is also important to note that 17% of the adult population has been there for less than a year — a fact that has important implications for the community workers and organisations on the estate. Creating and recreating a community with this amount of change is a much harder task, needing constant back-up and communication between new tenants and community organisations. Perhaps new residents need to be visited and introduced to the community organisations on a regular basis to ensure that they are in touch, not only with the council's services but also with the community as a whole.

7.7 We asked a series of questions about the general characteristics of our adult respondents. This is important since we have already reported that we know that over 50% of the adults on the estate have moved onto the estate since 1981. This must mean that all of the Census material from 1981 would be of little use in terms of representing the population in 1986.

The Inquiry has heard a wide variety of different figures describing the ethnic mix of the estate. At different times we have heard it described as three-quarters or two-thirds Black. The Middlesex Polytechnic team decided to ask their interviewers to categorise the race of the respondents. We received the following figures that we believe are representative of the adult population of the estate.

White	49
Black (West Indian/African)	42
Indian sub-continent	3
Other (e.g. Cypriot)	6

We must remember that this represents a sample of the adult population and in no way counts the children on the estate. We can guess at this by looking at the ethnicity of different age groups and roughly extrapolating the children under 16 from those figures.

7.8 Given the age differential we can compute that more than half of the children on the estate are Black (West Indian/African) – raising the overall ratio of the population to about half Black (West Indian/African) and half White. These figures are important since there have been a broad range of different estimates put forward as fact to us about the different proportions of Black people and White people – on many occasions the number of Black people has been exaggerated.

7.9 We asked the age of our respondents and again given the sample size feel confident that this will reflect the age of the adults on the estate.

	16–24	25–44	45 plus
% of the adult population	33	47	20

This population is different from the national average in so far as there are fewer older people. We found a fairly even distribution of the sexes.

	Women	Men
% of the adult population	52	48

HOUSEHOLD COMPOSITION

7.10 The folowing table represents the household composition of the estate.

	All Figures are %
Households with no children	56
Households with two children and two parents	25
Households with children and one parent	19

Roughly 20% of the households on the estate are single parent families. These have an ethnic breakdown of:–

	% of single parent families
White	32
Black (West Indian/African)	64
Others	4

7.11 **YEARLY HOUSEHOLD INCOME**
We asked about the average household income on the estate. For us to compute people's incomes in detail we would have had to concentrate upon a very wide range of questions about their assets

and expenditure. Since we wanted to look at a much wider range of opinions and attitudes we only asked one question about income: What is your average income in this household? If the answers were at all near the average it would not have been possible to draw any important conclusions. However, this was not the case. From the following answers we can quite clearly say that the estate is poor.

```
Yearly household income
      Under £3,000              35
      £3,000 – £7,999           38
      £8,000 – £11,999           7
      £12,000 – £14,999          2
      Over £15,000               2
                          No answer – 16
```

7.12 Comparisons around income are not easy to make. We must point out that given these overall income figures the economy of the estate is at a very low point indeed. This must affect the possibility of the estate generating its own economic salvation. As a consequence if regeneration is to occur there must be some significant outside input of resources.

7.13 EMPLOYMENT

We asked whether the respondent was in employment; whether someone else in their household was and whether there were two or more people in employment in that household. The answers were as follows:—

In employment	31%
Someone else in their household in employment	15%
Two other people in employment	2%

If we turn these percentages into actual numbers in employment (given 1063 households on the estate we can multiply by 10.5) we can compute that there are 330 respondents in jobs, 160 living in households where someone else is in work, and about 30 other people in employment. This means that, taking the estate as a whole, there are some 500–530 people in full time employment. With an adult population of some 1800 this is a very low figure for economic activity.

VOTING PATTERNS

7.14   We asked for the voting intentions of people on the estate. The months of April/May 1986 saw quite bitterly fought local election campaigns. Some Conservative councillors had called for the "blowing up" of the estate. As a consequence these statistics will reflect this political consciousness.

% voting for different parties as a percentage of those who declared a preference.

Labour	77
Conservative	9
Alliance	8
Other	6

These statistics represent a great deal of support for one particular party. If we also recognise that some 55% of registered voters voted in May 1986 then it is likely that the Labour Party received considerable votes from the estate.

7.15   "Monolithic" and "faceless" are two of the ways in which the estate has been described and these are words which carry with them pictures of isolation and fear. Consequently it was important for us to find out if residents knew other people on the estate.

How many of your neighbours do you know?

Most	A few	None
28	51	21

Social isolation is not great here. It is unfortunately the case in most of Britain's cities that a section of the population is isolated. If we were to ask the same question in any inner city area – council estate, terrace houses or semi-detached suburban – it is likely that the number would be the same or even greater. It is significant that over three-quarters of the population feel they know a few of their neighbours, with over a quarter who would claim "most". This shows that a large number of people have some social contact and over a quarter could be said to be fully integrated into the community. If these figures are at all abnormal they err on the side of integration and not isolation. Indeed, as will be seen later on (7.20), when we asked people about what they thought about problems on the estate, 53% thought unfriendliness was no problem at all.

WHO LIVES ON BROADWATER FARM – WHAT DO THEY THINK?

COMMUNITY ORGANISATION

7.16 We not only wanted to understand the extent to which people on the estate knew each other. We thought it was important to gauge the success or failure of the community organisations on the estate. In Chapter 3 we demonstrate the way in which these community organisations, and the Youth Association in particular, played a role in the regeneration of the estate. We feel they did this through a great deal of imaginative hard work. It is important, though, to gauge the extent to which they have the overall support of the estate. Consequently we asked a series of questions about the community organisations. We wanted to know whether people had heard of the organisation, whether they had been to a meeting in the last two months, whether they were members and what they thought of the quality of the service.

We specifically asked about six organisations that existed on the estate.

	Heard of	Been to meeting	Member	Quality of service (of those who had heard of)
% of all respondents	YES	YES	YES	GOOD/VERY GOOD
Broadwater Farm Youth Association	78	7	5	81
Mothers' Group	54	5	4	90
Under Fives	30	4	3	90
Tenants' Assoc.	66	8	8	73
BWFYA Co-op	41	3	1	91
Pensioners' Group	33	3	2	100

7.17 Looking at the figures for the Youth Association first, some important factors emerge. Firstly, over three-quarters of the estate had heard of the Youth Association – considerably more than any other group. Secondly, over four-fifths of those that had heard of the association thought it was either doing a good job or a very good job of work. Given the way in which the press has attacked the Youth Association, this represents a very high degree of support indeed. Whatever else is said about community organisation on the estate we feel we can say that the Youth Association has the support of the great majority of residents. It is equally significant that the other groups have a high level of support. While fewer people haver heard of them; those that have are pleased that they are working.

7.18 The question of active involvement is different for the Mothers' Group, the Under Fives' group and the Pensioners' Group — these exist to provide services for only a small part of the residents. Thus 5% of people had been to a meeting of the Mothers' Group in the last two months — a group of some 100 people. Since there are only some 450–500 mothers on the estate this represents a large proportion of this group. similarly both the Pensioners' and Under Fives' groups would not expect the active involvement of people who were not in that section of the community. The Co-op has been recently formed with very specific aims with regard to economic regeneration, and would not expect a mass involvement.

7.19 The active involvement of so few in the Tenants' Association and the Youth Association does need some further comment. Both organisations have spent much of the last four years bringing considerable resources to the whole estate. Many people have experienced the result of their campaigns through their significantly better housing and environmental conditions. We do not believe that a large proportion of the estate would have to be involved in these organisations for them to be able to claim representativeness. They obviously have the support of a large majority of residents and must not be judged by different criteria than we would judge other representative organisations. In 1986, British society is not one that has the active involvement of a very high proportion of its citizenry. We return in Chapter 9 to the need for more active involvement of people on the estate. People support organisations without attending their meetings.

PROBLEMS ON THE ESTATE
7.20 We wanted to know how people perceived the problems on the estate.

Are the following a big problem, a bit of a problem or not really a problem?:−

%	Not really	A bit of a problem	A big problem
Unemployment	2	4	94
Poor housing	40	18	42
The behaviour of the police	50	21	29
Poor street lighting	45	29	26
Poor schools	45	23	32
Poor public transport	41.5	25	33.5
Crime	21	22	57
Race relations	37.5	25	37.5
General unfriendliness	52	26	22
Not enough places for children to play	38	18	45
Not enough things for young people to do	24	19	57

First and foremost we must underline the answer about unemployment. The residents nearly all understand just how deeply this effects everyone. It is the nearest to a unanimous answer as exists in the whole survey. Secondly, all of the other issues have between three-quarters and a half of the estate feeling that they are a problem of some order. Crime and lack of youth facilities are seen as a big problem by some 57% of the estate. Residents clearly recognise the importance of lack of provision for youth as a part of its problems.

7.21 We will return extensively to the attitudes about crime. Here though, it is important for us to understand that people feel that there are *big* problems for people in living on the estate. Indeed in answer to the question − Do you like living on the estate? − 51% said yes and 49% said no. Given the labelling of the estate outlined in Chapter 2, and given the events of the last year, this is not surprising. It is an important element of people's lives, and one that *all* agencies must take into account. Many people in giving evidence to the Inquiry pleaded for a return to normal. It is essential that nothing stands in the way of this.

POLICE ACCOUNTABILITY
7.22 The issue of police accountability has become a matter of

central importance not just to the work of this Inquiry, but also within discussion about public attitudes to the police. We therefore asked a series of questions about who should decide policing in the locality.

Who should decide how a local area is policed?

	YES	NO
Scotland Yard	31	69
Local police station	68	32
Home Secretary	25	75
Local council	71	29
Local magistrates	21	79

7.23 It is undoubtedly the case, following the disturbances, that three of them played a role in deciding local policing of the area — Scotland Yard, the local police station and the Home Secretary. Two of these bodies are unwelcome to over two-thirds of the residents of the estate whilst the local police station is seen as acceptable. Constitutionally, local magistrates and the local council have no role to play in deciding local policing and whilst four-fifths of the estate were pleased with this state of affairs with regard to the magistrates, over two-thirds believe that the local council should play a role in policing decisions. This is higher than in any other survey about police accountability. This is obviously important for two different areas of our report. Firstly it does underline the fact that the London Borough of Haringey as an organisation is felt to be capable of deciding on social policy in a general sense. This is surprising because for many council estates one of the last organisations trusted by council tenants to be capable of running anything is their landlord. On Broadwater Farm this appears to be different. Secondly, and specifically with regard to policing matters, it is important to realise that people do feel that the local council should have a say — alongside of the local police station — in deciding policing policy. For a locality with such a troubled experience of policing, as well as one where the question of to whom the police should be accountable is an issue sharply contested by the police and local community groups, these aspirations are highly important.

7.24 If we compare this figure to the Islington Crime Survey — where only 8% of the population saw the council as having a role in the decisions about policing — we can appreciate this response about the London Borough of Haringey.

ASSISTING THE POLICE WITH THEIR ENQUIRIES

7.25 We wanted to know whether the residents of the estate would assist the police in a number of situations and we found that their response was very specific to different situations. "I would like to ask you how far you would be prepared to assist the police in certain situations. For each example would you tell me if you would be prepared to identify the people who did it, and whether you would be prepared to give evidence in court.?"

% of those that answer that they would

	Help identify	Give evidence	Would do neither
Youths smashing up a bus shelter	43	32	53
Youths knock a man down and take his wallet	63	50	30
A traffic accident where someone was badly hurt	76	70	14
A conversation between two people planning a break in	36	26	60

7.26 There is no simplistic and total rejection of either the law or the police force contained within these answers. Rather it demonstrates the way in which residents are quite prepared to help the police with their enquiries in certain areas. In particular they are prepared to help in those areas of crime that they feel the police are capable of dealing with. Over 80% of residents were prepared to help the police in a traffic accident; over 70% would assist in terms of a mugging, but under half would do anything about vandalism or conspiracy to burgle. It is insufficient explanation for the police or anyone to label the residents of the estate as "unhelpful" to the police – or against law and order. The reality is more complex and must be seen as in part a measure of the community's confidence in police efficiency.

HOW WELL DO THE POLICE PERFORM?

7.27 We felt that residents' opinions about police success would be an important part of their overall attitudes to the police. As a consequence we asked them how successful the police are at dealing with particular sorts of crime?

THE BROADWATER FARM INQUIRY REPORT

		Successful		
	Very	Fairly	Not very	Not at all
Racist attacks	5	21	38	36
Burglary in houses	6	30	43	21
Fights in the streets	9	53	29	9
Vandalism	6	27	41	27
Sexual assaults on women	9	28	36	28
Control of heroin dealing	10	25	34	31
Mugging and street robbery	8	28	40	23
Drunken driving	24	51	18	6
Violent domestic disputes	8	34	27	31

7.28 These of course are NOT actual success rates by the police but represent the estate residents' perception of police successes. As such they don't tell us anything about what police actually achieve, just what Broadwater Farm residents THINK they achieve, in a number of areas. Whilst nearly two-thirds of the estate feel that the police have some success in dealing with fighting in the streets and drunken driving, around two-thirds feel that they have little success in dealing with burglaries, vandalism, sexual assaults, the control of heroin dealing, street robbery and domestic disputes.

WHAT SHOULD THE POLICE CONCENTRATE ON?

7.29 In connection with this, it is important to understand the way in which the residents of the estate view those police tasks that they think are important. It is interesting then to compare this with the way in which the London Borough of Islington survey and the Policy Studies Institute survey for the whole Metropolitan area see policing issues.

% Prioritising these crimes for the police to deal with	BWF	ICS Islington	PSI Metropolitan area
Sexual assaults on women	84	70	79
Heroin control	69	59	40
Mugging	66	71	73
Domestic burglary	66	58	68
Racial assaults	59	39	
Bag snatching	30	25	
Drunken driving	27	44	
Cannabis	14	13	

Fraud	13	6
Theft from car	12	9
Football rowdyism	12	22
Vandalism	11	26
Prostitution	10	8
Office burglary	8	8
Street rowdyism	7	10
Shop lifting	2	3

7.30 Thus, over two-thirds of the people on the estate want the police to prioritise burglary, mugging, the control of heroin dealing and four-fifths the sexual assaults on women. Yet as we saw above, it is these same areas of concern that more than two-thirds of the estate feel that the police are not very successful in dealing with.

7.31 But if we compare this to the London Borough of Islington and the whole Metropolitan area we find a similar spread. People in London think the police should prioritise the safety of women from sexual assault; the problem of personal safety on the street and robbery in the street and at home. The one important and marked difference is to be found in the level of concern about the dealing in heroin from the people of Broadwater Farm. The deep anxiety about the problem of heroin dealing once more demonstrates a sharp sense of the necessity for its own self-defence against the deep dangers of hard drugs. It is inconceivable that a group of heroin dealers could survive within such a large community if they acted at all openly.

7.32 Equally the residents on the estate agree with the residents of Islington about those activities that the police spend too much time on such as prostitution, cannabis and shoplifting. Importantly, the estate is in line with these wider areas in making the sharp distinction between different sorts of crimes. There is no overall and simplistic rejection of law and order: there is no simplistic rejection of the police, rather there is a consistent attempt to protect themselves from crimes that they think are important alongside the belief that it is these areas that the police do not deal with. This must be of great importance to us since there is an attitude that we have outlined above which sees the residents of the estate as criminals. Our evidence is to the contrary.

HOW DO RESIDENTS VIEW POLICE ACTIVITY?

7.33 One of the ways of measuring the way in which the residents of the estate view the police is to ask them views they may have about police conduct in arresting people, obtaining evidence and obtaining a conviction.

Consequently we asked: When they are questioning people do you think that police officers ever....

	Never	Hardly ever	Sometimes	Often	Very often
Use threats to get the answer they want	29	7	35	20	10
Falsify statements made to them	29	10	36	15	9
Use unnecessary force when making arrests	28	7	35	18	12
Use violence in police stations	26	12	34	20	10
Plant evidence on people	34	12	34	13	7
Accept money as a bribe	43	20	28	5	4

7.34 This table must be of profound concern to everyone. Whilst it does demonstrate that a consistent level of 30% of residents believe that the police NEVER engage in malpractices, it also demonstrates that a majority of people on the estate believe that the police sometimes (or more often) use threats to get answers, falsify statements, use force and violence and plant evidence on people. These are very high figures indeed if we compare them to the PSI survey of London:–

% who believe that the police ...

	BWF	London
	Sometimes/Often/Very Often	
Use threats to get the answer that they want	65	Not Available
Falsify statements made to them	60	34
Use unnecessary force when making arrests	65	38
Use violence at police stations	64	38
Plant evidence on people	54	Not Available
Take bribes	37	56

These differences are very striking indeed. They mean that the people on the estate — with the exception of bribes — are considerably more likely than the rest of London to believe that the police engage in malpractice.

7.35 How does the estate have such a bad view of the police? The survey asked whether the respondent or a close friend had actually had direct experience of these malpractices. They were also asked whether they or a close friend had witnessed the malpractice. Compared with the PSI London Survey the results are most startling.

	BWF	London
Has the malpractice happened to you or to someone you know	60	12
Has it been witnessed by you or by someone you know	61	14

7.36 This means that some three-fifths of the estate's adults — that is about 750 people — have either experienced or witnessed or their close friends have experienced or witnessed police malpractices — compared to between 12 and 14% in London. This underlines the fact that their perception is based upon specific experiences.

7.37 Therefore a large proportion of the residents of the estate, whilst they have clear priorities about the nature of crime that has to be tackled, also feel that the police engage in malpractices two-thirds of the estate believe that the police engage in malpractices and two-thirds believe that they are ineffectual in dealing with those areas of criminality that are important for their safety, it is not surprising that half of the estate will not assist the police with their enquiries into certain crimes.

FAIRNESS AND THE POLICE

7.38 We also wanted to find out whether people saw the police's understanding of the issues on the estate as good and whether the police treated all sorts of people fairly.

Therefore the survey asked: Would you say that the police operating on the estate...

	Yes	No
Had a good understanding of the problems on the estate?	49	51
Treat people of all sorts fairly and equally?	49	51

7.39   We also asked people whether the police stopped and searched people without good reason. 43% said yes. Of these they believed that the categories of people that the police were likely to stop and search without good reason were:—

Black	95
Young	93
Men	67
White	51
Women	28
Old	10

This means that 40% of the estate believe that the police stop and search young Black people without good reason.

POLICING BY CONSENT

7.40   What does this range of answers mean for police/community relations? Firstly, it further underlines the fact that one-half of the people on the estate have little confidence in the way in which the estate is policed. This must undermine the effectiveness of policing since, as we have seen from other questions, people are unlikely to assist a police force that they think is unfair, lacks understanding of their problems, uses unnecessary force and falsifies evidence. Under these circumstances policing by consent is not possible since for those people, consent has been withdrawn.

7.41   Secondly, we must underline the fact that one half of the estate believes that the police do understand and are fair and for one-third of the estate they consistently believe that the police never engage in malpractices. It may be argued that having the support and confidence of one-half of the community is a good record. Yet in comparison to the survey carried out across the London Borough of Islington (ICS 1985), these figures are low. Some two-thirds of the people of Islington believe that the police never engage in malpractices. Even with figures such as these, there is a consistent minority who would have very little confidence. On the Broadwater Farm, from these figures it appears that between one-half and two-thirds of the estate have these worries.

WHO LIVES ON BROADWATER FARM – WHAT DO THEY THINK?

7.42   In the *Caribbean Times* of 13th June 1986, the Home Secretary made the following important points: –

"The police force in Britain is an instrument for protecting not coercing citizens. Policing in this country is based on the concept of the citizen in uniform. The police go about their duties in the vast majority of occasions unarmed. Such a philosophy of policing can only be successful if the police can draw strength and support from the community that they serve."

We also believe that this philosophy can only succeed if the police draw strength and support from the community and therefore view with alarm the fact that so many people on the estate have such bad experiences of policing that they find they cannot give it.

7.43   This issue was so important that we have categorised a range of answers by gender, age, and race. The following figures are categorised therefore by age across the top and gender and race down the side. Breaking down the answers to whether the police are fair or not: –

% Who believe that The police are unfair	16–24	25–44	45 plus	All
White men	67	56	10	48
Black men	75	48	55	59
White women	51	36	12	34
Black women	78	73	33	72

For the whole estate there was a feeling from 51% that the police were unfair. Here we can see the way in which age and ethnicity effect people's beliefs about the police. Young people believe they are unfair more than their relevant older categories – but so do Black people.

7.44   Looking at the question of malpractice by the police we can see this pattern re-emerge.

Do you believe that the police sometimes/often/very often threaten when questioning?

THE BROADWATER FARM INQUIRY REPORT

	16–24	25–44	45 plus	All
White men	60	76	45	67
Black men	75	78	65	72
White women	62	49	26	46
Black women	85	76	50	77

Three-quarters of young Black men and over four-fifths of young Black women believe that the police use threats. These numbers stay that high for the group up to the age of 44.

7.45 It is important to also gauge where these opinions came from. Do they come from direct experience or from direct witnessing?

It was asked whether this malpractice had happened to them or to a friend of theirs?

%YES	16–24	25–44	45 plus	All
White men	60	67	35	58
Black men	85	76	42	73
White women	65	35	35	46
Black women	81	60	50	69

It was also asked whether they or a friend of theirs had seen this happen?

%YES	16–24	25–44	45 plus	All
White men	71	61	33	58
Black men	88	78	33	73
White women	62	52	35	51
Black women	83	66	Not statistically significant	75

Again Black people had experienced or witnessed this malpractice consistently higher than the White group. This must represent in a different form the discriminatory policing discussed in our Chapter 3. Given the high proportion of people who have witnessed and experienced malpractice it is very likely that this group will experience the police as attacking them as a group. In this case the group is Black, under the age of 45, both men and women. The principal characteristic of this group is their colour.

7.46 We asked if people would be prepared to help the police if they overheard a burglary being planned. This is the percentage that said neither.

	16–24	25–44	45 plus	All
White men	71	69	41	62
Black men	68	50	62	58
White women	61	54	43	53
Black women	73	63	68	67

7.47 Over three-quarters of young Black people have had either direct experience of police malpractice or their friends have. A similar proportion have witnessed such malpractice – or their friends have. Under these circumstances it is very likely that these groups will be wary of assisting the police. If the police do want the support of such groups then they must stop policing in such ways as to cause Black people feel that they are the ones being targeted.

THE COMMUNITY VIEW OF CRIME

7.48 We have noted earlier on in our report that some senior police officers always believed that the estate seemed to represent a criminal entity. Does our evidence support this view? If over half the estate believe that police sometimes or more often act wrongly does this back up the view that the estate is outside the law?

We have already outlined the way in which people on the estate seek to involve the police in a different prioritisation in dealing with sexual assaults, mugging, burglary and heroin dealing. Not a list of activities that a criminal community would necessarilly arrive at. But perhaps one section of the community is different from another. Again this is simply not the case. If we compare the police priorities of young Black people with those of the estate we can see they have similar fears and worries.

Police priorities	Young Black people of BWF	BWF as a whole %
Sexual assaults	89	84
Heroin dealing	74	69
Robbery	54	66
Burglary	64	66
Racial attacks	72	59

7.49 We wanted to see if there was a difference between sections of the estate in their overall worry about crime. Here we break the statistics down by race, age and gender.

Is crime perceived as a problem/a big problem?

% saying yes	16–24	25–44	45 plus	All
White men	76	83	77	77
Black men	71	79	85	77
White women	93	75	82	82
Black women	81	75	Not statistically significant	77

Women tend to worry about crime more than men, but all sections of the estate worry about it. These figures contain no evidence that criminality can be a characteristic of the estate.

7.50 It is interesting to note the extent to which crime has been experienced on the estate. There has been an important new approach to this area of research — the study of "victims" carried out both by the Home Office and by independent researchers. They all uncover various amounts of unrecorded crime. Therefore, whilst no one has disagreed with the falling crime figures that the police produced and that we cite in Chapter 3, there is inevitably going to be some crime unrecorded. Consequently we asked the following set of questions. Has the following happened to you or to someone living in your household in the last 12 months? We compare this with Sussex Ward in Islington — one of the wards containing council estates and surveyed in the I.C.S.

% of respondents who are victims	BWF	Sussex Ward
Has your home been burgled	12	23
Tried to break into your home	13	Not available
Had your house vandalised	6	42
Had car/van motor bike broken into or stolen	6	7
Had car/van motor bike vandalised	6	52
Been mugged or robbed on the street	7	15
Been physically attacked	7	22
Been threatened with violence	9	Not available
Women been sexually attacked	2	10
Women been sexually pestered	7	Not available

WHO LIVES ON BROADWATER FARM – WHAT DO THEY THINK?

7.51 On Broadwater Farm, as elsewhere, there is a quantity of unrecorded crime, especially in the field of burglary and vandalism. However, the figures for Broadwater Farm are in every case less than the Sussex Ward in Islington. What does this comparison mean? At the very least, it means that we cannot classify the estate as a high crime area. There are whole wards in Islington where there are much much higher incidents of crime. Once more the survey cannot support the view that the estate is a criminal community.

7.52 We asked people whether they thought crime had gone down compared to five years ago.

Would you say that the following crimes are more common, less common, or about the same as they were five years ago?

	More common	The same	Less common
People being robbed and mugged in the street	35	10	55
People's houses being burgled	33	10	57
Vandalism and deliberate damage to property	36	13	51
Sexual assaults on women	39	11	50

Over one-half of the whole estate believe that every single crime mentioned has gone down in the last five years and of course it is important and significant that over one-third feel that it has gone up. However, if we compare these with Islington, the difference is most striking.

	More common	The same	Less common
Robbery/Mugging	61	28	12
Burglary	67	23	10
Vandalism	54	30	16
Sexual assaults	48	32	20

7.53 These differences in perception are very striking. Whilst one-half of the estate think that crime is less common it varies between one and two-tenths in Islington. Once more we must ask whether these perceptions can be about a criminal community?

7.54 However, we return to the important fact that 57% of the estate think crime is a big problem irrespective of whether it is actually lower than elsewhere or irrespective of whether they think crime has gone down over the last five years. We also asked people whether they believed crime was carried out by people on the estate or outside of it. 81% of the estate believed that crime was carried out by people from off the estate. Therefore, even for those people who believe that crime is a problem, a large proportion must see the criminals as coming from outside. Again hard evidence from people on the estate suggests to us that it cannot be seen as a community of criminals.

7.55 To further check we also asked a series of questions about those police tasks that were perceived as of major importance and received the following replies.

List in order of majority saying they were of importance...

Immediate response to 999 calls	93
Detection of criminals	80
Deterring criminals	68
Crime prevention advice	57
Contain rowdy behaviour	50
Controlling crowds	49
Check the security of shops and offices	41
Lost property	39
Road traffic control	38
Maintaining contacts with schools	36
Youth work	30

Once more it is difficult to imagine that these responses could ever come from a community of criminals. Would they be in favour of quicker responses to 999 calls, the detection of criminals and the deterrence of crime?

7.56 Yet in a simple sense the opponents of community policing may feel that they gain some support from these statistics, as they appear to reflect a demand for traditional policing. The estate wants crime responded to, deterred and detected; all traditional views of the policing role. They are not interested in police doing youth work, school work or the "softer view". Yet it is necessary to view these responses from the estate in the light of all of the others. The majority of people want crime to be dealt with quickly; they want the police to deal with certain crimes as a much higher priority than others, yet, they believe that these are the crimes that the police are not very successful in dealing with and two-thirds of them believe that the police engage in malpractices. Therefore whilst they recognise the importance of the "fight against crime" for their own security — two-thirds of them have little confidence in the police capacity to engage in that fight. Until police have gained that confidence it is unlikely that the residents will feel enthusiastic about the force's ability to increase Broadwater Farm's security.

7.57 D.A.C. Richards had said on *Diverse Reports* in October 1986:—

"It is the ill-doer, it is the person who is offending the law who objects to the presence of the police in the estate."

It may well be that this statement is meant to disarm all criticism of police activity on the estate lest the critic be labelled a criminal. Our survey demonstrates not only that there is considerably concern about the police activity but that this estate is also concerned about crime. It is evident that people other than criminals can be critical of the police.

Dining out in style . . . pensioners enjoy a hearty lunch in the Youth Association building on the Broadwater Farm Estate.

The Princess of Wales meets local community leaders during a visit to the estate in 1985.

To welcome the Princess to the estate local artist Tony Steele produced this drawing.

A winter dawn over the Broadwater Farm Estate.

An estate built on stilts . . . the dwellings were raised above ground level as a precaution against flooding.

◀ *Chairman of the Inquiry, Lord Gifford, Q.C.*

Rt. Rev. Philip Harvey, O.B.E. ▶

◀ *Rev. Canon Sebastian Charles.*

◀ *Dorothy Kuya.*

Dr. Paul Corrigan. ▶

◀ *Randolph Prime.*

Counsel to the Inquiry Anesta Weekes. ▶

◀ *Metropolitan Police Commissioner, Sir Kenneth Newman.*

PC Keith Blakelock, who died during the disturbances. ▶

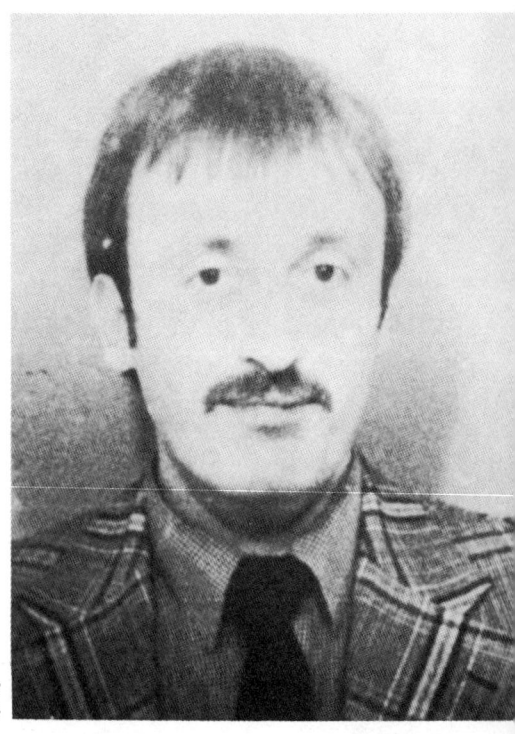

A witness gives evidence on day one of the Inquiry.

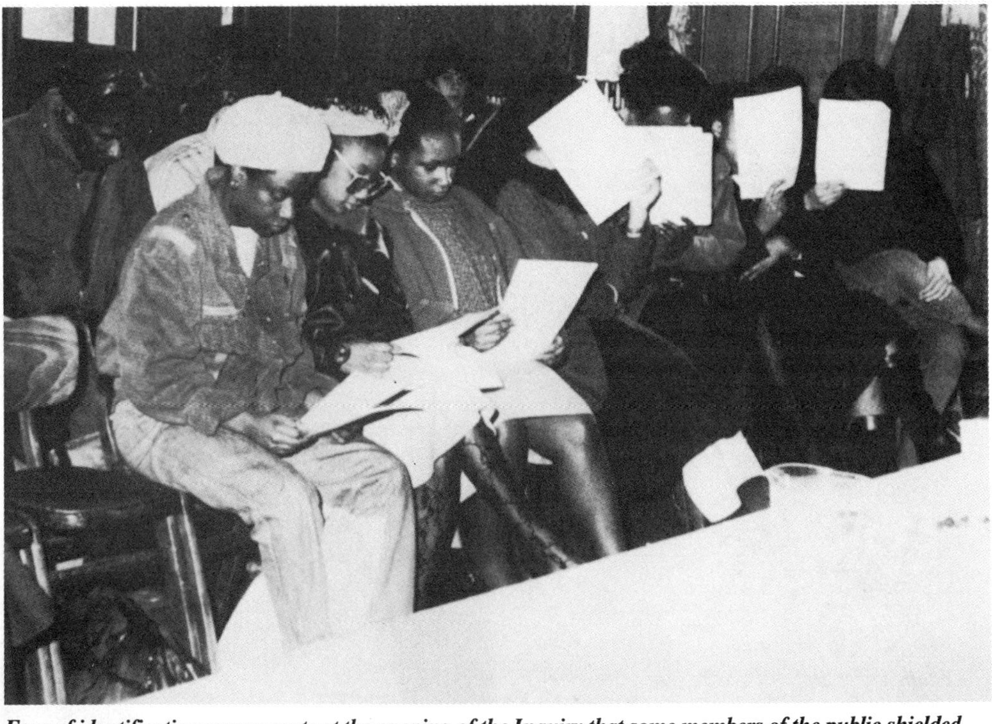

Fear of identification was so acute at the opening of the Inquiry that some members of the public shielded their faces from television cameras.

◀ *Clasford Sterling . . . his nose was broken during a clash with police.*

Youth leader Stafford Scott . . . told the Inquiry about aggressive behaviour on the behalf of beat officers. ▶

◀ *Dolly Kiffin . . . an indefatigable campaigner for the estate and its people.*

Martha Osamor . . . met angry youths after Mrs Jarrett's death. ▶

◀ *Mrs Cynthia Jarrett . . . collapsed during police raid.*

The Jarrett's house in Thorpe Road, Tottenham. ▶

The Disturbances reach their climax as vehicles are set alight to force back the ranks of police.

Injured Riot Police dash for emergency aid.

◀ *Bernie Grant . . . told youths violence is not the answer.*

Ernie Large . . . tested a theory on racist policing. ▶

Part 2

Chapter 8
LOOKING FORWARD – JUSTICE FROM THE LAW

WHY DID IT HAPPEN?
8.1   In this Chapter and the next we turn to the future. Before doing so we pause to review the evidence which has been related so far and to see what it tells us about the causes of the disturbances of 6th October. In Chapter 2 we described the growth of community organisations on the Broadwater Farm Estate, and their success in turning back what appeared to be a dreadful failure of municipal housing policy. That success is worth reporting on and learning from, irrespective of the events of October 1985; and in Chapter 9 we make proposals designed to recognise and build on that success, and to encourage the development of other self-reliant and forward looking communities. As we explain in the Chapter, the need to invest resources in developing such communities is based on social justice and on the general community interest. Investing resources in a community such as Broadwater Farm, whose members are ready to complement the investment with their own dedication and hard work, will generate more jobs, better living conditions, and a happier life for many people. Such an investment will not in itself avert conflicts with the police; nor has the absence of resources been in any meaningful sense a cause of those conflicts.

8.2   The reason for the fighting which erupted on 6th October with such appalling consequences for the police and the community, is to be found rather in the history which we have traced in Chapter 3 of failed initiatives in police/community relations; and in the dreadful sequence of events which started with the arrest of Floyd Jarrett and which continued until the clash at Willan Road. That clash as we have seen was between a group of youths who, along with many others, were full of sorrow and anger because a mother had died and because nothing effective was being done about her death; and a unit of police officers who were, with many others in reserve, heavily equipped, hostile to the people on the estate, expecting trouble to start, and ready at a moment's notice to quell it with force. Thus the disturbances came about because of an appalling state of distrust and hostility which existed on 6th October between the police and the people who lived in and frequented Broadwater Farm. To explain why that had come about had been the purpose of our analysis of events in Chapters 3 and 4.

8.3   Reviewing the salient findings of those Chapters, we can conclude that there would have been far less likelihood of serious disturbances if all, or even a few, of the following had taken place: —

(1) If the top leadership of the police in Y District had recognised, encouraged and responded wholeheartedly to the community organisations on Broadwater Farm.

(2) If serious efforts had been made both by the home beat officers on the estate and their superiors, to ensure that those officers knew, understood and respected the members of the Broadwater Farm Youth Association.

(3) If the contradiction between co-operative community policing and the incursion of intimidatory mobile units had been resolved by the local police command.

(4) If there had been goodwill on the part of both the police leadership and the council, to work together in setting up a consultative forum in which all interests in the borough were represented.

(5) If the police had come forward and discussed their concerns about policing on the estate at the Broadwater Farm Panel.

(6) If the drug pushers who began to appear on the estate had been arrested or otherwise prevented from committing their crimes on the estate.

(7) If the other community leaders who were available during the absence of Dolly Kiffin had been recognised and trusted by the police during August and September in order to resolve the problems which were developing.

(8) If there had been adequate procedures at Tottenham Police Station to prevent officers going off on a speculative and unjustified search of Mrs Jarrett's home, which in the event led to her tragic and untimely death.

(9) If — that tragedy having happened — the police authorities

had immediately acted to suspend the officers involved and to demonstrate their desire for the full truth about the tragedy to be uncovered.

(10) If during the evening of 6th October the police had maintained the restrained response which they had shown during the afternoon demonstration.

8.4 Examining these questions provides a much truer account of the ingredients of the disturbances than does a simplistic, and in our view misguided explanation that the disturbances were caused by wickedness or criminality. In saying that, we recognise that in the history we have outlined, things were done against the police which were reprehensible. In Chapter 3 we gave a similar description to the striking of a police officer with a bottle; to the striking of a police officer with a billiard cue; and to the stabbing of an officer with a knife − all criminal acts which happened on the estate in 1982 and 1983. We recognise also that police work is difficult and dangerous and that injury to (and even more the death of) a police officer generates a reaction among colleagues of both anger for what has happened and fear of what may happen to them. Relations can be poisoned between the police and the whole community of people which they see as being ready to do similar acts. We have shown that on Broadwater Farm the reprehensible things which were done were the isolated acts of particular individuals, and were not the acts of a criminal community.

8.5 Nor do we accept the explanation put forward by many newspapers, that the estate was seething with tensions which would have sparked a riot in any event, and that it only needed a "trigger" to set it off. On that view, the death of Mrs Jarrett is seen as the "trigger", but any other event might equally have served. Such an analysis seriously underestimates the magnitude of that tragedy. It was, so far as we know, unprecedented for an innocent Black woman to have died as a direct consequence of a police operation. When one adds together:

(1) − the shock and sorrow of that event;
(2) − the natural association of it with the shooting of Mrs Cherry Groce;
(3) − the distrust, justified in the event, of the mechanisms for investigating the tragedy;

THE BROADWATER FARM INQUIRY REPORT

(4) – the pre-existing bad relations between rank and file police officers and people on the estate;
(5) – the accumulated bitterness of years of experienced malpractice, as confirmed strikingly for the Broadwater Farm residents by our survey;
then the ingredients of an uncontrollable confrontation were present. Without the first three factors, all stemming from the death of Mrs Jarrett, we do not believe that the disturbances would have occurred, as we explained at the end of Chapter 3.

8.6 But even then, that confrontation might have been averted, and was for a time averted, by a strategy of controlled policing. What finally happened was the worst possible provocation – the blocking of the free movement of people leaving the estate to go to the police station, as their practice had been at other such times. Many Black people have spoken to us powerfully about how they have been constricted all their lives – by inequalities of education, by discrimination in employment, by the abuse of stop-and-search and other police powers. On the estate in particular the fear had taken a physical shape. One witness told us that in discussions among the youth about the police on the estate "there was always this dread that the police could hem them in". With the deployment of riot police at every entrance, spreading out and blocking the roads, that dread became reality. For even though some people were allowed in and out during the evening of 6th October, the evidence is that the vast majority of young Black people were not allowed to leave by the roads off the estate from about 7.00pm onwards.

8.7 As we described in Chapter 6, the consequences of the disturbances have been horrendous. The intensity of the fighting and above all the death of a police officer, have for many police officers been a confirmation of everything bad which they believed about Broadwater Farm. The immense scale of the arrest and search operation has put the community in fear and has caused people to believe, with reason, that they are the targets of exceptional surveillance and oppressive action. Criminal trials will continue for many months, causing hardship and anxiety for those on trial and their families. Many people are involved in the Broadwater Farm Defence Campaign, which aims to give support and assistance to those on trial and their families. While the trials continue, it is difficult for either the community or the police to do anything other than relive the conflicts of the past. If abnormally heavy sentences are imposed, the bitterness will endure still further, and the task of reconstruction and reconciliation will become even more difficult.

8.8 Even so we must look forward. As we showed in Chapter 7, people on the Broadwater Farm Estate remain very anxious about crime; but they have limited confidence in the capacity of the police either to solve crime or to act fairly and lawfully towards them. One witness, Mrs Scott summed up the sentiments of many other witnesses, when she articulated in a sentence the problem which must somehow be resolved:—
"I would really like to be able to respect the police."

8.9 We therefore approached the question "What can be done?" with some anxiety. We have made it clear that we are not equipped to draw up a comprehensive blueprint for the resolution of police/community relations in Haringey. Many who have read the preceding Chapters will have more experience of policing than any of us and may have better proposals to make. We have been limited by time and the amount of expert research which we can assimilate. We propose therefore in this Chapter and the next to reflect some of the proposals which have been put forward in evidence, and to add proposals which seem sensible to us after all we have heard. We do not express them as recommendations, but rather as proposals which can be discussed, improved, and acted on by people who in many different ways have responsibility for the welfare of the community.

POLICING IN TOTTENHAM
8.10 From April 1986, Chief Superintendent Alan Stainsby was appointed Chief Officer of the Tottenham Division. The only role which he played in the events which we have narrated was that on the evening of 5th October he came over from Enfield, where he was then Chief Officer, to take charge temporarily at Tottenham after the death of Mrs Jarrett. He behaved with complete correctness in going at once to 25 Thorpe Road to express his sympathies to the Jarrett family and to tell them of the decision to set up an investigation under the supervision of the P.C.A. On 6th October Chief Superintendent Couch had returned, and so far as we are aware Chief Superintendent Stainsby was not involved in any of the policing decisions which took place on that day. We have also noted that he attended a meeting of the Broadwater Farm Panel soon after being appointed, and

presented a written report. He has met with Dolly Kiffin and other representatives of organisations on the estate. He has expressed his desire, in principle, to see a substantial reduction of the level of policing on the estate. Coming in at this time he has a heavy burden of responsiblity to bear, and we wish him well.

8.11 The task can be summarised as the task of introducing genuine community policing into Tottenham. Both police officers and members of the public talk often of the need for "policing by consent" — but what does that mean? The term "community policing" has become so hackneyed that it may be useful to use another term to describe what we have in mind — "co-operative policing", by which we mean a policing strategy by which the police at all levels co-operate (on a basis of mutual respect and equality) with those various agencies which represent the community, in order to deter and detect those crimes which the community believe to be priority evils.
evils.

8.12 There are several elements in that definition. First there must be **genuine co-operation** — which means a real exchange of information about the problems which are troubling either police or community, and about the operations which may have to be mounted to deal with them. The experience of the drug pushers on Broadwater Farm must never be repeated. There, both police and community wanted action, but there was no dialogue about how it should be taken. There is much which can be discussed about the tactics of dealing with particular kinds of crime, without jeopardising the effectiveness of the operations themselves. Chief Executive Roy Limb, who has had close experience of dialogue both with the police and community organisations, gave this view about what was needed:—

"There is no doubt that we have to get into much closer consultation with the police. I have great hopes that the new Chief Superintendent of Tottenham is of a similar mind, and that there will be many three-cornered meetings between the various bodies — the Tenants' Association, the Youth Association and so on — on Broadwater Farm and the council and the police to discuss operational matters. I put it as crudely as that. What I mean is the way in which policing is carried out, because that's the thing that is of concern to the people down there."

LOOKING FORWARD: JUSTICE FROM THE LAW

8.13 Secondly, the co-operation must be **on a basis of mutual respect**. The people of the community must be prepared to see police officers as individuals – citizens in uniform with a difficult job to do. Equally the police must be prepared to listen to and learn from local people talking about the problems of their community, and to act on what they have learnt. Co-operative policing does not mean a public relations front.

This key factor of respect was emphasised by George Martin of the West Indian Leadership Council: –

> "I have no confidence that they will change, but if they do listen to people like myself who have been telling them this for years, then the first thing they have to do for us to change this thing round is to demonstrate absolutely clearly, both in the street and in the police stations and wherever they speak, that they regard Black parents – adults, as human beings. My feeling is that there is no respect in the police station or on the streets."

8.14 Thirdly, the co-operation has to be **at all levels of the police force.** One of the most startling revelations in our inquiry was the statement of Woman Police Sergeant Gillian Meynell to Tricia Zipfel, consultant to the Department of Environment, that she had rarely been on the estate, had never met with Dolly Kiffin or any other key people, and was not allowed to meet with community groups. Tricia Zipfel herself compared the change in strategy which is needed to the changes pioneered by her own project: –

> "To get the people at the front end of management on the ground where it matters, so that they can actually deal face to face with the people that they are serving there and then."

While there are differences between housing management and policing there is the same important principle involved in both. All the people who take day to day decisions affecting people's welfare must have a close co-operative relationship with all of them, for if not, the decisions will be taken in ignorance. Liaison with the community must not be shunted off to the community liaison officer.

8.15 Fourthly, the co-operation must be **with the organisations which represent the community.** It is not for the police to choose who represents the community. This means, for example, that the organisations on Broadwater Farm must be accepted as having a legitimate status in the local liaison process. It means also that the council's police sub-committee should be listened to and responded to when it takes some initiative on behalf of the council about the policing of the area. As we observed in Chapter 3, it does not infringe any sacred principle for the police to work with a council police committee. Unlike any other organisation, the council has a known representative status as the body chosen by the majority of the electorate. We saw in Chapter 7 that 71% of the people in Broadwater Farm believed that the council ought to be involved in policing decisions. Without conceding any constitutional ground, the police should be able to give expression to that wish. We note with interest that Chief Superintendent Stainsby, in his first address to the Community and Police Consultative Group on 15th May, said that he recognised the importance of the local election results and had already had a meeting with Councillor Grant.

8.16 Finally, co-operative policing means discussions designed **to deter and detect those crimes which are the priority concerns for the community.** We have heard during the Inquiry of two different concepts of policing which are said to be in oppostion: "hard" policing or "soft" — a police force or a police service. But we do not believe that there is a contradiction between co-operative policing and law enforcement. As our survey has shown, the Broadwater Farm community wants positive and effective police action against crimes which they deplore. A high priority is put by Black people and White, young and old, on the need to prevent heroin dealing, sexual assaults, mugging and burglary. They also consider that the police are unsuccessful in dealing with these crimes. While the police have an overall duty to enforce the law, they have in practice a huge area of discretion in the way resources are used. If the police are seen to neglect these priority areas and to spend time on, for example, shoplifting or road tax offences, resentment in the community will continue. Co-operation therefore means discussing what are the priorities and how they should be tackled. It should also include local C.I.D officers and district support unit officers, as well as the home beat team. Any good understanding which might be built up by the home beat officers could be destroyed if, when serious crimes occur, a separate and alien team of officers become involved.

8.17 We are acutely aware that it is one thing to state principles and quite another to implement them. We have seen how ideas which were held by Chief Superintendent Couch were sometimes unacceptable to his colleagues and some of his subordinates. We see three principal ingredients in the programme which is needed to make co-operative policing a reality in Tottenham:—

(1) A programme of education and training of officers of all ranks in the skills which are needed for co-operative policing in a multi-ethnic community.

(2) A commitment demonstrated by the top ranks of the police leadership through the ranks downwards to eradicate oppressive and racist policing.

(3) A system of consultation and accountability which is effective to secure changes in policing strategy when the community is seriously dissatisfied with the service which it is receiving.

A COMPREHENSIVE TRAINING PROGRAMME

8.18 The need for training was voiced by many witnesses, including Mrs Scott:—

"It's up to the government to do these things, but they have got to give their police more training and they have got to put them in the right way, give them the proper training as to handle Black people in general."

And Arthur Lawrence:—

"Better training in their understanding of other ethnic groups would go some way to resolve some of the problems. At one time they used to be some visits by police to youth clubs and all that; somewhere along the line that broke down."

And a Black woman:—

"The training for the police is vital. Talking to certain policeman, men who are well meaning in many respects, they don't know what racism is at all. They just have it and they do not realise how much it's affecting other people."

And Tricia Zipfel, drawing on her experience of housing management, described how when people are the "old guard type", then "they damned well have to be trained into new attitudes, new approaches, and new styles of management that are appropriate."

8.19 This need for training is underlined by the fact that Metropolitan police officers are not recruited out of the communities which they are to serve. According to a report by Andrew Tyler in *Time Out* magazine on 14th May 1986, around 70% of officers are recruited from outside the greater London area. In their training period, they are based in a police section house. Another aspect of the problem is expressed by a Black officer in the article who

THE BROADWATER FARM INQUIRY REPORT

described the effects of this total non-contact with the real community:–

"With eight hours a day in the section house, three or four drinking and the rest on duty, it gets to the stage where it's embarrassing for them to meet people who aren't policemen. It gets so they can't cope with ordinary people and that they come to actually detest any group apart from themselves. Hard drinking and hard bragging about sexual conquests are prerequisites for being accepted as 'one of the boys'. If they do have to mingle, like go to an Asian community on house inquiries, they'll come back and slag and slag about how much they stink. And it isn't a small minority, it's the core of the group, I'd say, aged from 18 to 25."

8.20 Senior officers, who should be playing a key role in cracking down on racist and sexist attitudes appear often to condone and encourage them. The pages of the Policy Studies Institute report *Police and People in London*, which was commissioned by the Metropolitan Police and involved actual observation by researchers who were attached to the Metropolitan Police over two years, reveal case after case of such behaviour by high ranking officers. These are some examples:–

"When (a researcher) worked with one crime squad, one of the first things the uniform sergeant told him was that he thought he would have to get rid of the WPC in the squad, since none of the men wanted to work with her."

"It was a Detective Chief Inpector who said in an interview that 'Asians are incapable of telling the truth.'"

"One of the officers giving the briefing for a large public order event managed to indicate that he sympathised with PCs who found Black people ridiculous even while he was saying that the PCs should not call them 'monkeys' as this might cause trouble."

"It was a Chief Inspector who (in the aftermath of the Black People's Day of Action) worked himself up into a frenzy of hatred against Black people and orchestrated a session of absurd racist talks with a large group of PCs in the canteen."

"A Commander in a sensitive area spontaneously spoke at length (to a researcher) about the alien, unintelligible and threatening nature of the West Indian way of life: while some of the points he made were individually valid, what he had to say was, taken as a whole, an expression of hostility towards West Indians, especially since he had nothing to say in their favour. It was quite clear that this Commander had little sense of common humanity with the

LOOKING FORWARD: JUSTICE FROM THE LAW

West Indians who form an important part of the local population."

8.21 In only one of the ten divisions which the researchers studied did they find senior officers who were prepared to exercise their leadership in combatting racism. Their description of this division is worth quoting:—

"In one of the divisions that we studied, the senior management team (chief superintendent and superintendent) were clearly very anxious to establish and maintain good relations with members of ethnic minority groups locally. They showed this by giving their own attention to any events or incidents that might act as a focus for racial tensions. They also spent a considerable amount of their time getting to know prominent people belonging to the ethnic minority groups locally. They were well aware that there was a great deal of racialist talk among PCs on the reliefs; they certainly did not appear to condone it and they made a (partly successful) attempt to stop it while the researcher was there. Although the racialist talk continued the PCs were well aware of the policy of the senior management, especially their insistence on giving support to the Asians when under threat from skinheads and supporters of extreme right-wing organisations. This policy was often commented on, was resented by some, but was put into action. It was significant that the researcher saw a potentially explosive incident involving West Indians successfully defused in this division."

8.22 These quotations, from a study made as recently as 1981 – 1983 indicate the magnitude of the task. From the evidence which we have summarised earlier, we have no doubt that these attitudes are as prolific in Tottenham now as they were in 1981 – 83 in the areas studied by the researchers. To change them requires first, an absolute commitment from the senior officers in Tottenham, supported by the deputy assistant commissioner at area level. For example, since it will be necessary to use substantial police time in the training and retraining of officers, it may be necessary to have support from outside Tottenham to cover essential policing duties. We have seen how vast numbers of officers were brought into Tottenham from outside in October to December 1985 to deal with was seen to be a crisis. The crisis of racism and alienation from the community amongst police officers is at least as desperate.

8.23 In 1983 the Working Party on Community and Race Relations

THE BROADWATER FARM INQUIRY REPORT

Training for the Police published its report. It had been set up by the Police Training Council, and its recommendations were accepted by the Home Office. Among its findings about the attitudes of police officers was the following, with which we fully agree:—
"Many officers, of course, appreciate the need for the police to offer a full range of services and take pride in discharging all their functions in a thoughtful and professional manner. There is, however, a tendency for some, particularly in inner-city areas, to regard their task as more or less exclusively one of law enforcement. Such a narrow conception of their role can lead officers to exercise their discretion without regard to the effect of their actions on long-term relations with the public, and to regard themselves as representing an authority apart from the community. Officers who focus exclusively on law enforcement may, in addition, assume that all individuals with whom they come into contact are criminally inclined, and take a disparaging and moralistic view towards high crime areas (and the local populations) where the generally accepted means of social control may be relatively difficult to apply."

The Working Party's general conclusions about existing police training methods were strongly critical:—
"There are a number of serious weaknesses in present 'in-force' training. Not all forces give training in community and race relations and few give training to ranks above sergeant. The aims of such training as is given are generally unclear and unrelated to the practical requirements of the police service. The most serious defect in the content of present training is that it consists, for the most part, simply of information. A narrow range of methods is used and neither the training nor individual officers are assessed. Training is not organised to maximum effect. Expertise and materials available, while adequate for present training, will not be so in future."

The Working Party made a series of recommendations both for in-service training and for the training of probationers, designed to rectify this serious situation.

8.24 In some areas of the Metropolitan police at least, this need for intensive training at all levels is beginning to be recognized. In a paper presented in September 1984 to the Cranfield-Wolfson Colloquium on models of police/public consultation in Europe, Commander Alexander Marnoch, who was in charge of the Lambeth district from

LOOKING FORWARD: JUSTICE FROM THE LAW

1981 to 1985, described the introduction of new training programmes. He said it was impossible to exempt police from some of the blame for the alienation of the Black community, in that wrongful attitudes had all too often been seen as confirmation of prejudice and the catalyst of public disorder. He continued:–

> "We must ensure that the men who come (to Lambeth) are well trained and carefully selected. For this reason, the training programme for our officers has been enhanced and the element that we call "policing skills" has been increased, with a view to ensuring that officers project the right attitude to elicit the right response. A recent addition to the programme for Lambeth has been the development of a district training unit which, in addition to providing normal "on the job" training, would be used for specialist "policing skills" development, with the accent very much on the needs of the community. We anticipate that in the next three years this emphasis on training will increase even more and that the unit will come into its own, providing training for probationers, senior constables and detectives. We have established a coherent and logical strategy for introducing new recruits to the district. The street duty course takes up the first ten weeks of a probationer's career and aims to teach not only local geography and characteristics but to involve the probationer in operational policing in a guided situation. We have effectively attained the six months' training period Scarman suggested – indeed it is 30 weeks – while community relations training for senior officers and experienced constables is greatly featured."

8.25 We welcome this approach in Lambeth, but we question to what extent the recommendations of the Working Party have been taken seriously in Tottenham. We certainly believe that a training unit similar to that in Lambeth is needed in Tottenham, and that − for a start − all the home beat officers to be attached to Broadwater Farm should attend, however "experienced" they are. We believe that such in-service training programmes must involve both local community representatives and non-police experts in a teaching role. We believe that the training of probationary officers must be completely reviewed and greatly extended in length. The present 20 weeks at the training college at Hendon is a very short period, in which it is impossible for a trainee to understand, let alone master, the difficult skills needed to serve the public well, such as an understanding of civil liberties, an understanding of human relations, and an understanding of community organisation.

8.26 After the initial period the 'training' of probationers seems too much to involve the use of probationary officers as extra police numbers, without any real learning programme. Many other professions require a period of placement for trainees in places where they can gain necessary experience. Specifically we note that Chief Superintendent Stainsby in his address to the Community and Police Consultative Group said that he was approaching the local authority regarding the placing of probationers after their initial training. He said: —
"I would like to attach them to bodies in the local authorities sphere for them to study the social impact of policing."
We can think of no better place for such attachments to be started, than at the Neighbourhood Office and the Youth Association on Broadwater Farm Estate, and we believe that, if the plan was seriously discussed with community representatives, they would work with it.

8.27 A comparison between the schemes described in Commander Marnoch's paper and the divisional reports issued by the Tottenham police shows how inadequate has been the attention given to training in Tottenham. In 1984 a divisional strategic plan for Tottenham was published. The foreword stated that: —
"The strategy includes an element of quality of service to the public, which is hoped to provide for a better quality of life for Tottenham and a closer police/community understanding."
The plan contained not one reference to training. The divisional report for 1985 contained one reference to in-service training: —
"Our fifth objective was to improve the overall skill and effectiveness of police officers from Tottenham divisions. To achieve this aim a series of one day training courses was organised for community beat officers where lectures and talks were given by speakers with relevant knowledge."
It is our belief that courses lasting one day for a limited number of officers only scratched the surface of the problem that we have described. The 1986 report states generally that the force's goal for 1986 is to improve the service to the public by a number of methods, of which the very last in the list is training. There is however no further reference to training in the report, and nothing to indicate that any further attention has been given to the training of officers in the necessary skills which they lack.

A COMMITMENT TO ERADICATE OPPRESSIVE AND RACIST POLICING
8.28 Training is only part of the answer. An equally important part is

LOOKING FORWARD: JUSTICE FROM THE LAW

supervision and discipline. The need for the most senior officers to know what abuses are going on and then stamp on them was stressed by Norton MacLean, Principal Youth Officer for Haringey: —

"If the senior management in the police were really committed to changing things, then I feel lots of people in the community will go more than half way in meeting them. Now they can demonstrate this commitment by actually prosecuting to the fullest hilt of the law the officers who break the rules."

Mr Jarrett made the same point: —

"We won't trust the police until we get a written statement going across the whole world saying that any policeman caught telling lies should have been sacked or been dismissed or been disciplined."

8.29 The problem however is that police officers have so much individual discretion to enforce the law as they think fit, that senior officers can evade responsibility by pleading ignorance. Stopping people in the street, calling in district support units, obtaining search warrants — to take three areas where we have evidence of abuse — are all done by junior officers with minimal supervision. We have seen how DC Randall was able to carry through the search of Mrs Jarrett's home with little or no questioning from the duty officer Inspector Clarke. The Chief Executive Roy Limb spoke of this lack of awareness on the part of the senior officers of what was going on:–

"One thing was clear to me, though I cannot say it was ever admitted by the police, and that was that sometimes the right hand did not know what the left was doing. There were a number of different police forces at work."

Mr Limb said that was a familiar experience to him as a senior manager, and often he does not know that certain things are happening "until some councillor kicks me up the backside". For police officers who have the potential to do more harm to the individual than almost any local authority officer, to be out of control in this way is unacceptable. We have seen how, on the findings of the P.S.I. researchers, racist behaviour was condoned and instigated at the level of very senior ranks. We believe therefore that tackling racism and the abuses which flow from it, is a priority which requires clear and strong leadership from the Chief Superintendent of Tottenham himself, with firm and public backing from all ranks above him up to and including the Commissioner of Police.

8.30 How can this be done? We are sorry that we could not have heard from Chief Superintendent Stainsby himself whether he thought that

THE BROADWATER FARM INQUIRY REPORT

there was a need for a commitment to eradicate oppressive and racist policing, and if so how he proposed to carry it through. We asked the Commissioner of Police a number of questions about racist behaviour in our letter of 6th May 1986. He did not answer them. In our view such a commitment would have to include:–

(1) A requirement that over a reasonably long period, no house search or arrest warrant should be applied for without the authority of the Chief Superintendent, or some officer delegated by him in cases of emergency;

(2) A stipulation that every stop-and-search of a person in the street be reported to the Chief Superintendent with a full reason why it was done. In this connection we mention the answer given by the Home Office to Lord Gifford's question:–

"How many people were stopped and searched by police officers in the Tottenham area during each month of 1985; of what ethnic origin they were; and in how many cases the stop was followed by an arrest?"

The answer was that in the first three months there were 867 stops resulting in 175 arrests; and in the last nine months there were 413 searches followed by 51 arrests. After April the basis of recording changed and it seems that stops were not recorded. Information on the ethnic appearance of those searched was not collected centrally. These are worrying statistics, especially as many of the arrests are likely to have been "knock on" offences (See paragraph 3.5). Hundreds of people who were innocently going about their lawful business have been stopped, and have suffered the humiliation of a public search.

8.31 These requirements should be accompanied by guidance from the Chief Officer that there should be no stops of Black people on "hunches" that they were up to no good; no fishing expeditions to the homes of Black people who were rumoured to be criminals. Search powers should be used only where they was clear evidence of specific crimes. The requirements would also need personal leadership from senior officers; for example, there are many opportunities at briefings before officers leave the police station for senior officers to ram home the message that racist and oppressive behaviour will not be tolerated. We understand that in other police divisions in London such methods have been effective in reducing the number of oppressive searches. The need to justify a search in the face of probing questions of a Chief Superintendent should be a deterrent even to the most racist constable.

8.32 Similar constraints will have to be placed upon the district support units, which are about to be reorganised as a new form of Special Patrol Group serving the whole of a police area. They will be known as Territorial Support Groups. Their job is a difficult one. They have to wait or drive around, often for long periods, until called out to help out in some emergency or some special operations. They usually have no knowledge of the people to whom they are sent. It is therefore vital that they should be under control. The experience of the day when district support units left the Spurs' ground and moved into Broadwater Farm looking for something to do, must never be repeated. Once again we would suggest that the control must be imposed by direct supervision from the appropriate Area and Divisional Chief officers, to whom all operations of these units should be reported. The aim must be that officers who call in such units without good reason, and officers in the units themselves who abuse their power, can be called to account and disciplined. The ill-effects of using these units where they are not needed cannot be overstated: Vernon Moore of the West Indian Leadership Council, put the point succinctly in saying to us:–

> "The deployment of "meat wagons" in certain areas should be decreased in order to dispel the psychology of fear which the Black community is currently experiencing."

8.33 Over and above these specific suggestions, we call for a ruthless determination to eradicate racism from the police force. Community development officer Laxmi Jamdagni made this call in clear terms:–

> "I think the single biggest issue here is police racism and the short term and long term effects that that is having."

The Commissioner's Report for 1985 tells us that there has not been a single substantiated complaint of racial discrimination since racial discrimination became a specific disciplinary offence in 1984. To us that speaks volumes, not only about the hopelessness of the police complaints procedure, to which we return below, but about the low level of commitment to take racism in the police force seriously. We urge the senior officers in Tottenham to prove by every means at their disposal – by publicity, by example, by training, and by discipline – that disrespect and ill-treatment of Black people because of their colour will not be tolerated under their command, and will be punished.

8.34 We mention in this context the question of the recruitment of Black police officers. It is in our view fallacious to suppose that recruiting drives for Black officers will help to combat racism. The converse is the case — cracking down on racism will make a job in the police force considerably more attractive to many Black people. They will be far more ready to serve in an organisation which respects them as people, which does not abuse them or degrade them, and which will give them the opportunity for promotion in accordance with their abilities. Our own view is that we want to see Black people playing a full part in all walks of life, including the police. Advertisements and campaigns aimed at potential Black recruits are to be welcomed, but they will not significantly increase the number of Black officers unless the Metropolitan Police Force at all levels is clearly seen to be attacking the racism within its own ranks.

POLICING BROADWATER FARM
8.35 The proposals set out above could be implemented on the Broadwater Farm Estate in a way which would, over a period of time, effect major improvements in relations between police and residents. First, we believe it to be essential that there are no officers being drafted in from other divisions outside Tottenham to be part of the Broadwater Farm patrol. Secondly, the members of the home beat team must be introduced to the people of the estate which they are policing. This will require most careful liaison and discussion with both the representatives of community organisations and the police. Many people in the community have almost lost hope that police officers will respect them as equals, and on the other side we understand that there is a reluctance on the part of police officers to serve on Broadwater Farm, which is still branded in their eyes as a violent and anti-police community. But if, as we have been told, the members of the home beat team have been selected with care: and if, as we believe, the community organisations will respond to a dialogue which is seen to be genuine, then it can be done. The community is entitled to know, and we think wants to know, who its police officers are. Pat Ford, former chair of the Tenants' Association, said this of the present situation:—
> "They are still very erratic as they are in their vans, and they are in and out, and you get them very thin on the ground one minute and loads the next. If they are going to have 12 here, I think they should have 12 here, and I think that we should know their faces, and I think they might stand a chance then."

It must also be very difficult for the home beat officers to be patrolling in a community whose prominent members are unknown to them, and where they feel estranged and on edge. We would leave it to discussions between senior officers and the representatives of community organisations to determine exactly how and when such contact should be made. The attendance of some of the home beat officers at the Broadwater Farm panel would be very helpful.

8.36 It is not for us to say precisely how many police officers should patrol Broadwater Farm. It is evident that for 16 officers to patrol 1063 dwellings is out of proportion to any other neighbourhood policing operation. Spread over Tottenham, the same ratio would require about 1000 community beat police officers for the whole of Tottenham, whereas in reality there are only about 200 constables in the division for every kind of work. People in other neighbourhoods are entitled to ask why they cannot have a greater share of community beat policing for themselves. Even so, it is not just the numbers but also the attitudes and behaviour of the officers which mattered. In our survey 65% said that they thought the existing numbers were about right or too few. Sixteen officers who understand and work with the community, and who do not call in reinforcements for every minor policing job, will create far less trouble than eight who are hostile and aloof.

CONSULTATION AND ACCOUNTABLITY
8.37 We believe that the present legal position whereby the Home Secretary is the police authority for London should be changed, and that London should have a police authority of elected representatives. At present it is virtually impossible for any effective democratic control to be placed upon policing in London. Norman Atkinson MP, who declined to give evidence to the Inquiry but spoke to three of us privately, said that we could refer to his experience of how difficult it was to raise any questions about policing strategies on behalf of his constituents. When he raised the matter with the Home Secretary, he would normally be answered by a Minister of State saying that it was an operational matter for the Commissioner. Many other public servants, such as teachers and social workers, are able to maintain strong professional standards in dealing with individual problems, while being accountable to elected bodies for the financing and policy direction of their service. In the same way, even though police officers as trained experts should have a discretion in how the law is enforced, their budget and general priorities should be determined by a body of elected representatives which can call them to account. Without that, the interpretation of the public interest is left entirely to a

Commissioner of Police, who is not accessible to MPs or responsible to a public mandate. That is not the democratic way.

8.38 However we do not enter further into the debate about what sort of elected police authority, with what powers, there should be. There is a crisis of confidence in the police in Tottenham today, and it must be tackled within today's legal framework. That means making use of the arrangements for consultation between the police and the people of the area which are required by Section 106 of the Police and Criminal Evidence Act 1984, which we quoted at paragraph 3.49.

8.39 The Home Office has published guidance on the arrangements for local consultation in the Metropolitan Police District. Paragraph 7, dealing with membership and organisation, starts as follows: –
"If a group is to have the confidence of the local community as the focus for local consultations on policing matters, it is essential that its membership should be as representative as possible of that community. Groups should be accessible to the public so that the community in its widest sense can make a constructive contribution, as well as the police, elected representatives and statutory agencies . . . The formation of sub-committees to consider particular problems or initiatives could involve representatives from the community who are not members of the group itself."

8.40 The Haringey Police and Consultative Group first met on 31st October 1985, and its constitution and standing orders were adopted on 9th January 1986. Members of the Inquiry attended the two following meetings on 13th March and 15th May. It was quite apparent that the Group was not representative of the Haringey community. Eric Clarke, chair of the group, accepted this in his evidence to us: –
"What is missing basically is the Black element in any numbers and the Black element is quite a strong element within Haringey. We had the Standing Conference and a couple of bits and pieces, which are good bits and pieces, but no, I wouldn't think we were representative of the electors of Haringey at all."

He believed that the biggest inhibiting factor to Black organisations joining was the attitude of the Borough Council which had not taken part. In a dialogue with a number of Black members of the public who intervened during his evidence, his position was that the group was open for them to join, and if they wanted the group to concern itself

LOOKING FORWARD: JUSTICE FROM THE LAW

with the grievances of the Black community, it was for them to come along and voice them. They however were saying that for the Group to be acceptable it must show itself ready to deal with the injustices suffered by Black people, and of this they saw no sign.

8.41 It is necessary to examine how the present situation has come about. If the intention of the group was to bring together as wide a range of community interests as possible, in accordance with the Home Office guidance – it would have had a list of 1,200 organisations in Haringey to call upon. Both the Haringey Council and the Haringey Council for Voluntary Service have compiled extensive lists of all organisations in the borough and these lists are updated regularly. The Haringey Council for Voluntary Service has computer-based lists of 1,200 organisations from which can be retrieved any groupings of organisations required for a particular type of mailing. The council's community affairs department produces an updated directory regularly.

8.42 The initiative for the present Consultative Group first began on 6th June 1985 when an exploratory meeting took place, at which according to D.A.C. Richards "a good section of community representatives were invited". In fact the conveners of that meeting appear to have written to only 60 organisations, and did not consult either the Haringey Council or the Haringey Council for Voluntary Service about other possible invitees. They appear to have made no real efforts at initially inviting a great many of the Black and minority ethnic organisations, of which there were approximately 230, even though the Black and minority ethnic communities' population is about 44% of the borough. According to the information which we have received, only 17 such organisations were invited. Only two women's organisations were invited, even though women are among the most vulnerable people in terms of criminal attacks and abuse. The initial list of invitees comprised mainly neighbourhood watch organisations, tenants' organisations and long established groups such as the Church, Council of Churches, London Transport, and the Probation Service. There were 21 organisations present at the exploratory meeting, of which six appear to be minority ethnic organisations. The chair Eric Clarke told the Inquiry that the membership is now 100, most of whom are neighbourhood watch schemes. Dudley Dryden, who attends the Group on behalf of the West Indian Standing Conference, and is one of the very few Black

people to attend, gave us his view of the Group at its present stage: —
"I do have some concern about the Consultative Group. I think the base needs to be broadened for greater representation of the people in Haringey, and not just as it stands at the moment, but is early days and we have yet to see the base being broadened. Otherwise it will have a voice just in one concept only. When I am there at the moment I am like a voice in the wilderness, but sometimes the voice in the wilderness does get results."

8.43 The constitution as at first drafted contained as one of the nine aims of the group: —
"To monitor the incidence of racial attacks and harassment in general within Haringey and to discuss the police methods for their alleviation and investigation."

When the constitution was adopted, this was amended to substitute "personal violence" for "racial attacks." It must be said that the senior police officers who were present supported the idea that the monitoring of racial attacks should be one of the aims of the group. However, the amendment, carried by a meeting composed almost entirely of White people, has caused a concern about the commitment of the group to anti-racist policies which we find entirely reasonable. This concern would not have been allayed by the passing at the next meeting of a motion worded in weak and general terms that the group "wishes to record their commitment that all their efforts and endeavours will be based on a policy of equal opportunities irrespective of race or sex."

8.44 The Middlesex Area Probation Service, in their written submission to the Inquiry, gave this summing up of the performance to date of the Group which has so far been meeting: —
"The mood of the meeting is populist, and anger is directed primarily against Haringey Council. The majority of members present show little awareness of the feelings and problems experienced by the young and by ethnic minorities in the borough. Some of the decisions taken by the Group show an unwillingness to accommodate the views of disadvantaged and minority groups. The Group is unable to offer any constructive criticism of the police."

8.45 However, the council has also a serious responsibility to bear for the present situation. We have said above (3.51) that in our view the council indulged in obstructive tactics when first invited to hold discussions about the consultation arrangements. It deprived itself of the opportunity to insist on a truly representative membership list, and a constitution which would be acceptable for the whole community. With all the information at its disposal it would have been in a strong position to have negotiated to set up the Group on a constructive basis. Its absence has encouraged the Group to become, as we have ourselves seen it, the anti-council gathering described by the Probation Service, where any support for the council is greeted with boos. At its meeting on 15th May 1986, the Group issued an ultimatum that it would appoint council representatives itself, if the council had not done so by the next meeting on 17th July.

8.46 It is our firm view that this state of affairs does no service either to the police or to the community at this critical time. It can only be ended if there is an open mind and a readiness to re-think on all sides. The Group itself should be prepared to make a fresh start, and to throw open its organisation to help every group which wishes to join. A public campaign to draw in members from all parts of the community would create confidence in the Group and enable it to establish wide and important links into the community. There are a number of key agencies in the borough, such as the Haringey Council for Voluntary Service, the West Indian Leadership Council, the co-ordinating bodies for Asian and other ethnic minority and womens' organisations, with whom the Group could co-operate in making the campaign effective.

8.47 But the re-thinking should go further than membership and extend to the structure of the Group and its meetings. At present it meets every two months, for two hours only, unless the meeting decides otherwise. A considerable portion of that time is taken up by reports from the two chief superintendents of Hornsey and Tottenham. Within that framework it is not easy to see the Group being able to grapple effectively with matters of serious complaint. There needs to be a readiness to meet more frequently, (the Lambeth Consultative Group meets twice a month) and to create sub-groups which can deal more informally and carefully with issues of particular concern.

8.48 In the longer term, the Consultative Group should have funding which enables it to employ its own staff and provide information and service to its members independently of the police.

THE BROADWATER FARM INQUIRY REPORT

The guidance states that costs, which are covered by the Home Office, should be small. We know of at least one Consultative Group in London which has secured funding to cover the costs of its own office and staff. The problems of Tottenham certainly deserve priority for the funding of effective consultative arrangements.

8.49   We also urge the council for its part, to enter as a matter of urgency into discussions with the Group with a view to participating fully in its work. The council has potentially an important representative role to play. The councillors who would most logically be appointed would be the members of the police sub-committee. We have heard evidence from members of that committee representing both the major parties on the council. We have been informed that frequently the decisions of the sub-committee are taken by a consensus of both parties. If a matter of concern were brought from the sub-committee on a bi-partisan basis to be raised at the Consultative Group, there would be powerful pressure on the police to deal satisfactorily with that matter of concern. Moreover the council maintains a Police Research Unit. The information which the unit has gathered would be at the disposal of council representatives on the Consultative Group, and could be used to support a demand for a new policy or a request for further information.

8.50   We questioned Councillor Grant about his attitude as leader to the council's relations with the Consultative Group. His answer deserves careful attention:—
> "I think that we should take part in the Consultative Group providing that the Consultative Group is representative of the people in the borough. At the moment the Consultative Group is made up, as I understand it, of something like 80-90% of neighbourhood watch schemes. There is little or no representation from Black and minority ethnic groups in the borough, of which there are literally dozens. There is no representation to any great extent from some other community groups within the borough, women's groups and so on. I think that if the Consultative Group were to become representative, then the council should take part, even though politically we disagree with the whole way in which it was set up. I think we should concede that point and we should take part, providing it's representative. Secondly, I think the Consultative Group will need to make a clear anti-racist statement and that I believe has been thrown out by the Consultative Group.

They have refused to consider the question of racism at all within their work. As I understand it, even the police were quite happy to have a reference in their objectives to an anti-racist police policy, fighting against racial harassment and so on. Even the police were quite happy with that, but the Consultative Group couldn't bring themselves to agree to that particular statement. But if those two things are agreed, I think we should take part in it."

We have recognised the force of both of the points made by Councillor Grant in this answer. If the Consultative Group is unwilling to respond, then we believe that the Metropolitan Police would be obliged to dissolve the present unrepresentative group and start again with a wider forum.

8.51 We emphasise, that in the interests of utilising this process of consultation for the benefit of all the people of the borough, flexibility and restraint will be needed on both sides. The first and most immediate piece of restraint will need to come from the Group at its next meeting on 17th July. We believe that it must drop its "ultimatum" to the council. In the first place, the Group has no right whatsoever to appoint council representatives; only the council can do that. In the second place, we hope that all concerned will want to digest the findings and proposals of this report, before travelling a step further down the road of provocation and disunity. It may then be possible for a genuine and constructive dialogue to begin.

THE PREVENTION OF DISORDER

8.52 On 7th October 1985, the Commissioner of Police Sir Kenneth Newman made the following statement in relation to the decision not to use plastic bullets the night before:—

"But I wish to put all the people of London on notice that I will not shrink from such a decision should I believe it a practical option for restoring peace and preventing crime and injury. I would have hoped not to have had to express that thought but yesterday evening's events have made it a regrettable possibility."

This was a chilling threat. We are sure that Sir Kenneth was keenly aware of the anger of his own men at the experiences of 6th October. He had himself visited the scene in the middle of the night. He may have felt the need to give them reassurance that they would not be left unprotected. Even so, the words in our view would have been better left unsaid, for they increased public perception of a police force concerned only to subdue disorder with even greater force. We urge the Commissioner to take no further steps to make that threat a reality. We agree with the statement which was made to us by Dudley Dryden of the West Indian Standing Conference:—

"I would like to say something about the presence of plastic bullets, water cannons and CS gas. They are not going to be a solution to the problems. Because if a person is cornered they definitely intend to fight back and fight back in a very vicious and ferocious way. Examples over the years and hundreds of years tell us that to put more pressure on persons who have already been pressurised, that is not the solution. The solution to the problem is to get around the table in an amicable way with the community and have the matter being sorted out."

8.53 Since October 1985, the Metropolitan Police have introduced Londoners to "Riot City" — a mock-up of an urban area where police officers simulate riot conditions and throw petrol bombs and missiles at each other. It appears that all police officers are to undergo training there. We find it frightening that police officers are being put through training for urban warfare without any concentrated effort being made to give them training also in the understanding and conciliation of urban conflicts. It is said that plastic bullets would be introduced only as weapons of last resort, but the experience of Northern Ireland has shown that they can rapidly become used as a standard way of dispersing a hostile crowd. Two members of our panel have had eye-witness experience in Northern Ireland of police officers firing baton rounds at bystanders who were jeering at them, before any hostile move had been made, provoking the very violence which they were intending to deter. The Northern Ireland experience also tells us that plastic bullets can and do kill innocent bystanders. We therefore oppose any use of plastic bullets. The more that such weapons are available and are used, the more an attitude of mind develops, both among police and other people, that it is necessary for sections of the community to be at war with each other, with one section — the police — being armed as if to put down an enemy.

POLICE COMPLAINTS
8.54 We have stated in paragraphs 4.52 to 4.54 our belief that the Police Complaints Authority failed lamentably in its investigation of Mrs Jarrett's death to satify a large section of the public, including ourselves, of its independence and impartiality. What is striking about the investigation is that the responsibility for that failure must be laid

squarely at the feet of the Authority itself and not of the investigating officers. We know from the evidence given to the jury, essentially what it was that the investigating officers discovered. On the basis of what they discovered, there was a clear case to recommend disciplinary action, but the Authority took the decision not to do so. Thus the argument which many put forward that complaints against the police must be investigated by an independent body would not have affected this case. If the Police Complaints Authority had had the power to investigate the case themselves, instead of merely supervising the investigation, it is likely that they would have come to the same conclusion. The problem is that the members of the Authority, although lay people, appear to have no idea of what standards of conduct are expected by reasonable members of the public. They expect that a police officer conducting a search who so carelessly pushes past a woman standing peacefully in a doorway of her house, that she falls and dies, will be disciplined.

8.55 We believe that it would be better for there to be a completely independent authority for the investigation of complaints against the police. However, the Police Complaints Authority is a newly established body and we have to consider the future on the basis that it will remain. In the case of Mrs Jarrett's death it could have fulfilled the valuable function of insisting that disciplinary action was taken. It would then have been for the Commissioner as the disciplining authority, to have satisfied the public that he was committed to dealing with police misconduct. As it was, the Authority, who knew that there had been intense concern and anger expressed about Mrs Jarrett's death, exonerated the officers completely. They have seriously lost credibility and public confidence. Having failed to act on this complaint, one wonders what trust can be placed in them by others whose complaints are less publicised. The case of Mrs Jarrett's death in our view calls into question whether the members of the Authority who were party to the decision should continue to hold their responsible public office.

POLICE INVESTIGATIONS
8.56 We have raised in Chapter 6 a number of questions about the fairness and the legality of many aspects of the investigation which began after 6th October. Although the new law was not in force, that investigation tells us a lot about how the powers under the new law will be used. For example, we saw how the police on a number of

THE BROADWATER FARM INQUIRY REPORT

occasions applied to the Magistrates Court for a remand in police custody for three days, and how in the great majority of cases, those applications were granted. The new law allows detention for up to 96 hours provided that a Magistrates Court grants a warrant of further detention after 36 hours. We fear that it will become customary for magistrates to grant such warrants in cases such as this, and we address a particular appeal to the magistrates below.

8.57 We have seen also how blatantly the police acted to deny a person being interrogated, the right to have the assistance of a lawyer. It was intended that under the new law the right to the assistance of a lawyer was automatic from the outset, except in the very exceptional case where it was feared that the lawyer might pass a message (perhaps inadvertently) which would alert other suspects or harm other people. We fear that the exception under the new law will become used in as standard a way as that under the old. We believe that the right of an arrested person to consult with the lawyer of his or her choice is fundamental. If police officers refuse to respect that right, which is now enshrined in law subject to an exception which would occur rarely, then it is imperative that the courts protect it. Clear rulings are needed from the courts that a "confession" made after the wrongful refusal of access to a lawyer, will not be admitted in evidence.

8.58 As far as other abuses are concerned, such as oppressive questioning, intimidation, and threats, the new law provides that if a confession has been obtained by the oppression of the person who made it, or in consequence of anything said or done which was likely to render the confession unreliable, the court shall not allow the confession to be given in evidence. The difficulty with that, is that the judges who make such decisions are inclined to believe the police officer rather than the suspect when there is a conflict of evidence as to what was done. It is difficult to devise any set of safeguards which would be guaranteed to provide redress in every case of improper behaviour. But there is one obvious protection against abuse which should be obligatory in a technological age — the introduction of video recordings of police interviews. We find it to be something of a perversion of priorities that whereas sophisticated technology is available to the police for them to store and retrieve vast quantities of information on computer, the simple device of a tape recorder has not been installed except as an experiment in a few police stations.

LOOKING FORWARD: JUSTICE FROM THE LAW

8.59 There is another scheme which is already in operation in three parts of London, the introduction of "lay visitors", i.e. lay people who have the right (recognised by the police) to be admitted to any part of a police station at any time of day or night, without prior notice, in order to inquire whether suspects are being properly treated. We note that in the Report of the Commissioner of Police for 1985 it is stated that: —

> "At the time of the street disorders in Lambeth the lay visitors were immediately on hand to examine the way in which those arrested were being dealt with."

It would have been of crucial assistance to some of the people who were in custody for days, in the months following 6th October, for lay visitors to have entered all the police stations where they were being held in order to report on what was happening to them.

8.60 Such a scheme would be a considerable improvement upon the existing liaison officer scheme operated by the Haringey Council for Community Relations. That is a scheme whereby members of a panel of liaison officers maintained by the H.C.R.C. visit police stations if they are invited to do so either by a police officer or by a detained person, in order to defuse tense situations and ensure proper treatment. The scheme may well have had valuable results when it was first launched in 1974, but it has fallen into virtual disuse. We were told that it was only used about twice a month, and was not made use of by anybody during the period of the interrogation of persons detained after 6th October. The natural body to administer a lay visitors' scheme would be the Community and Police Consultative Group – if the group were operating effectively as a representative of all sections of the Haringey community. Certainly, such a scheme could only operate if the lay visitors were fearlessly independent people who were prepared to complain to the highest quarters if they came across abuses. It could be one of the priorities of a reconstituted and fully representative consultative group to set up a sub-committee to work with the police in the setting up of an acceptable scheme for Haringey.

8.61 Separate from the question of the treatment of detained people, is the question of how their relatives and friends are treated when they inquire about their welfare. Whatever the arguments about the rights of people who are being questioned, it is totally unacceptable to be disrespectful to their relatives and to deny them information. As a matter of common humanity it should be appreciated that the anxiety of relatives, particularly over the detention of juveniles and young adults, will be acute. There should be standard procedures whereby relatives who telephone or visit the police station can be given accurate information about what is happening. Failure to observe those procedures should be a matter of misconduct. Here again the introduction of a lay visitor scheme would be of value.

COURTS OF LAW
8.62 If the rights of the individual are abused by the police, the only recourse available is to complain to the courts of law. However we have not heard of any case during the course of the investigation after 6th October in which the court intervened effectively to curb the abuses about which complaints were being made. Indeed we have recorded (paragraph 6.29) one occasion on which a high court judge washed his hands of the matter of complaint and claimed that he had no jurisdiction. We would appeal to magistrates and judges to recognise that they are expected by the public to be impartial arbiters between the police and the accused, who appear before them as innocent persons because they have not been proved guilty. Magistrates do have powers which they can exercise if it is reported to them that the police have used oppressive methods. They have the power to refuse to issue warrants of further detention under the new law; and to refuse to allow applications for remands in police custody. If magistrates supinely acquiesce in whatever the police require, then the courts of justice as well as the police become the objects of cynicism and disrepute.

8.63 We find the use of the power to remand a defendant into police custody to be particularly sinister. Normally, if bail is refused, the defendant is remanded in custody to a prison, where police officers have no right to enter and question him or her without consent. When the remand is into police custody, the defendant remains in the police station and will be questioned at any time. Therefore, a remand into police custody authorises a further period of detention for questioning over and above the limits which Parliament has laid down. We believe that this law should be changed in the light of the Broadwater Farm experience, so that such remands could only be ordered in cases where the defendant agrees (as is sometimes the case when a person is giving information to the police about other accomplices). So long as the present law remains, we urge magistrates not to allow such remands when they are objected to by the defence.

8.64 The need for vigilance in the defence of civil rights, extends also to members of the legal profession. They have the power – by the arguments they raise in court, by alerting the press to attend the public courts, and by making statements where necessary out of court – to ensure that violations of their clients' rights do not go unnoticed. If just and proper redress cannot be obtained from the courts, then the responsibility lies with the lawyers, who understand what legal principles are being breached, to alert the public to the injustice of the case.

8.65 The other judicial proceeding with which we have been concerned has been the Coroner's Court. We have stated in Chapter 4 that the inquest into the death of Mrs Jarrett was conducted with exemplary fairness. However there are two potential sources of injustice relating to Coroner's Courts which must be rectified. First, in an age in which the right to legal aid for representation in serious cases has been accepted, it is a scandalous anomaly that no legal aid is available to the relatives of the deceased to be represented at an inquest. As we have stated above, the Jarrett family were fortunate in having able barristers and solicitor to represent them without a fee. Secondly, there is no good reason why the rules should preclude the legal representatives of the interested parties from directly addressing the jury about the verdict which they wish the jury to bring in. It is a basic rule of natural justice that the case of every affected party should be heard. The fact that the Coroner's inquest has some of the features of an inquisitorial procedure is no reason for denying that right.

EDUCATION IN LEGAL RIGHTS
8.66 All the proposals made in this Chapter have been concerned to ensure that the basic rights of the citizen under the law can be protected from abuse by the agencies of the law. It is far easier for those abuses to occur if citizens are ignorant of what their legal rights are. In Britain there is no written constitution or bill of rights which sets out fundamental rights in a way which can be easily understood. The extent of individual rights and the extent of police powers can only be understood by reference to a complicated body of statutory and judge-made law. Accordingly we see, as have some of the

witnesses to our Inquiry, a real value in introducing into the secondary education system – as an obligatory part of the curriculum – a course of education in legal rights and police powers. The course could be extended to include law and politics, so as to cover elections and political parties, central and local government, as well as legal rights and powers of the police. These are topics which at present occur only incidentally (for instance in social studies courses) in the normal school curriculum. If they were compulsory, they would inform not only those who will have to deal with the police, but also future police officers, of their rights and duties under the law.

Chapter Nine
LOOKING FORWARD – BUILDING A SELF RELIANT COMMUNITY

9.1 In Chapter 2 we traced the decline and revival of Broadwater Farm. We decribed a community of people who succeeded, in co-operation with the council and other agencies, in improving their living environment against all the odds. In paragraph 3.53 we spoke of the optimism which showed through the headlines of the Youth Association magazine in June 1985. In the 12 months since then, the disturbances and their consequences have over-shadowed the success. But the council and other agencies which supported Broadwater Farm in the past have not changed their attitudes to the estate. On the contrary, they favour new projects to the extent that resources allow. And the people of Broadwater Farm, in evidence to us and in answer to our survey, have been stressing the problems and making proposals for dealing with them.

9.2 We believe that the achievements of Broadwater Farm in recent years must be extended and developed. The self-reliant spirit of the Youth Association and other organisations cannot be guaranteed to continue whatever the circumstances. It is vulnerable to a combination of factors – lack of resources, police action, the despair of community leaders, the apathy of residents. If it were crushed entirely the social consequences would be grave. We do not make a simplistic link between deprivation and rioting, for the cost of unemployment and poverty can be paid in many other ways. But there is a connection: as Ernie Large said: –
> "If you take unemployment and poverty and top them up with oppression, you are likely to light a fuse, and that goes for any community anywhere in the world, if you add those ingredients together. And that is what is perceived to have been happening with the Black community in Tottenham."

9.3 In concentrating on Broadwater Farm and its immediate neighbourhood we in no way intend to imply that it should have special treatment over and above other neighbourhoods in Haringey or elsewhere which have similar needs. There are ways in which Broadwater Farm is exceptional. Its organisations have proved themselves able to make maximum use of the resources which were available. Its organisations have been led principally by Black people and have earned the support of the vast majority of residents, Black and White. These are considerable achievements, but in directing our proposals to Broadwater Farm we do not wish to exclude other areas. On the contrary we believe that much of what we propose would also have beneficial effects if applied to other areas of high unemployment and poor facilities.

9.4 Apart from the need for co-operative policing, the needs which have been voiced to our Inquiry can be summarised under five headings:
1. Resources and support from central government.
2. Investment and support for projects which will generate employment.
3. Continued development of community facilities.
4. Better education for children and adults.
5. Fair reporting in the media and an end to the undesirable label put on the estate by other agencies.

9.5 We stress that in this chapter we do not provide a complete blueprint for action in these fields, but rather a number of signposts to further discussion, in which we hope the people of Haringey generally, and of Broadwater Farm in particular, will be involved. Indeed the common thread of the topics covered in this chapter is that those who have power to make decisions affecting a community of people must consult with them, listen to them, learn from them, and modify their preconceptions accordingly. We ourselves have gone through this process. The experience of this Inquiry has confirmed for us that people addressing serious problems have experiences and ideas which those with any influence must treat with serious attention. Dolly Kiffin illustrated the point vividly for us with the aid of the carafe of water and plastic cup on the table beside her:—

LOOKING FORWARD: (2) BUILDING A SELF RELIANT COMMUNITY

"They must not come down to any community and just say, I am going to give you this bottle. Because the people might not want the bottle, they want this cup. They should be able to ask the people, what do they want? and then the people tell them that they want the cup."

THE ROLE OF CENTRAL GOVERNMENT
9.6 Different government departments have developed very different approaches to the Broadwater Farm Estate. We have noted earlier on the important work of the Priority Estates Project in not only helping to develop community organisations but also ensuring that those organisations have a voice in the Department of the Environment. We have also noted the personal interest which Sir George Young, Minister of State at the Department of the Environment, has shown in the successful innovations in housing management on the estate. On the other hand the Home Secretary seems to have taken very little interest in the estate as a community of residents when he visited police units around the estate in March 1986.

9.7 But the major impact of central government on housing and other local authority services has been caused by government policies on public expenditure — in particular, rate support grant penalties and rate capping. The amount of government contribution to Haringey's expenditure which has been cut back through the operation of these policies since 1979 has been massive. It has inevitably had an effect upon both the physical fabric of Broadwater Farm and the facilities available for the community. We have noted that the Department of the Environment in 1980 concluded that it would probably be necessary for the estate to be blown up. We believe along with Tricia Zipfel that the fact that it was not blown up is mainly a vindication of the community organisations on the estate. However the cut-backs reveal a striking inconsistency: the Department of the Environment's controls on spending were contributing to the very decline which the same Department's Priority Estates Programme was working to avoid. We believe, therefore, that there must be a considerable increase in the investment of public money in the areas of greatest deprivation and that this must be effected through the elected local authority rather than through a number of unrepresentative bodies.

9.8 There has been one specific and important anomaly in government expenditure which has affected Haringey in a discriminatory way. This concerns the status of the borough within the Urban Programme. Different local authorities have a different status within this programme, which means that they can claim a greater or lesser amount of government grants. The most favoured status is Partnership status, accorded to three London Boroughs, and after that Programme status, accorded to four London Boroughs. Haringey, although the sixth most deprived borough according to the Department of the Environment's own indicators (colloquially known as the "misery league"), has not been accorded either Partnership or Programme status. The achievement of Programme status would bring something between four and five million pounds into the deprived areas of Haringey in urban programme grants. The council's finance officer said in evidence to us about the rejection of Haringey's representations: --

"It is very difficult to understand why, because we feel that a strong case has been made. On the DOE's own measures of deprivation Haringey is rather more deprived that a number of authorities which do have Programme status."

We urge the Government to recognise the needs of the people of Haringey; and to grant Programme status to Haringey without delay.

9.9 There have also been inconsistencies in the way in which finance is distributed from central government. Recently, in June 1986, an application made by Haringey to the Department of the Environment's Urban Housing Renewal Unit was granted. As part of this application around half a million pounds has been allocated for housing improvement on the Broadwater Farm Estate. We welcome this significant input of financial resources. But the half million pounds has to be spent within the current financial year. This means that the building design team, which is now based on the estate for the purpose of listening to the ideas of local people, does not have time to carry out effective consultations about how the money should be spent. The borough is faced with the choice of either failing to spend much needed resources, or spending them without proper consultation. John Murray, of the council's Building Design Service, explained the problem in terms with which we agree —

"We must have economic planning over about three years. Even

LOOKING FORWARD: (2) BUILDING A SELF RELIANT COMMUNITY

the District Auditor had said that it is impossible for councils to plan in this way. It is obviously impossible on Broadwater Farm for us to do it sensibly because decisions are rushed, and foolish decisions are made, but rather than lose the money people will attempt to spend it."

9.10 Another area of direct impact of government policy concerns the funds available for spending by local authorities on economic development schemes. The only effective legal power possessed by local authorities for investment in business or co-operative enterprises is that given by Section 137 of the Local Government Act 1972 to spend amounts up to the product of a 2p rate in the pound on any projects which are considered beneficial to the borough and which are not otherwise authorised. Valuable use of this power has already been made to fund co-operatives on Broadwater Farm. But there are too many calls on the limited funds allowed by law. Haringey along with many other authorities in London has called on the government to double the amount which the council could spend on economic development schemes under this power, and we agree. Given the crushing unemployment which we consider below, it must be sensible for local authorities to have the greatest possible discretion to prioritise employment-generating schemes.

9.11 We emphasise that our ability to consider detailed overall policies for central government towards urban priority areas has been limited both by time and by the locally based nature of our Inquiry. The ideas discussed in the preceeding paragraphs are those which would have the most direct impact upon Broadwater Farm, but they are not comprehensive. The report of the Archbishop of Canterbury's Commission on Urban Priority Areas (*Faith in the City*) has made a more thorough examination of policies for such areas, and we broadly agree with its conclusions and recommendations.

THE CREATION OF JOBS
9.12 Being unemployed within British society is an experience of personal humiliation and social isolation. Even if many friends and relatives are also out of work, there are powerful social forces which underline the insecurity of being without a job. For the people of Broadwater Farm, household incomes are very low. 69% of the adults in our survey were without full time employment. Whilst for young white men aged 16–24, 47% were unemployed, whereas for young

Black men the figure was a terrible 83%. 94% of the adults see unemployment as a big problem. Many residents both young and old talked of the appalling effect of being without a job on the young people of the estate. We do not have to prove that unemployment has a disastrous effect on people's lives, nor that there is a growing lack of employment opportunities in the Broadwater Farm area. But while few people on Broadwater Farm have jobs, many would readily respond to a worthwhile job. Adeyemi Hinds, development worker with the Broadwater Farm Youth Association Co-operative, described the position:–

"The situation here is that there is a lot of bored people about, but at the same time there is a tremendous enthusiasm for getting things done, or to actually do something."

9.13 The people of the estate have demonstrated their ability to work hard at community regeneration. We are sure that they want to work hard also at the provision of employment opportunities. But just as we have seen the necessity of external intervention and assistance in other areas, the same is true of economic regeneration. As we show in paragraph 7.12 the residents of the estate possess minimal resources, hardly sufficient to enable them to purchase bare essentials, let alone provide the base for new initiatives and jobs. The estate needs external resources linked to internal initiatives and labour, to enable economic regeneration to take place. Leonardo Leon, treasurer of the Residents' Association, described how the potential was there to be tapped:–

"This place is a very effective work place. You have many problems here, but what struck me when I came is you also see people with a will to change things. Whatever we do here could be a test case, a showpiece for the country and for our communities."

9.14 The major loss of jobs in recent years has come from the reduction in the size of the manufacturing sector. Given the nature of employment in Haringey (some 44% of employed Haringey residents are employed outside the borough) it is necessary to look at the London economy as a whole. Some 534,000 manufacturing jobs were lost in London between 1971 and 1981. Within Haringey we know that the decline in industry is twice that of Brent, and unemployment was the highest in any borough in outer London in January 1986. In 1981 the Department of Employment's Labour Force Survey found that Black workers were in general concentrated in manufacturing

LOOKING FORWARD: (2) BUILDING A SELF RELIANT COMMUNITY

industries as opposed to other sectors: 27% of West Indian men compare to only 12% of White men worked in that sector. Consequently the contraction of the manufacturing sector has hit Haringey harder than other boroughs, and Black people harder than White.

9.15 It would be useless for this Inquiry to recommend that private enterprise should re-invest in the Haringey area in defiance of the logic of profits. National and international competition has undermined the economy base of London. However, local government can have an effect upon local private sector employment. Local authorities contract for a great many goods and services, and are in a position to insist that companies with whom they contract employ local labour. This would represent an extension of the practice of contract compliance, that is to insert conditions in contracts to require contracting companies to adopt policies for equal opportunities and good race relations. Positive action imposed by the power of the public purse could encourage private corporations to take a more responsible attitude to both local and ethnic employment. To be fully effective this proposal would need changes in the legislation which requires competitive tendering, but even within the existing law there are ways of persuading private companies to employ local labour, as Leonardo Leon told us:—

"We have been working on the idea of building workshops under some of the blocks. Now we got some building companies coming to us, and I remember in one meeting they put plans to us, and a youth there said 'all right, how many people are you prepared to employ from the estate on the project?' And they said, because they wanted to get the tender, 'we are prepared to employ anyone.' And he said "But how many will be working as assistants to the architects, not just bricklayers and painters? How many people are you prepared to train for two or three weeks, so they can learn a proper job, be more professional?' and they were surprised and they said 'we will consider it'."

This example shows the power of dialogue with local people. If the ideas whereby conditions are inserted in contracts being discussed at that meeting were implemented, it would be to the benefit both of the private employer and of the people of the estate.

9.16 The largest employers of labour in Haringey and in London generally are in the public sector. It is impossible to construct any plan for employment without taking that sector into account. The London Borough of Haringey has continued to increase employment opportunities throughout the past six years: but we question the extent to which these opportunities have been available to ethnic minority applicants.

9.17 As they have been keeping and maintaining ethnic records of their workforce for some time, we would expect that they would be taking the necessary positive actions that would ensure a more equitable distribution of employment opportunities.

9.18 We turn next to the field of small businesses and co-operatives, which as a form of employment regeneration has considerable support from the residents of Broadwater Farm. People see running their own business or playing a part in a co-operative as not only providing a job but giving some element of control over their work. Over the past few years there have been a number of co-operative enterprises started on Broadwater Farm with support from the council's Economic Development Unit. Grants have been made to the Launderette (£44,187 plus £2,500 loan); the Photographic project (£39,000); and the Youth Association for the development of the Co-operative (£25,880 plus £3000 loan). Such grants were of great significance in enabling projects to be launched. But limited as they were by the constraints of Section 137 (see paragraph 9.10) they can only be a small part of the solution to the estate's investment needs. We have received criticisms of the Economic Development Unit to the effect that they are unnecessarily bureaucratic in their operation. We learned also from the evidence of the Economic Development Unit's officers that they have in 1985/86 fully achieved their target of allocating 40% of available funds to enterprises run by Black and minority ethnic people. We urge the council to continue this priority, and to continue to fund enterprises on the estate to the limit.

9.19 However, the role of a local authority is necessarily limited. The problem in this field is the provision of finance capital to provide a base for economic development. Traditional sources of finance have failed to provide such a base. Banks and other private financial institutions claim that the business enterprises put forward are not ones which can guarantee a return for their depositors. Accordingly the initiatives have been left to public agencies and the results so far achieved have been minimal in comparison to the scale of the problem.

LOOKING FORWARD: (2) BUILDING A SELF RELIANT COMMUNITY

9.20 Because of the overwhelming importance of economic regeneration, we decided to commission a study from the consultancy firm Equinox into the possibilities for the development of small businesses and co-operatives on the estate. Their report merits detailed study by all involved in the consideration of this question. They identified the principal elements which are necessary for enterprise development as being: —
1. The availability of willing entrepreneurs; the report traces the pattern of discrimination against Black entrepreneurs, and describes the various structural forms which a business can adopt.
2. The need for profitability and a sufficient market.
3. The need for adequate capital and credit; the report identifies the various schemes operated by central and local government to provide loans or guarantees for businesses which would find difficulties in raising capital on the private market.
4. The need for management and technical expertise: the report criticises the lack of hard business know-how in the economic development units of local authorities which try to give advice in this field.

The report also identifies certain possible business projects which we discuss below.

9.21 The agency which has recently been set up on Broadwater Farm to promote economic development is the Broadwater Farm Youth Association Co-op Limited. The ways in which the co-operative will participate in particular economic projects is still under discussion, and the Equinox report offers a number of possible structures. It seems to us that two initiatives — one already under way, the other only in the planning stage — are central to the capacity of the co-operative to promote significant economic regeneration. First the co-operative is in the course of carrying out a skills survey on the estate. This will give two important sets of information. First, the skills which people living on the estate possess will be known. In economic terms we will know the full extent that labour power on the estate can be used to create wealth. Secondly, the survey will reveal the numbers of people on the estate who not only want to develop their skills working for other people, but who also want to act as entrepreneurs themselves. Both sets of information, which are not yet gathered in a form that we can take account of, will be of great assistance in making economic plans for the estate.

9.22 The other necessary foundation for development would be the establishment of a financial holding company as a part of the co-operative. The co-operative has a wealth of possible ventures for the community, but it lacks finance and technical back-up. The lack of capital is the most pressing problem. To obtain that capital the co-operative will need an organisational base, together with a high level of financial skills. In the United States there are examples of responsible finance capital and other organisations assisting inner city groups to develop by providing their skills without charge. We believe that the same could be true in Britain, given a similar commitment to social responsibility by financial institutions.

9.23 There is space on the estate for the physical location of small businesses. The council has put forward a plan for building a number of workshops under the walkways along Willan Road. Because of the construction of the estate, there is space for such workshops without interfering with the residential amenities. The Department of the Environment is presently determining whether to support this plan: we would commend it strongly as a most appropriate use of space and as an essential prerequisite to the generation of employment.

9.24 A further element in the back-up needed would be a specially designed training programme. Since the estate will have a full analysis of available and potential skills, together with several possible marketable ideas, the necessary training programme for managerial and craft skills should be easy to construct. Many of these programmes should be carried out on the estate itself. The workshops could also provide a base for training. We would hope that the two further education colleges run by Haringey and the two local polytechnics in Middlesex and North London would be able to provide staff time in this venture. All four institutions have a specific brief for the involvement of the community in further and higher education. Broadwater Farm, where the community has a clear view of what it needs, would provide a prefect opportunity to demonstrate that commitment.

9.25 Lastly, but most significantly, there are already a number of specific ideas for co-operative developments on the estate. Three co-operatives have been formed: the launderette, the fruit and vegetable shop, and the hairdressing salon have all managed to establish themselves at a time when many small businesses were

LOOKING FORWARD: (2) BUILDING A SELF RELIANT COMMUNITY

struggling to survive. There are three further organisations in existence which are in the process of becoming co-operative ventures. First, the photographic project has provided a useful service to the estate, and could be the basis of further training. Secondly, the sewing and dressmaking project has established itself over several years as a part of the life of the estate, and is now in a position to develop an organisation of home workers for the machinists that live on the estate. Finally, the restaurant in the Youth Association already provides meals for residents, and could develop a catering service for events within the borough.

9.26 For the future, there are no less than six other possible ideas that have emerged in discussion between the people of the estate and the consultancy firm Equinox: —

(1). **A radio station and music studio.** People are not only interested in listening to music or radio, but they are also very capable of making it. In other areas of high unemployment, notably Sheffield, Consett and Sunderland, recording studios have been built; the studio in Sheffield is of the highest international standard. A well run studio is likely to attract artists from outside the estate and the borough to come in and use the facilities, using musicans on the estate as session artists. Radio is an area where Black people are under-represented although they form a sizeable target audience. The Home Office is at this moment monitoring a scheme to provide very local radio licenses, and we believe that a radio station would be a project that will be well received by the residents of the estate. A sound proofed studio would have to be built which could be used for both these ventures.

(2). **A radio controlled mini-cab service.** A number of people on the estate own cars which could be used for the provision of a mini-cab service, which could be particularly viable if it obtained contracts from public organisations.

(3). **A motor repair and servicing garage.** Again this service could make use of skills already existing on the estate. Potential customers could be drawn from large public organisations which own fleets of cars, such as the council. It could be expanded to include a used car supermarket.

(4). **A construction company.** Construction remains one of the real possibilities for the estate to develop a labour-intensive industry. The area surrounding the estate has a constant demand for housing improvement. The estate itself has also continued to need reconstruction. All the money spent on the estate may well assist in improving the environment, but it does not provide local jobs. There was particular ill feeling expressed to us about a recent contract for painting the concrete pillars under the blocks which did not involve any local people. A local construction company would change this. The company could act as a contractor for work by the council, although members of the co-operative are aware that discussion would have to be held with the council's direct labour organisation in order to secure amicable agreement about the distribution of council work.

(5). **Light assembly and repair facilities in high technology.** There is considerable interest in using one of the workshops for the assembly and repair of computers. A major computer company could be encouraged to become involved as partners in the development of this idea, helping to train young people on the estate for careers in computer repair, which is now becoming a growth area.

(6). **A supermarket or mini-market.** The shopping precinct on Tangmere has never been fully developed as an economic unit, and many of its shops are at present empty. A comprehensive shopping centre would be of great value to residents on the estate, but it would be unlikely to be profitable if it only sold to people on the estate. People would have to be attracted from outside. In terms of car parking this is quite feasible; the problem is to challenge the reputation of Broadwater Farm as an undesirable place to visit.

9.27 These six ideas are further discussed in the Equinox report. Clearly a great deal of further work is necessary before any of them could be put forward as a feasible project. The exact structure of such businesses needs careful thought and consultation, and we would wish to ensure that in the selection and development of enterprises on the estate there was not a dominance of participation by men to the exclusion of women. The ideas are imaginative, and they indicate the determination of residents to construct employment opportunities. But their ideas and commitment are not enough to bring about the reality. Private and public enterprise, both nationally and locally, need to take these hopes and projects seriously. They need help with finance, expert advice, and markets. People on the estate have moved this far through their own efforts; it is vital that their efforts should not be ignored by those in the outside world who have the power to help.

LOOKING FORWARD: (2) BUILDING A SELF RELIANT COMMUNITY

THE ESTATE AND ITS ENVIRONMENT
9.28 Building a large council estate represents an enormous organisational task. It calls upon a wide range of professional and craft skills. A thousand-dwelling estate like Broadwater Farm could only be successfully completed in a few years, if all of these skills were deployed to the highest standard. In fact, as we have noted, there were physical problems resulting from design errors in the construction of the estate which have had, and continued to have, an impact on the lives of the residents. However, the council in building the estate built no facilities which were adequate to enable a community of residents to develop. We have seen at Broadwater Farm how new residents were arriving all the time, adjusting to a new environment, nearly all of them living on an estate for the first time, needing assistance and services which were not there.

9.29 We have seen that four factors coincided to save Broadwater Farm from total decline. First, there were members of the local community who were prepared to start from nothing and retain their hope against all the odds. Secondly, there were a number of trusted local community leaders who at crucial points were catalysts in the organisation of change. Thirdly, the local authority was willing to change its structures and to admit great errors in its previous actions. Fourthly, there was skilful support from outside from the Priority Estates Project of the Department of the Environment.

9.30 What of the future? We have seen that the majority of residents are still concerned about the lack of facilities on the estate. There remains nowhere for people to go who do not fit into the activities of the Youth Association or the Mothers' Project. A proper community centre is an essential next step. Funds have been allocated, and discussions about its location and design will take place with the design team of the council's Building Design Service. Sheila Ramdin, chair of the Residents' Association, explained her ideas for the new centre: —

"Activities for the young, old, and middle-aged. We used to have a bingo session downstairs for the old age pensioners in the social club. When we build this new place we want to have a place where people can come with their kids and relax and have a drink. There should be a place where the kids can go and play. Probably there would be keep-fit, dance classes, bingo sessions again, and if people wanted to hire the place for private dos, they could."

Leonardo Leon made the point that a new community centre should be for the whole area, not only for the estate:—

"If it is ever built, I don't think we will mind if it is placed on the fringes of the estate. We would like ourselves to be in charge and to administer it. But we are working not only for the estate but for the whole area."

In this connection we were pleased to hear the evidence of Anne Musselwhite, who represented the Mount Pleasant Residents' Association, and who said that she and her association would be pleased to be involved as a user of a community centre situated in an accessible place.

9.31 We have received other proposals for specific amenities on and around the estate. There is a proposal which has already been broadly approved for an arts workshop in one of the Tangmere shops. Some people have expressed the need for a doctor's surgery, which was originally part of the design of the estate. There is a need also which many people have spoken of, for a bus service to go through the centre of the estate. If as we believe an adequate case in terms of demand is made out, we can see no reason why London Regional Transport should not meet this need. Where a community of three thousand people have access roads running through, and the level of car ownership is low, it would seem logical for a bus service to go down those roads and serve that community. If LRT does not respond, then a private mini-bus enterprise could well be valuable on the estate, travelling at regular intervals to the High Road and to Wood Green.

9.32 We spoke in Chapter 2 of the grave under-use of the Lordship Recreation Ground, which had been brought to our notice particularly by the Haringey Sports Council. This is an amenity which many housing estates would much desire to have on their doorstep. We understand from the Community Affairs Department that they have over some years proposed a major leisure and environmental package for the Recreation Ground but nothing has been done, partly through lack of resources, and partly perhaps because the Recreation Ground has not been high on the priorities of the community. But we feel that with imagination and pressure from the community there could be much more benefit to be derived by the people of the estate from this important open space.

LOOKING FORWARD: (2) BUILDING A SELF RELIANT COMMUNITY

9.33 In relation to all these specific ideas it is not our business to speak for the community, for they are well capable of speaking for themselves. The essence of the message to be learned from the last few years on Broadwater Farm is that participation of residents in all aspects of the development of an estate is essential if acceptable and successful decisions are to be taken. It is no good at all to have council estates with well organised community groups unless they can play a full part in the management of the affairs of the estate. It is towards this goal that a policy of full decentralisation must be aimed. The Neighbourhood Office and the Broadwater Farm Panel have made considerable progress to this end. People are beginning to feel that they have a say. They are beginning to feel that their Neighbourhood Office will represent them against the faceless council bureaucrats. They have plans to develop their own expertise on the estate, and as we have seen, to provide their own employment organisations. We would urge the council to develop this policy of decentralisation of power as fully as possible. In particular the powers of the Broadwater Farm Panel over the disbursement of finances on the estate should be extended. One of central government's main arguments against increasing local government expenditure is that money is in some way lost and does not get spent on the sort of activities that it is meant to be spent on. We believe that the more local communities, in conjunction with their local authority representatives, can play a role in the expenditure of resources, then the more likely it is that they will be targeted most accurately to the greatest areas of need.

9.34 So far as the financing of community organisations themselves is concerned, we applaud the allocation of grants which have been made in the past to the Youth Association and other bodies. As we have described in Chapter 2, the funds granted have been well used. We note however that some of the community groups have complained that they were given insufficient grants, in addition to their basic expenditure needs, to employ the necessary accountants to assist them in carrying out their tasks. We would urge all grant giving authorities to make sure that as well as providing the money for service expenditure they also provide sufficient top-up to allow community groups to obtain the professional back-up for the organising of their accounts.

9.35 Finally we should make some comment on the housing allocation policy of the council. Between 1976 and 1981 there were some six separate reports put before the housing committee which proposed different kinds of modification to the policies for allocating tenancies on Broadwater Farm. There were a number of problems common to all these reports. First, they have all been unable to deal with the issue of racism in housing allocation because the statistics based upon ethnic monitoring of housing allocation did not exist. We know from reports from other London boroughs that racism is one of the important components of some housing allocation policies, and it seems quite possible that it is so within the London Borough of Haringey. But we do not know, because the important commitment to ethnic monitoring of this system has not been carried out. Until this happens with all housing statistics, it is going to be impossible for the council adequately to implement an anti racist housing policy. We are aware that housing officers were recommending ethnic record-keeping since at least the mid 1970s, and we are surprised that nothing effective has yet been done. We urge the council to take this in hand without delay.

9.36 The second common feature of allocation policy on Broadwater Farm is that the council in attempting to engage (as one of their reports stated) in social engineering, caused considerable restriction of choice, and in the event failed to achieve the desired balance. For once the initial estate population has come together through the first allocation, people's choices to move onto and out of the estate are taken on the basis of a number of factors which the council cannot directly control. For example once the estate gained the reputation of being an unpleasant place to live, many people refused to move onto the estate because of that reputation. And therefore the estate became tenanted, particularly, by homeless people who were given no choice. To change the mix of people on the estate would have required changing that reputation, which in turn would mean dealing with the conditions which had brought the estate a bad name. Since this was never taken on board, the many changes in housing allocation over the late 1970s and early 1980s were simply affecting people at the very margin who had little choice in any case. For the overall pattern was that, in their anxiety to fill the voids (the empty flats on the estate) the council was pushing people in who had no choice but to accept the offer made to them.

9.37 The changes in allocation policy, particularly the decision to give homeless people a second choice, have had some marginal effect upon the estate. However the real changes in the nature of the estate have come about through a much more comprehensive housing policy relationship between the people on the estate and the housing management office. Quite simply, people will want to be allocated a tenancy in an estate which is well run, well maintained, and has good community facilities. Housing allocation policy has to be part of a much wider housing framework. We note that housing allocation policy in Haringey is being comprehensively reviewed at this moment, with a discussion document being considered by tenants' associations and other relevant bodies. We would urge full member involvement, and also full consultation with organisations on the estate, in the allocation of housing on Broadwater Farm.

PARTICIPATION IN EDUCATION

9.38 The inquiry has received reports and held interviews with senior staff of the Haringey College, the Tottenham Technical College, the Adult Education Institute, and a number of primary and secondary schools including all the schools on the estate, as well as receiving written and oral evidence from the council's Education Service. The material which we have received suggests that many school leavers and older youth on the Broadwater Farm estate are resentful of formal education and schooling, because of their past school experiences. The education system has failed young Black people in particular. Teachers with whom we spoke considered that while Black pupils were as intelligent and creative as White pupils, many left school with poor literacy in written English, and with little understanding of the formal techiques and application of scientific knowledge. The potential which many people possessed was not developed by the schools that they attended nor by further education, where there is a lower than average take-up compared with other areas.

9.39 There was a report published in 1984 by HM Inspectors on *Educational provision and response in some Haringey schools*, which presented a "rather depressing picture". They noted a higher than average incidence of non-attendance; disruptive and unacceptable behaviour; and undemanding work. They found that careers education was generally underdeveloped, and the transfer rate to further education was lower than in other authorities. Examination results in GCE 'O' Level and CSE were disappointing. Their overall conclusion was that "with a few notable exceptions, the quality of the education being received by older junior and secondary pupils ranged from mediocre to poor". The picture was particular gloomy for Black pupils. A local Black Pressure Group on Education was formed in 1975 because, in the words of the group, "a lot of us saw that the education system in Haringey was not catering for the Black children that are born here".

9.40 We have not been able to study the education system in Haringey in such depth as to be able to offer a comprehensive programme for tackling the serious problems that exist. However, we have no doubt that for Haringey's Education Service there is an urgent need for actions which will make a reality of the council's firm anti-racist position. These actions should include: a thorough scrutiny of the curriculum to eradicate racist bias from school studies and promote an anti-racist and a multi-cultural approach (making full use of the resources of the Multi-Cultural Curriculum Resource Unit); in-service training of teachers in countering racism; and a commitment to positive action to recruit Black people as teachers and other staff at all levels.

9.41 It was accepted by the Education Service in their evidence to us that there were few Black teachers in Haringey schools in proportion to the numbers of Black people in Haringey. The exact position is impossible to state because of the failure of the Education Service to carry through a policy of ethnic monitoring of teachers. In the context of Broadwater Farm, this under-representation was plainly apparent to us. In the junior and infant schools adjacent to the estate there were no Black teaching staff before October 1985. Councillor Martha Osamor, who became chair of the schools sub-committee in May 1986, spoke strongly on this issue:—
> "The need for us to have in schools, teachers that represent the community of that particular school becomes very, very crucial. Because if we don't, our young people will grow up and come out with nothing. Not coming out with a proper education, but also coming out confused. So what I personally hope to see within the school is for us to see a radical change within the structure, being from the nursery upwards."

9.42 We also believe that the Education Service must take planned initiatives to go out to community organisations and involve people in consultation and discussion about the service which is being provided.

LOOKING FORWARD: (2) BUILDING A SELF RELIANT COMMUNITY

We doubt whether the existing parent/teacher structures are adequate for this purpose. People on Broadwater Farm have felt that the arrangements for consultation and public participation, which have been so successfully adopted in the Housing Management field, have not been attempted in the field of education. For example, at the local level, personnel involved in education services which are relevant to the estate should be represented at inter-agency meetings and at the Broadwater Farm Panel meeting. There they could discuss the problems with many community representatives who include not only parents but others, such as ex-students, who would have a valuable input. At a borough level, there are many minority ethnic organisations who ought to be involved in a dialogue about the effectiveness of the education service for the children of their communities.

9.43 So far as the various stages of education are concerned, we are clear that the provision of facilities for the under-fives is still inadequate and needs to be extended. The Willan Road Day Nursery has made a remarkable contribution, but much more is needed. So far as primary and secondary schooling are concerned we are not in a position to make particular recommendations over and above the important comments which we make about anti-racist policies and about consultation.

9.44 Given the shortcomings of the education service in the past the role of further and adult education is crucial. It is here that we feel there is a particular need for dialogue between community organisations on the estate and educational personnel. There will soon be available the results of the skills survey carried out by the Youth Association Co-operative. Once skills have been identified, there will be a need to consider how they can be extended and made marketable. Specific programmes tailored to residents on the estate can be elaborated. We are aware that there are courses available at the Tottenham Technical College and the Haringey College which could be of immense value to Broadwater Farm residents. In the event, not many men attend; whilst a lot of women enrol, there is a high drop out rate. The causes for this must be discussed and dealt with. As in all other fields, the more that those responsible for the provision of the education service can come into Broadwater Farm and discuss problems face to face, the more that there will be a constructive take-up of the important courses which they provide.

MEDIA REPORTING

9.45 Finally, the people of Broadwater Farm ask for fair recognition in the outside world of who they are, what they have done, and what they hope still to achieve. Several people saw this Inquiry as the means of redressing a gross distortion for which they held the mass media responsible. H. Gordon of the defence campaign said this:−

"What I would like to see from the Inquiry is truth come out. I would like see all that has been achieved brought out, the fact that we had Princess Diana come down here, or the programmes that were set up on the estate, how well it was progressing because the community had actually worked. I would like to see all that printed up and stated. It would go a long way to easing some of what's being said, and would take out from me a lot of real anger at some of the things that have been said about Broadwater Farm. Because I do feel angry."

9.46 In our view the anger was justified. We have examined the coverage a total of 25 newspapers for the period from October 1985 to May 1986; 15 were national papers, four were local, three provincial, one London-wide and four ethnic minority. In Chapter 6 we summarised the reporting of the disturbances and the estate itself. We noted how a series of racially slanted reports described the estate as the place where Whites and Asians lived in fear and vilified Councillor Grant as a figure to be hated and ridiculed. We noted that in contrast to the prominence given to PC Blakelock, his life and his family, Mrs Cynthia Jarrett was virtually ignored. There were no reports of the comments of her family and friends about the sort of person she was and why she came to this country. This coverage left the reader no opportunity for empathy and understanding.

9.47 Towards the end of October some of the national press began to direct its attention to Dolly Kiffin under various headlines: **"Dolly and her Dynasty"**, **"The rise and rise of Dolly Kiffin"**, **"Dolly's club cash under the spotlight"**, **"Police probe a riot estate's godmother"**. A systematic campaign of defamation of Dolly Kiffin was orchestrated and still continues. It appears to be intended to discredit her and remove her from her position of trust in the Broadwater Farm Youth Association. It may also be an attempt to destroy the Youth Association itself. One such report led directly to a Fraud Squad investigation of the accounts of the Youth Association and other organisations on the estate. We cannot comment on this investigation

LOOKING FORWARD: (2) BUILDING A SELF RELIANT COMMUNITY

in any detail as it still continues, except that we record that the integrity of the officers of these organisations has been praised by many witnesses who have been directly concerned with them.

9.48 The impression gained through all the reports since 6th October has been that there was no positive relationship between Black and White people on the estate at all. There was no mention of the excellent meal service for the mainly White elderly, and other activities which White people attended at the Youth Association building and in other places around the estate. There was nothing said of how the campaign to improve the estate, which was spearheaded by the Tenants' Association and Youth Association, had created a great deal of work which had benefitted White people as well as Black. It has meant more White cleaners, caretakers, repair workers and staff at the housing office. The press did not mention that a great many of the people who are working on the estate, many of whom also live there, are White and Asian people who have spoken warmly and positively about their relationships with Black people. Nothing was said about the fact that many of the families on the estate are inter-racial, or are living in multi-racial households. The press set out to emphasise contrast and divisions.

9.49 Black organisations, who over the past few years have been able to receive for the first time, grant aid from central and local government, are now being held up as irresponsible and untrustworthy. There is talk of "unscrupulous local leaders" receiving grants and stirring up racial hatred and riot. Individuals have been defamed, and the public, having no other source of information but the press, tend to accept the information given by the press about particular people. In one article, Dolly Kiffin was described as "just an ordinary West Indian mother with her own talents but without the intellectual capacity to run a high profile political campaign". They say "she has been manipulated by the far left". So we are faced with another stereotype, and that is of the Black person who is not really as clever and as able as he or she seems to be. If a Black person shows the immense ability, commitment and toughness that Dolly Kiffin has done, it is implied that there must be someone manipulating her, because according to the stereotype Black people do not possess such qualities.

9.50 Our report has shown in detail much of what has in fact

THE BROADWATER FARM INQUIRY REPORT

happened during and since the disturbances. The information which we obtained could have been gathered by the press if it had made the effort to do so. When the press chooses to campaign on social issues and carry out major investigations into areas of social concern, it has a first class ability to ferret out information and to bring about change. We remain confident that the press can play an active, positive and critical role in improving race relations and community relations and we believe it has the right to express itself about areas of concern. We believe however it should do so with responsibility and with regard to the major influence it has for change for better or for worse.

9.51 In 1975 the National Union of Journalists laid down its first set of guidelines for journalists. Two of these were: only mention someone's race and nationality if strictly relevant; and resist the temptation to sensationalise issues which would harm race relations. These were added to in 1977 when a joint agreement between the National Union of Journalists and the National Graphical Association stated that:—

"Freedom must be conditioned by responsibility and acknowledgement by all media workers, of the need not to allow press freedom to be abused, to slander a section of the community or to promote the evil of racism."

We would urge that the N.U.J guidelines and the N.U.J/N.G.A agreement be rigorously enforced and to become a disciplinary matter in those unions. The Press Council should adopt similar principles and implement them against proprietors who breach them. Furthermore the unions and the Press Council should be monitoring press coverage of sensitive issues and major public disturbances.

9.52 We are concerned not only with the adults of today but with the adults, Black and White, of tomorrow. There has been major research done, which was summarised by Sara Goodman Zimet in her book *Print and Prejudice,* in these terms:—

"When characters belonging to minority groups are presented in a favourable light the attitudes of readers moved in a positive direction. However when characters belonging to minority groups were presented in an unfavourable light attitudes of readers moved in a negative direction...The research shows that the more attractive and desirable the models, the greater the likelihood that the reader will be able to identify with them personally and therefore feel positively towards those characters'"

LOOKING FORWARD: (2) BUILDING A SELF RELIANT COMMUNITY

We fear for the children who are being presented with negative images of Black people through the press – images which teach a Black child to feel undervalued and to be ashamed, and which teach a White child the so-called superior values of Whiteness. We believe that the ordinary White British person would be more ready to accept the ideas of racial justice and of equal opportunities if these were properly explained and not negatively sensationalised.

CONCLUSION
9.53 We have enjoyed complete independence in the conduct of this Inquiry. We now present our Report to the Council of the London Borough of Haringey, and at the same time to the people of Broadwater Farm Estate and to the wider population of Haringey. We regret the reasons which led to the Inquiry being set up, but we have been privileged to have been part of it. We have each gained in knowledge and understanding from what we have heard and read. We have seen how the human spirit can face real and desperate problems and overcome them. We conclude our work believing that although Broadwater Farm last October passed through the most tragic days of its history, there are people enough on the estate, in the surrounding area, in council offices, in the police service, and elsewhere, who have the courage and ability to help build a united and successful community for the future.

LIST OF WITNESSES AT THE PUBLIC HEARINGS
(In the order in which they gave evidence)

Name	Organisation
Dolly Kiffin	*Founder, Broadwater Farm Youth Association.*
Stafford Scott	*Youth Worker, Broadwater Farm Youth Association.*
Mr Jarrett	
Floyd Jarrett	
Clasford Sterling	*Vice President, Broadwater Farm Youth Association.*
Harry Adams	*Youth Worker, Broadwater Farm Youth Association.*
Millard Scott	*Volunteer Worker, Broadwater Farm Youth Association.*
Neale Coleman	*Neighbourhood Officer, Broadwater Farm.*
Andy Sansom	*Caretaker, Broadwater Farm Estate.*
Russell Simper	*Estate Supervisor, Broadwater Farm Estate.*
Beverley Scott	
Joanne George	*Social Services Community Worker.*
Rupert Downing	*Social Services Community Worker.*
Michael Hutchinson-Reis	*Social Worker, Broadwater Farm.*
Gabriel Black	*Solicitor.*
Cliff Ford	*Sweeper, Broadwater Farm Estate.*
John Lea	*Building Design Service, London Borough of Haringey*
Councillor Narendra Makanji	*Chair of Finance Committee, London Borough of Haringey.*
Richard Williams	*Finance Department, London Borough of Haringey.*

THE BROADWATER FARM INQUIRY REPORT

Councillor Bernie Grant	*Leader, London Borough of Haringey.*
Ann Musselwhite	*Mount Pleasant Residents' Association.*
Mr Kemp	
Mrs Kemp	
Councillor Mitchell	*Conservative Councillor, London Borough of Haringey.*
George Martin	*West Indian Leadership Council.*
Vernon Moore	*West Indian Leadership Council.*
Tina Kent	*Social Worker, Welcare.*
Leonardo Leon	*Treasurer, Residents' Association, Broadwater Farm.*
Tricia Zipfel	*Consultant, Priority Estates Project.*
Jeff Crawford	*Senior Community Relations Officer, Haringey Community Relations Council.*
Chris Kavallares	*Chair, H.C.R.C.*
Hyacinth Moody	*Chair, Police Liaison Committee, H.C.R.C.*
Leslie Cohen	*Secretary, Police Liaison Committee, H.C.R.C.*
Eddie Wedderburn	*Hon. Secretary, H.C.R.C.*
Maureen Bailey	*Officer, Haringey Independent Police Committee.*
T. Lenney	*Chief Education Officer, London Borough of Haringey.*
R. Jones	*Deputy Chief Education Officer.*
G. Kerr	*Education Officer for Further Education.*
M. Moncombe	*Education Officer for Schools.*
M. Tolhurst	*Assistant Education Officer for Further Education.*
Reverend Wheaton	*Minister, Miller Memorial Methodist Church.*

LIST OF WITNESSES

Ernie Large	*Former Councillor, London Borough of Haringey.*
Ronnie Roach	*Senior Playleader, Broadwater Farm Play Centre.*
Councillor Peter Chalk	*Labour Councillor, West Green Ward.*
Michael Keith	*Researcher, St Catherine's College, Oxford.*
Jonathan Cave	*Head of Economic Development Unit, London Borough of Haringey.*
Peter Wiess	*Deputy Head, Economic Development Unit, London Borough of Haringey.*
Frank Newall	*Housing Allocation Officer, London Borough of Haringey.*
Debbie Wilde	*Officer, Police Research Unit, London Borough of Haringey.*
Eric Clarke	*Chair, Haringey Community and Police Consultative Group.*
Tony Ward	*Officer, Inquest.*
Dave Leadbetter	*Officer, Inquest.*
William Trant	*Director, Community Development Project, West Indian Standing Conference.*
Dudley Dryden	*Representative of West Indian Standing Conference.*
Mr Charles	*Membership Officer, West Indian Standing Conference.*
Sheila Ramdin	*Chair, Residents' Association, Broadwater Farm Estate.*
Cllr. Martha Osamor	*Chair, Police Sub-Committee, London Borough of Haringey.*
Andy Shallice	*Researcher, Runnymede Trust.*
H. Gordon	*Representative of Broadwater Farm Defence Campaign.*

THE BROADWATER FARM INQUIRY REPORT

Mary John-Baptiste	*Outreach Worker for youth/women, Haringey Independent Police Committee.*
Gwen Bart	*Solicitor.*
Arthur Lawrence	*West Indian Leadership Council.*
Roy Limb	*Chief Executive, London Borough of Haringey.*
Howard Simmons	*Head of Community Services, London Borough of Haringey.*
Reverend Ackroyd	*United Reform Church.*
Reverend Ashworth	*Catholic Church.*
Reverend Evans	*Anglican Church.*
Mr Norton	*Salvation Army.*
Mrs Norton	*Salvation Army.*
Reverend Goodridge	*Community Church of God.*
Reverend Scott	*Redemption Church of God.*
Reverend Ingledew	*Church of England.*
Laxmi Jamdagni	*Community Development Officer, Broadwater Farm.*
Councillor Steve Banerji	*Former Chair of Police Sub-Committee, London Borough of Haringey.*
Nick Wright	*Head of Police Research Unit, London Borough of Haringey.*
Caroline Ricketts	*Officer, Police Research Unit, London Borough of Haringey.*
John Murray	*Building Design Service, London Borough of Haringey.*

List of People Interviewed

Pat Ford	*Former Chair, Tenants' Association, Broadwater Farm.*
Evelyn Oldfield	*Community Worker, Area Management to Tottenham, London Borough of Haringey.*

LIST OF WITNESSES

Norton McLean	*Principal Youth Officer, London Borough of Haringey.*
Mike Bates	*Youth Worker, London Borough of Haringey.*
Wesley Mendonca	*Former Community Development Worker, Broadwater Farm.*
Barry Simons	*Former Senior Housing Officer, London Borough of Haringey.*
Malcolm Sargison	*Former Social Services Community Worker, Broadwater Farm.*
Ann Sargison	*Former Chair Broadwater Farm Tenants' Association.*
Mr Ewell	*Senior Education Welfare Officer, London Borough of Haringey.*
Mr Reid	*Senior Education Welfare Officer, London Borough of Haringey.*
Dr Williams	*Principal, Tottenham Technical College.*
Adeyemi Hinds	*Co-operative Development Worker, Broadwater Farm Youth Association Co-op*
Mike Cummins	*Race Relations Policy Adviser, London Borough of Haringey*
Salem El-Doori	*Architect, London Borough of Haringey.*
Julian Ruddoch	*Former Community Affairs Officer, London Borough of Haringey.*
Hugh Sutherland	*Carpenter, Repairs Service, Broadwater Farm.*
David Whitfield	*Journalist.*
Nadine Finch	*Former Community Development Worker, London Borough of Haringey.*
Pat Tonge	*Former Councillor, London Borough of Haringey.*

THE BROADWATER FARM INQUIRY REPORT

Joy Shriver	*Head of Home Helps, Tottenham.*
Reverend Rushmore Smith	*Minister, Westbury Avenue Baptist Church.*
Mr Smith	*Headteacher, Northumberland Park School.*
Mr Fitzpatrick	*Head of Youth Training Scheme, Haringey College.*
Mr Jackson	*Multi Cultural Curriculum Support Group, London Borough of Haringey.*
Mr Evans	*Headteacher, Langham School.*
Mr Baker	*Headteacher, Moselle School.*
Mr Veronique	*Adult Education Service.*
Wendy Forest	*Youth Training Scheme Officer, Tottenham College.*
Juliet Burdett	*Head of Homeworkers, Broadwater Farm.*
Mr Kennedy	*Area Chief Officer, London Fire Brigade.*

In addition we conducted full interviews with 40 people who asked not to be named.

The list does not include those interviewed who later gave oral evidence.

INDEX

Adams, Harry, 89.
Adams, Mr, 74, 75, 78.
Allan, PC, 67, 70, 72-75, 78.
Anderson, Tony, 36.
Anderson, Diane, 46.
Atkins, Robert, 36.
Atkinson, Glenys, 50.
Atkinson, Norman, 207.

Banerji, Steve, 93.
Bart, Gwen, 136.
Bates, Mike, 58, 90.
Betts, PC, 48.
Birmingham City Council, 3.
Black on Black, 43.
Black, Gabriel, 136, 137, 139.
Blakelock, PC Keith, 3, 8, 9, 117, 119, 126, 128, 146, 240.
Blom, Tracey, 66.
Bonham Carter, Mark, 4.
Bowell, Sergeant, 71, 72, 74.
Brixton, 4, 37, 61.
Broadwater Farm Defence Campaign, 131, 148, 192, 240.
Broadwater Farm Infants' School, 17, 129.
Broadwater Farm Junior School, 17, 109, 129.
Broadwater Farm Panel, 30, 54-55, 207, 235, 239.
Broadwater Farm Tenants' Association, 16, 19, 20, 24, 29, 31.
Broadwater Farm Youth Association, 8, 13, 24-29, 33, 34, 39-42, 49, 50, 57, 59, 93, 94, 120, 123, 150, 157, 158, 175, 221, 233, 235, 241.
Broadwater Review, 56.

Caribbean Times, 167.
Carnell, Bernard, 81, 82.
Casey, PC, 67-75.
Caton, PC Roger, 98.
Clarke, Eric, 90, 208, 209.
Clarke, Inspector, 69, 71, 72, 74, 77, 78, 203.
Coleman, Neale, 30, 32, 41, 54, 60, 63, 125, 149.
Commissioner of Police, 4, 9-11, 52, 53, 55, 81, 82, 112, 115, 143, 205, 207, 213, 217.
Couch, Chief Superintendent, 39, 40, 41, 44, 48, 50, 51, 54, 58, 59, 62, 63,

74, 87, 90, 92, 104, 111, 112, 116, 119, 124, 193, 196.
Crawford, Jeff, 90.

Daily Express, 124.
Daily Mail, 124, 125.
Daily Mirror, 124, 125, 140.
De Geneste, Superintendent Henry, 39.
Department of the Environment, 13, 18, 32, 223, 224, 233.
Dickinson, Commander, 38, 42-44, 49, 53, 54, 55-56.
Director of Public Prosecutions, 83.
Diverse Reports, 44, 132, 173.
Downing, Rupert, 58, 132, 146.
Dryden, Dudley, 209, 214.

El-Doori, Salem, 14.
Equinox, 8, 12, 229, 231.

Fletcher, PC, 74.
Ford, Cliff, 50, 59, 64, 101, 104, 125.
Ford, Pat, 150, 206.
French, Chief Superintendent, 112.

Gardiner, Mr, 70-73, 84.
Gee, Inspector, 39, 40, 62.
George, Joanne, 6, 19, 28, 58, 100, 132, 149.
Gifford, Lord, 5, 9-11, 52, 113, 127, 143, 204.
Glenarthur, Lord, 113, 143.
Gordon, H., 240.
Grant, Bernie, 24, 30, 47, 48, 50, 54, 55, 93, 95, 125-129, 212, 213, 240.
Greater London Council, 27, 28, 29.
Groce, Mrs Cherry, 4, 61, 62, 64, 96, 176.
The Guardian, 126.

Handsworth, 3, 61, 64, 127.
Haringey College, 230, 237, 239.
Haringey Community and Police Consultative Group, 55, 56, 114, 145, 208-213, 217.
Haringey Community Relations Council, 36, 53, 202.
Haringey Council for Voluntary Service, 209, 211.
Haringey, London Borough of, 4, 6, 12, 29-34, 52-56, 160, 208-213, 228, 233-237, 238.

INDEX

Haringey Sports Council, 17, 234.
Harris, Ralph, 67.
Henry, Mike, 117.
Hinds, Adeyemi, 226.
Holland, PC, 45.
Home Secretary, 3, 4, 52, 53, 207, 223.
Hornsey Journal, 19, 34, 36, 38.
Hutchinson-Reis, Michael, 37, 122, 138, 145, 147, 148, 149.

Inter-Agency Working Party, 31.
Islington Crime Survey, 151, 160, 162, 163, 166, 170-172.

Jamdagni, Laxmi, 190.
Jarrett, Cynthia, 3, 4, 6, 8, 62, 65-88, 89, 97, 125, 126, 128, 175, 176, 192, 215, 204, 240.
Jarrett, Floyd, 6, 66-70, 74, 84, 85, 87, 90, 174.
Jarrett, Michael, 77, 78, 90.
Jarrett, Mr, 35, 65, 88, 203.
Jarrett, Patricia, 65, 73, 75-78, 82, 83, 87.
Jeffers, Chief Superintendent, 112.
The Job, 12, 112.
John-Baptiste, Mary, 148.

Kavallares, Chris, 90.
Keith, Michael, 106, 108.
Kennedy, Mr, 96
Kerr, Howard, 140.
Kemp, Mr, 107, 116.
Kemp, Mrs, 62, 107, 116.
Kiffin, Dolly, 15, 22, 25, 26, 27, 28, 31, 33, 34, 36, 40, 42, 45, 50, 57, 59, 60, 61, 62, 87, 90, 93, 97, 117, 118, 120, 121, 175, 194, 195, 222, 240-242.

Large, Ernie, 15, 23, 42, 47, 48, 90, 148, 206.
La Touche, Panchita, 139, 140, 150.
Lawrence, Arthur, 62, 93, 99, 101, 109, 111, 116-121, 197.
Lawrence, Sharon, 93.
Leadbetter, Dave, 66.
Leon, Leonardo, 31, 104, 106, 107, 226, 227, 234.
Limb, Roy, 15, 17, 27, 33, 40, 43, 47, 48, 52, 58, 61, 74, 90, 91, 93, 117, 119, 145, 194, 203.
Local Government Act 1967, 225.
Lordship Recreation Ground, 17, 28, 234.

McLean, Norton, 37, 57, 203.
Mail on Sunday, 88.
Makanji, Narendra, 43, 55.
Marnoch, Commander, 200.
Martin, George, 88, 93, 94, 99, 101, 116-121, 195.
Meynell, Sergeant Gillian, 42, 59, 62, 64, 195.
Middlesex Area Probation Service, 146, 220.
Middlesex Polytechnic, 8, 12, 34, 151, 152, 153.
Mikkides, Andreas, 90.
Mitchell, Andrew, 48, 114, 123.
Moore, Vernon, 93, 99, 101, 116-121, 205.
Moody, Hyacinth, 90.
Morning Star, 126.
Moselle School, 17, 109.
Moyle, Roland, 91.
Murray, John, 16, 225.
Musslewhite, Anne, 234.

National Graphical Association, 242.
National Union of Journalists, 242.
Newman, Sir Kenneth, 9-11, 124, 126, 213.
New Society, 111.

Osamor, Martha, 39, 87, 88, 93, 94, 99, 238.

Parsons, Sergeant, 67, 68, 70, 71, 72, 74, 75.
Paul, Dr David, 80.
Platt, Steve, 111.
Police and Criminal Evidence Act, 71, 81, 131, 208.
Police Complaints Authority, 4, 6, 10, 66, 73, 81-87, 90, 91, 193, 214, 215.
Police magazine, 12, 13, 50, 59, 60, 62, 63, 97, 110.
Police Review, 12, 114.
Policy Studies Institute, 51, 162, 164, 165, 198, 203.
Press Council, 242.
Princess of Wales, 13, 29, 32, 240.
Priority Estates Project, 32, 223, 231.

Ramdin, Sheila, 15, 119, 121, 135, 147, 149, 231.
Randall, DC, 65, 69, 70, 72-78, 81-84, 203.
Richards, Deputy Assistant Commissioner, 3, 7, 9, 14, 39, 44, 52, 56, 60, 62, 63, 64, 90, 91, 93, 97, 98, 102, 103, 105, 112, 113-115, 116, 123, 133, 144, 173.

INDEX

Riot Damages Act 1886, 130.
Rowe, Chief Superintendent, 112.
Runnymede Trust, 137, 141.

Sansom, Andy, 27.
Sargison, Malcolm, 23, 24, 25, 26, 47.
Scarman, Lord, 4, 5, 37, 38, 55.
Scott, Mrs Beverley, 35, 95, 98, 133, 134, 193, 197.
Scott, Millard, 47, 59, 90.
Scott, Roger, 45, 46.
Scott, Stafford, 23, 24, 29, 41, 49, 89, 90, 93, 94, 100, 104, 134.
Shallice, Andy, 137, 141, 142.
Shorthouse, John, 89.
Simmons, Howard, 26, 110, 112.
Simons, Barry, 21, 25.
Simper, Russell, 18, 20, 27, 45, 62, 147.
Simpson, Assistant Chief Constable, 71, 81, 83.
Sinclair, Superintendent, 41, 112.
Solley, Stephen, 67, 68.
Somerville, Dr, 79, 80.
Stacey, Superintendent, 39, 40, 58, 59, 60, 62, 74, 116, 120.
Stainsby, Chief Superintendent, 55, 87, 88, 145, 193, 196, 202, 203.
The Standard, 124.
Sterling, Clasford, 23, 25, 29, 46, 47, 59.
Stratton, PC, 20, 45, 47.
The Sun, 125.
Sutherland, Hugh, 147.

Taylor-Woodrow, 14.
Time Out, 182.
The Times, 125.
Tottenham Technical College, 240, 237, 239.
Tottenham Weekly Herald, 19, 25, 33.
Trant, William, 22, 93.
TV Eye, 116.
Tyler, Andrew, 197.

Waldorf, Stephen, 89.
West Midlands County Council, 3.
Wheaton, Rev John, 142.
Whitfield, David, 118.

Wilde, Debbie, 101, 105, 135.
William C. Harvey School, 17, 109.
World in Action, 59.
Wright, Nick, 43, 61, 92, 93, 101, 105, 109.

Young, Sir George, 13, 27, 33, 223.
Young, Dr Jock, 8.

Zimet, Sara Goodman, 227.
Zipfel, Tricia, 13, 32, 41, 42, 195, 197, 223.